Essential JavaScript™
for Web Professionals

Prentice Hall PTR
Essential Guide Series

THE ESSENTIAL GUIDE TO DATA WAREHOUSING

Agosta

ESSENTIAL JAVASCRIPT FOR WEB PROFESSIONALS, SECOND EDITION

Barrett

THE ESSENTIAL GUIDE TO WEB STRATEGY FOR ENTREPRENEURS

Bergman

THE ESSENTIAL GUIDE TO THE BUSINESS OF U.S. MOBILE WIRELESS COMMUNICATIONS

Burnham

THE ESSENTIAL GUIDE TO TELECOMMUNICATIONS, THIRD EDITION

Dodd

THE ESSENTIAL GUIDE TO WIRELESS COMMUNICATIONS APPLICATIONS, SECOND EDITION

Dornan

THE ESSENTIAL GUIDE TO OPTICAL NETWORKS

Greenfield

THE ESSENTIAL GUIDE TO INTERNET BUSINESS TECHNOLOGY

Honda & Martin

THE ESSENTIAL GUIDE TO COMPUTER HARDWARE

Keogh

THE ESSENTIAL GUIDE TO NETWORKING

Keogh

THE ESSENTIAL GUIDE TO COMPUTER DATA STORAGE: FROM FLOPPY TO DVD

Khurshudov

THE ESSENTIAL GUIDE TO DIGITAL SET-TOP BOXES AND INTERACTIVE TV

O'Driscoll

THE ESSENTIAL GUIDE TO HOME NETWORKING TECHNOLOGIES

O'Driscoll

THE ESSENTIAL GUIDE TO KNOWLEDGE MANAGEMENT: E-BUSINESS AND CRM APPLICATIONS

Tiwana

THE ESSENTIAL GUIDE TO APPLICATION SERVICE PROVIDERS

Toigo

ESSENTIAL GUIDE TO XML TECHNOLOGIES

Turner

THE ESSENTIAL GUIDE TO STORAGE AREA NETWORKS

Vacca

THE ESSENTIAL GUIDE TO MOBILE BUSINESS

Vos & deKlein

THE ESSENTIAL GUIDE TO COMPUTING: THE STORY OF INFORMATION TECHNOLOGY

Walters

THE ESSENTIAL GUIDE TO RF AND WIRELESS, SECOND EDITION

Weisman

Essential JavaScript™ for Web Professionals

Dan Barrett

Prentice Hall PTR
Upper Saddle River, NJ 07458
www.phptr.com

A Cataloging-in-Publication Data record for this book can be obtained from the Library of Congress.

Editorial/Production Supervision: Faye Gemmellaro
Senior Managing Editor: John Neidhart
Cover Design Director: Jerry Votta
Manufacturing Manager: Alexis Heydt-Long
Marketing Manager: Bryan Gambrel
Editorial Assistant: Brandt Kenna
Interior Design Director: Gail Cocker-Bogusz

 © 2003 Pearson Education, Inc.
Publishing as Prentice Hall PTR
Upper Saddle River, NJ 07458

Prentice Hall books are widely used by corporations and government agencies for training, marketing, and resale.

For information regarding corporate and government bulk discounts, contact:

Corporate and Government Sales: (800) 382-3419 or corpsales@pearsontechgroup.com

All products mentioned herein are trademarks or registered trademarks of their respective owners.

Printed in the United States of America

10 9 8 7 6 5 4 3 2 1

ISBN 0-13-100147-7

Pearson Education Ltd.
Pearson Education Australia Pty., Ltd.
Pearson Education Singapore, Pte. Ltd.
Pearson Education North Asia Ltd.
Pearson Education Canada, Ltd.
Pearson Educación de Mexico, S.A. de C.V.
Pearson Education—Japan
Pearson Education Malaysia, Pte. Ltd.

Contents

Introduction

Welcome! This book is something I wish I had had when I was first starting out with JavaScript. At that time, there were basically two types of instructional books on the market: 1,200-page tomes of seemingly arcane knowledge and books that were overly simplified and lacking in practical information. Unfortunately, there were no books that were informative and at the same time provided instruction that could be used quickly and effectively in real-world situations.

This book guides you through JavaScript using examples taken straight from situations that are faced every day during Web site construction. It starts with simpler examples and becomes quite sophisticated with the scripting toward the end of the book. If you're a novice, it's probably best to start at the beginning and work up to the projects in the later chapters. A lot of what is accomplished in the more advanced chapters builds off of what is learned in the first chapters of the book.

◆ How This Book Is Laid Out

Chances are that at least some of you picked up this book when your boss called you into his or her office and showed you a Web site that made use of JavaScript. You were then told in no uncertain terms that it was your job to implement the same or similar functionality on your company's Web site. Believe me, I know how this goes, "No problem," you respond, while saying to yourself, "Gee, I'd better learn JavaScript and fast!"

This is often the way in which we expand our skills: We are given a job, and if we don't know exactly how to do it, we quickly learn how. In keeping with this real-world model, this book is split into two main sections. In each main section, we create and/or upgrade the Web sites for one of two fictitious companies.

In the first three chapters, we revamp the Web site of Shelley Biotechnologies, a fast-growing biotech startup. Each chapter has at least one project that consists of commonly used JavaScript solutions that range from easy to moderately difficult. At the end of each chapter are more advanced exercises that you can complete on your own to expand your skills. In the second half of the book, we make some much-needed additions to *Stitch Magazine's* Web site. *Stitch* is a popular fashion magazine that is trying to get the online version up to the same par as the hardcopy version of the magazine. The examples are, for the most part, more advanced than those found in the first section and show you some of the powerful things you can do using JavaScript.

The exercises in the book are designed to give you a solid foundation in JavaScript on which you can build as you continue to use it. You will find that more often than not there is more than one way to do things in JavaScript.

As an extra bonus, we have created a Web site where you can go to download all of the code and images needed to follow along with each project in the book. You can only learn so much from reading how to do something; the true way to learn is to get your hands dirty and do the work. The companion site for this book can be found at *http://www.phptr.com/essential/javascript/*. I encourage you to go to the site and work along with the real code as you move through each project.

◆ An Introduction to JavaScript

What Is JavaScript?

For those of you who are new to the world of Web development and are perhaps learning JavaScript in conjunction with HTML, a quick rundown of what JavaScript is may be in order. JavaScript is

Netscape's built-in cross-platform scripting language. Like HTML, it works on all platforms. JavaScript, however, allows you to enhance the functionality of your Web pages by embedding applications directly into your HTML. You can use JavaScript to build applications that range from adding interactivity to your pages to interacting with databases. Although Netscape created JavaScript, it has become an integral part of creating Web pages, and all of the major browsers, including Internet Explorer, support it in one fashion or another. When Microsoft first implemented support for JavaScript (which they labeled Jscript), it was buggy and unreliable. As JavaScript became more prevalent, it was decided to take a shot at standardizing the language so that all implementations would share common functionality. The standardized version of the language was put together by ECMA, an international standards body. As of Internet Explorer's (IE) 4.0 release of Jscript and Netscape's release of version 1.3 of JavaScript, both implementations are ECMA-compliant. Of course, as newer versions of IE have come out, Microsoft has introduced new extensions, most of which are not supported in any versions of Netscape lower that 6x. This constant bickering between the companies has made the life of the Web developer more challenging, to say the least. Often, you will find the perfect solution to a problem only to later realize that the solution is supported only in one of the two browsers; then you must go searching around for a solution for the other browser. This is one of the biggest drawbacks to using JavaScript; however, with the release of Netscape 6.x, the gap between the different implementations has closed a bit. Now all we need to do is wait until all of the Internet's users have upgraded their browsers to the latest and greatest versions. On second thought, don't hold your breath on that. For the foreseeable future, these differences are something we are going to have to deal with; lucky for you, we have come up with several ways to handle these issues. We will use them throughout the book when we have to treat code differently for the different browsers.

With the whole can't-they-just-get-along speech out of the way, let's look at the methods by which JavaScript can be implemented on the Web. There are two methods that you can use to include JavaScript in your Web pages: client-side and server-side. Both methods share the same basic language set. This core language defines a base set of objects and features that work in both client-side and server-side applications. Each method also has extended objects and feature sets that only apply to it.

Server-side JavaScript applications are stored on the Web server and must be called up from each page that wishes to access them. Using this method gives you two advantages. First, you are using the server's processing power to run the script, so if it's a really beefy script, your server can probably process it faster than the user machine. Second, by using server-side scripts, you have better access to the other applications running on the server. That being said, however, client-side scripts make up at least 90 percent of the scripts you see on the Web. If you really want to get into server-side applications, there are other more robust languages on the market that would better serve your needs, so in this book, we focus on client-side JavaScript.

Client-side JavaScript: How it Works

Client-side JavaScript applications are scripts that are embedded directly into your HTML pages and are executed by the user's browser as it loads the page. When the user's browser calls up an HTML page with JavaScript embedded in it, the browser's JavaScript runtime engine is called to interpret the script, which it reads from top to bottom, executing statements as it goes.

One of the main advantages of using client-side scripting is that the script is able to detect and make use of user-initiated events, such as changes to a form or the mouse rolling over a particular graphic. The script is then able to use that information to call other parts of the script, and all of this can be done without going back to the Web server and grabbing more information.

Now that we know a little bit about the different methods of JavaScript, let's look at how the language is set up. You can pretty much break the language into two sections, the first being objects and the functionality that deals with them, and second, the language elements that let you manipulate them. We don't want to get too deeply into these at this point, but a quick look at what each section consists of will be helpful as we start our scripting.

In the first section, we can find the following:

- Objects—JavaScript is an object-oriented language. Each element of a browser and the Web pages they display are stored in objects, which are made up of properties and have methods that can be used to access and modify them.
- Top-Level Functions and Properties—These are functions and properties that apply to all objects.

- Event Handlers—These are code structures that let JavaScript react to events that take place on a Web page.

The second section contains the following:

- Statements—Statements are predefined instructions executed by calling keywords using the proper syntax.
- Operators—Several types of operators are found in JavaScript, including assignment, comparison, arithmetic, bitwise, logical, string, as well as special operators. Operators enable you to perform operations on JavaScript objects and their properties.

This is just a brief look at how the JavaScript language is arranged. How these different parts of JavaScript all come together to create our scripts will be revealed throughout our projects. Before we move onto our first project, a quick word on some of the limitations of JavaScript is in order.

What JavaScript Can and Can't Do

While the applications that you can create using JavaScript are limited only by your imagination, there are several things that you cannot do. Most notably is accessing or controlling the user's machine. For security reasons, writing to a user's computer is severely limited. Only through the use of a cookie can you store any data on the user's machine, and even then you are limited to a simple text file. This protects users from scripts that might do their computers harm or allow unscrupulous programmers access to personal information.

A security feature called the Same Origin Policy also restricts the access of a script from one origin access to certain properties or files at other locations. For example, if you have a script located at *http://www.yoursite.com/test.html* and it tries to access certain properties of an HTML page located at *http://www.theirsite.com/test.html*, the Same Origin Policy will deny your script access. The properties that the Same Origin Policy restricts are shown in Figure I–1.

These two areas cover the main restrictions that you will find when writing JavaScript applications. I am sure you will find yourself at times trying to use an object or property to do something that can't be done, but those limitations are less restrictions than just a matter of learning the structure of the language.

Objects	Restricted Properties
images	src, lowsrc
document	anchors, applets, cookie, domain, elements, embeds, forms, lastModified, length, links, referrer, title, URL
layer	src
location	All properties except for x and y
window	find

FIGURE I–1 Same Origin Policy restrictions.

As you read this book, if you think of a possible solution that may differ from the examples, give it a shot; you can often stumble onto a solution that others may not have thought of. With all that said, let's get on with the learning.

Acknowledgments

I would like to thank the Academy . . . Oh, wait, wrong speech. But seriously, I would like to thank my wife, Kristin, for her support and understanding not only over the course of writing this book the first time, but putting up with me as I updated it for the second edition.

Thanks to my family, my parents, Chuck and Judy, and my brother, Rick, all of whom put up with me having my nose in a book for most of my childhood. See, I told you good would come of it some day.

I would like to thank Dan Livingston and Micah Brown for thinking of me when this project initially came along, and another round of thanks to Dan and Dominic Correa for doing the technical review for the second edition. Thanks also to Karen McLean and John Neidhart, my editors, and all the rest of the gang at Prentice Hall.

I'd also like to thank some friends and colleagues who helped in some fashion with the writing of the book. First I'd like to thank Kelly Salamanca for picking up the slack at my "real" job while I worked on the second edition. Next, thanks go out to Leon Atkinson for the idea of the Searchable Designer Database—if you're interested in PHP check out this guy's book. I'm telling you he's a big brain on feet, the man knows what he's talking about. Finally I'd like to thank Darryl Hahn for the "top" and "left" thing . . . you know what I'm talking about.

About the Author

Dan Barrett is co-owner of Smashing Pixels, a hardcore Web design firm located in the San Francisco Bay Area. He has worked for several large Web agencies whose clientele includes Hewlett-Packard, Novell PeopleSoft, Restoration Hardware, Electronic Arts, and Pacific Bell. His sites have won numerous awards, including several International Web Page Awards and Macromedia's Flash Site of the Day. When he is not sitting in front of his monitor working on Web sites, chances are that Dan is "destroying" his house while practicing his home improvement skills. He currently lives in the San Francisco Bay Area with his wife, Kristin, two dogs, and by the time this is published, a first child.

1 Dynamism and Detection

IN THIS CHAPTER

- Project I: Browser Detection and Cloaking—Dynamically Generating Platform-Specific Content
- Project II: Dynamic Content Creation—Printing Out the Copyright Information and Last-Modified Date
- Recap
- Advanced Projects

You've landed the job programming the Web site for Shelley Biotechnologies. At the moment, its site is okay, but very static, and your new boss has brought you on board to bring it up to speed with the competition. Before you begin to soup up the site, however, the boss wants you to look at an issue that has been raised by some people who have been browsing the site. The site is currently using Cascading Style Sheets with Dynamic HTML (CSS/DHTML) to specify what the font size should be for the text on the homepage. Users who are viewing the site with Netscape Communicator 4.x on the Macintosh are seeing the fonts at a different size than those using Internet Explorer or those using a Windows-based computer (see Figure 1–1). While this may seem like an insignificant problem, the boss is nothing if not a stickler for details, so this looks like the perfect opportunity to start putting JavaScript to work.

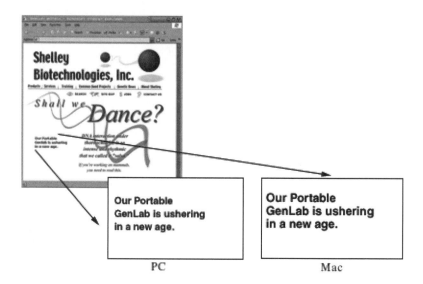

FIGURE 1–1   Font differences on the different platforms.

One of the most useful aspects of JavaScript is that it allows you to see what platform and browser are being used to view a site. We will use this technique throughout our projects in this book. By using the information we gather about users and their equipment, we can have the browser print out a different size font for the affected Mac users.

◆ Project I: Browser Detection and Cloaking— Dynamically Generating Platform-Specific Content

Even though you may not have had much experience with CSS/DHTML, because there is only one font style specified on the homepage, it's pretty easy to figure out how to change the size of the problem text. We simply change the point size of the font attribute.

```
<style type="text/css">
    .homePageText {
    color : #000000;
```

```
font : 9pt Arial, Helvetica;
font-weight : normal;
}
</style>
```

Unlike traditional HTML, where you change the font size by either adding or subtracting from a default size, with CSS/DHTML you can specify a point size for a font much as you would within a document editor such as Microsoft Word. Currently, the font is set to 9pt. After playing around with the existing HTML, you have concluded that in order for the page to look the same on Communicator 4.x for the Mac, you need to up the point size by two to 11pt. Currently, the CSS information is embedded directly into the homepage; however, this is not the only way to specify styles for your HTML page. You may also link to an external file that holds your CSS definitions. To solve our problem, we create two separate files to hold CSS style definitions, one for Communicator 4.x for the Mac and another to be used for the rest of the browsers. Then, using JavaScript, we determine which browser and version the user is viewing the page with and embed the proper CSS file.

For this first script, there are three main parts: First, we must create the two CSS files to be used in the project. Next, we must find out some details about the users equipment, such as the platform he or she is on as well as the browser and version being used to view the site. Finally, we need to have the browser dynamically print out the code to embed the proper CSS file into the homepage.

Creating External CSS Files

Creating the two CSS files is actually really simple. First, open up your favorite text/HTML editor and open a new blank document. The first file we create is the one for Communicator 4.x for the Mac, all that needs to go into the file is the single style definition with a font size of 11pt.

```
.homePageText {
color : #000000;
font : 11pt Arial, Helvetica;
font-weight : normal;
}
```

Save this file as *styles_mac_4x.css*. Congrats—you've created the first of our two files. To create the second file, simply repeat the steps above, but insert a font size of 9pt instead of 11pt, like so.

```
.homePageText {
color : #000000;
font : 9pt Arial, Helvetica;
font-weight : normal;
}
```

Save this file as *styles_default.css*, and with that, we are done with the first part of the project. The next step is to start writing our script.

Debugging JavaScript Code

Before we get into adding the script to our page, it's a good idea to take a few minutes and talk about the debugging of JavaScript code. Whether you're a beginner or you've been coding for years, I guarantee you will run into mistakes in your code. Sometimes it seems you spend more time chasing down bugs in your code than you do actually writing the script.

There are three types of errors that you will run across when writing JavaScript: syntax errors, runtime errors, and logical errors.

Syntax errors are the most common error that you will find when scripting. These errors generally result from a typo or misspelling. Other causes for syntax errors could be the wrong case, a missing quote, or missing IDs or names. The browser generally finds these errors when a page is first loaded.

Runtime errors occur during the execution of a script and arise when you try to have JavaScript do something that it can't do, such as divide by zero.

Logical errors are probably the most elusive and frustrating error of the three. They occur when the programmer has a script do something that results in an incorrect outcome. Probably the most common logical error for beginners is using the assignment operator (=) to compare two values instead of the comparison operator (==). When this is done, the left-hand value is assigned the value of the right-hand value instead of the two of them being compared.

There are several ways to help track down your errors. One of the easiest is to use an editor that has the ability to recognize

```
47
48     // function to turn on rolled over graphic
49     function on(pic)  {
50         if (document.images)  {
51             document.images[pic].src=eval(pic + "On.src");
52         }
53     }
54
55     // function to turn off rolled over graphic
56     function off(pic)  {
57         if(document.images)  {
58             document.images[pic].src= eval(pic + "Off.src");
59         }
60     }
61
```

FIGURE 1–2   Example color coding of syntax.

most syntax errors. Editors such as HomeSite and Dreamweaver color code your scripts (see Figure 1–2) and line numbering. Most browsers' built-in error handling lets you know the line number where it found an error, so by seeing the line numbers, you can more easily track down your problems. Color coding makes it a lot easier to spot syntax problems such as missing quotation marks. These editors, however, generally won't help you recognize runtime or logical errors.

Both Internet Explorer and Netscape offer some level of built-in debugging. Netscape comes with a JavaScript Console that you can use to find expanded information, such as the type of error and the line number on which the error occurs. To bring up the console in version 4.x and lower, simply type

```
javascript:
```

into the location box of the browser. If you are using version 6.x of Netscape, look under the Tasks –> Tools menu for the JavaScript Console. Internet Explorer offers the ability for the browser to pop up a message window with a short description of the error when it finds a problem with a script. To turn this feature on, go to Internet Options under the Tools menu, then choose the Advanced tab, click "Display a notification about every script error," and make sure the "Disable script debugging" is not checked. Of the two, I find that the Netscape version is much more helpful.

Even though it is a certainty that you will make some errors when writing your scripts, you can follow a few simple rules to help reduce those errors:

1. Indent your code. Every time you come to a new language structure, indent again. This will make it easier not only to find errors in your code structure but also to read it.

2. Comment your code. It's much easier to find errors if you are able to identify what each section of code is supposed to be doing by inserting small descriptions for each section of code. That way, if you are having a problem with a specific function, you'll know where to find that code.

3. Use well-thought-out naming conventions. Nothing is more infuriating than having to go in and fix the code of someone who used gibberish names for variables and function names. Use short descriptive names for your variables and functions; this will not only make it easier for someone else to come work on your code, but it will also help you out. Imagine revisiting a script you wrote two years ago and having to figure out exactly what the function "bisnosh" does.

Inserting a Script into Your HTML

Now that the "write clean code" lecture is out of the way, let's write our first script. The first step to writing any JavaScript is to tell the browser that the code you are putting into your Web page is not HTML but a JavaScript application. Once it knows this, it will send the information that follows to the JavaScript runtime engine, which will execute the script. For most scripts, we accomplish this by enclosing the scripts in the `<script>` tag, like so.

```
<script>
    . . .
</script>
```

There are several other ways in which you can embed your scripts into your HTML:

- You can specify an external file that contains your scripts.
- You can specify a JavaScript expression as a value for an HTML attribute.
- You can embed your scripts within some HTML tags as event handlers.

Using the `<script>` tag is by far the most common method—we will go over some of the others later in the book when we use JavaScript with images and forms. If the browser finds JavaScript outside of a `<script>` tag or not used in one of the other methods, your script will be treated as text to be printed on the screen and your script won't work.

As new versions of JavaScript come out, properties and expressions are added to the tools available in the language. If you use these new features in your scripts and a system with an older browser loads your script, chances are good that it will receive an error and your script will not work correctly. In order to check for this, we can add an attribute to our `<script>` tag to tell the browser what version of JavaScript we are coding for. When the user's browser gets to the script, it will check to see if it supports the version we specify, and if not, it will skip over the script. We accomplish this by using the LANGUAGE attribute of the `<script>` tag.

```
<script language="JavaScript1.3">
    . . .
</script>
```

This addition to the statement tells the browser that if it does not support version 1.3 of JavaScript, it should not continue with the script. This method takes care of cloaking for JavaScript-capable browsers; however, it is possible that some users are on older browsers that do not support JavaScript at all. You can solve this by putting all of your code in between HTML comment tags.

```
<script language=" JavaScript1.3">
<!-- Code after this will be ignored by older browsers
...
Stop hiding the code here -->
</script>
```

Now we know how to put our scripts into our HTML. However, before we get into the script in earnest, an understanding of the hierarchy of JavaScript is in order.

JavaScript Objects and Hierarchies

When your browser loads an HTML page, the JavaScript engine automatically creates a set of objects based on the content of your HTML. It keeps these objects in a hierarchy (see Figure 1–3), which then can be used to call on or reference the objects and their properties. Most of the scripts we write in JavaScript will either reference, change, or create objects. Understanding how to get at them is a must, so having a strong grasp of the hierarchy is a necessity.

The WINDOW object is at the top of the JavaScript hierarchy; this object is the actual window in which your browser appears. The descendants of the WINDOW object are its properties and are also objects themselves that can have descendants. For example, if you have an image called product on your page, then product is an object of the type image, and that image object is a property of the DOCUMENT object, which in turn is a property of the WINDOW object. Study the diagram above to learn what the main objects are and where they lay in the hierarchy. A glossary of all of JavaScript objects and their properties is located in Appendix B.

To reference an object in JavaScript, you must call not only the object itself but all of the objects above it in the hierarchy. Here's an example of how you would refer to the object of our image, product:

```
document.product
```

To call on a specific property of an object, you follow this same model and just take it a step further down the hierarchy. Calling on the source property of the product image looks like this:

```
document.product.src
```

You will notice that the WINDOW object was not included as the first object in the preceding examples. If you do not specify a specific window, JavaScript automatically assumes that you are referring to the window in which the document is loaded. The only time that you need to specify the window is when you are trying to access objects that exist in another window or frame. At this point, you should have at least a basic understanding of the JavaScript hierarchy; as we continue with the examples in this book, that understanding will increase.

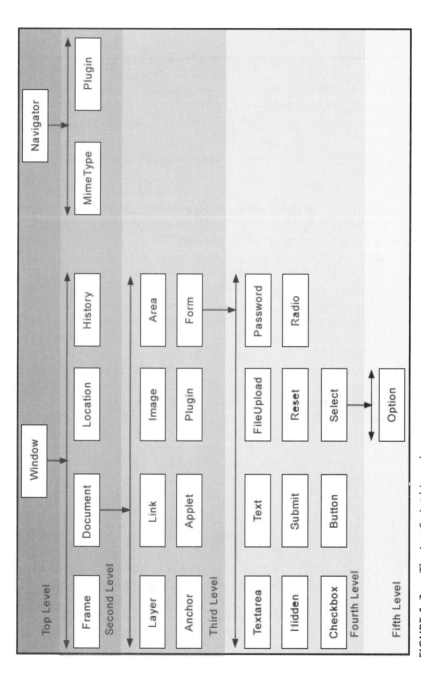

FIGURE 1–3   The JavaScript hierarchy.

9

VARIABLES

There is one other concept that you need to get under your belt before we move on to the first line in our script: variables. Variables play a very important role in scripting of any sort, and JavaScript is no exception. A variable can be thought of as a container with a user-defined name in which you can store information.

To create a variable, you use the `var` statement, like so.

```
var varibleName;
```

Once you have created a variable, you can assign a value to it, and from then on you can simply call the name of the variable to access the information it contains. You can also change the value the variable holds at any time. As an example, let's say you have a Web page that has a photo on it. Each time the user clicks on a "next" graphic, the photo changes to the next image in a list of 10 pictures. For this to work, you need to keep track of which picture the person is viewing, so you create a variable called `whichPic`, and when the page initially loads, you assign it a value of 1. Then, each time the user clicks on the "next" button, you add a value of 1 to the existing value. Using this method, you can keep track of where the user is at in the list of pictures. This is just a simple example of how you could use a variable. As we continue through the book, you'll find that variables will become one of your best JavaScript friends.

DETECTING BROWSER AND PLATFORM PROPERTIES

I know I've said it before, but we are now ready to start writing our script. In most cases, we will put our scripts into the `<head>` of the HTML page. However, you can just as easily place a script into the body of the HTML if you need the script to execute at a specific location on the page. For this project, we insert the script in the `Head` of the HTML. Here is a section of the HTML code showing the location at which we will place our script.

```
<html>
<head>
    <title>Shelly Biotechnology</title>

**** OUR SCRIPT WILL GO HERE ****

</head>
```

Now that we know where to put our script into the HTML code, let's insert the first chunk of script.

```
<!-- Begin JavaScript to embed the proper CSS file
depending on platform -->

<script language="JavaScript1.2">
<!-- Code after this will be ignored by older browsers

    // Assign the user information to a Variable
  . . .
// Stop hiding the code here -->
</script>
```

Let's dissect this first bit of code line by line and figure out what is going on. First, we insert an HTML comment to tell those reading the code that what follows is a JavaScript and to give them a general idea of what this script will do. There are times when within a single <script> tag there will be scripts that do several different things, so in such cases you should supplement your general description by placing a more detailed description of each part within the <script> tag near each different section.

Next, we put in the opening <script> tag, as we discussed in the beginning of the chapter. After the <script> tag, we started the HTML comment line, which hides our code from non-JavaScript-capable browsers. These second two lines are at the beginning of all the scripts we write, so get used to seeing them.

The next line is a JavaScript comment; as in HTML, you are able to add notations to your code to help make your scripts easier to follow. There are two ways to insert a comment into your JavaScript. The first (the method that we use here) is to start a line of code with two forward slashes.

```
// Text on this line is treated as a Comment
```

In this method, any code that follows the slashes on that single line is treated as a comment and won't be interpreted as code to be executed. The second method is used when you want to insert a comment that spans multiple lines. To do this, you enclose your comment between the symbols /* and */. Here is an example of this method.

```
/* This an example of a comment
    that spans multiple lines of code */
```

As we write our scripts, we will use these JavaScript comments to identify each major section of the code and specify its basic purpose. After inserting the comment, we left some space for the next part of our script. Whenever you see

. . .

in our examples, you'll know that we will be adding more script to that area.

Next, we inserted the closing HTML comment that will stop hiding code from the non-JavaScript-capable browsers. You will notice that we started this line with the two slashes that specify a single-line JavaScript comment; we put this in because the JavaScript engine doesn't recognize a closing HTML comment. Finally, we inserted the closing `</script>` tag, which tells the browser that we are done with our script.

The next part of our script captures the information about the user's browser and platform.

THE NAVIGATOR OBJECT

Let's insert the next portion of our script.

```
<!-- Begin JavaScript to embed the proper CSS file
     depending on platform -->

<script language="JavaScript1.2">
<!-- Code after this will be ignored by older browsers

     // Assign the user information to a Variable
     var platform = navigator.platform.substr(0,3);
     var browser = navigator.appName;
     var version = navigator.appVersion.substr(0,1);
     . . .

// Stop hiding the code here -->
</script>
```

All three of the next lines deal with the NAVIGATOR object. This is the object that is created to hold information about the user. In this case we are interested in three different aspects of the user's machine: the platform being used, the browser being used, and the version of the browser. The three properties of the NAVIGATOR object that we need to access are appName, which holds the name of the browser that the user is on; appVersion, which tells us what version of the browser the user has; and platform, which tells us what platform the user's computer runs on. Let's go over these three lines of code one by one and see how we gather our information. First, we need to find which browser the user is on.

```
var platform = navigator.platform.substr(0,3);
```

We use the basic assignment operator (the = sign) to assign the value of the platform property to a variable called platform. Several new things are happening on this line of code, so let's break it down and take a closer look at what is going on.

There are three basic things going on in this one line of code. First, at a top level, we are using an assignment operator to set the value of the left-hand operand to be the value of the right-hand operand. We also have things happening on both sides of the operator: On the left-hand side, we are creating a variable, as in our example. On the right-hand side, two things are happening: First, we are calling on the platform property of the NAVIGATOR object; this property holds the string value that tells us which platform the user is on. If the user is on a Windows-based machine, the value of navigator.platform will be either Win32 or WinNT. If the user is on a Macintosh computer, it will return the value macintosh.

We are not really interested in finding out which version of Windows the user is running, so it would be great if we could find a way to condense the value returned to just the first three characters: Win if it is a Windows-based machine or Mac if it is a Macintosh-based machine. This way, whichever version of Windows the user is running, a single value would be assigned to our platform variable. Luckily for us, there is a way, and it is the second thing that is happening on this side of the operator. The substr() method returns a specified number of characters from any given string. Because we know that the first three letters returned from all versions of Windows are the same, this is perfect for us. The syntax for the substr() method is as follows:

```
string.subtsr(start,length);
```

with start being the position of the character you wish to start with, and length being the number of characters that you want the method to evaluate. In the preceding code we tell the substr() method to start at the first character and go until the third. When referencing the position of anything in JavaScript, keep in mind that 0 is the first position in a list. The assignment operator will now be putting either Win for Windows-based machines or Mac for

Macintosh machines into our variable `platform`. You will notice the last thing on the right-hand side is a semicolon; this is used to tell the JavaScript engine that it has reached the end of the line.

The next line of code gathers the name of the browser the user is viewing the site with.

```
var browser = navigator.appName;
```

We declare a variable named `browser`. By putting the value of the `navigator.appName` property into it, we will most likely get values of either `Netscape` or `Microsoft Internet Explorer`. Finally, we get to our third line of code, where we will gather the version of the browser used.

```
var version = navigator.appVersion.substr(0,1);
```

This line is similar to the first line that we used to gather the platform of the user. We again use the `substr()` method, but this time we are only interested in the first character of the `appName` property. The value that will be returned when a user is on a Macintosh using Netscape 4 or below will be 4 or less. Since this is the browser that we want to cloak for, this will work perfectly for us. If you want to cloak for other browsers, you may need to gather more than just the first character.

Conditional Statements

We now have the information necessary to put in our next piece of code. We use the values of the variables as tests in a set of `if` statements to determine which font size we want on our page. An `if` statement is a conditional statement that says if a specific condition is met, go ahead and execute the code that follows; otherwise, skip down to the next statement.

We use an `if_else` statement to test the value of `platform`. Let's take a quick look at the syntax of an `if_else` statement.

```
if (condition1) {
    statements1
}
else {
    statements2
)
```

In the preceding syntax, `condition1` represents any expression that will return a value of `true` or `false`. If `condition1` is `true`, the JavaScript engine will execute the code contained in statements1. If, however, condition1 is false, the JavaScript engine skips over statements1 and executes statements2. The if statement is one of the most commonly used structures within JavaScript, and we will see a lot of it throughout the book. Let's put in the next section of code that contains our if statement.

```
<!-- Begin JavaScript to embed the proper CSS file
     depending on platform -->

<script language="JavaScript1.2">
<!-- Code after this will be ignored by older browsers

     // Assign the user information to a Variable
     var platform = navigator.platform.substr(0,3);
     var browser = navigator.appName;
     var version = navigator.appVersion.substr(0,1);

     // An if statement used to print out the proper css
file
     if ((platform == 'Mac') && (browser == 'Netscape') &&
(version <= 4)) {

     . . .

     } else {

     . . .

     }
// Stop hiding the code here -->
</script>
```

In the if statement in the preceding code, we tell the JavaScript engine to first look at the value of the variables platform, browser, and version, and if they are all equal to the values that we specify, then execute the statements that follow; if not, then skip down to the statements contained in the else portion of the code structure. Let's take a closer look at the first line where the test takes place. We first compare the variable platform to the value Mac. Notice that we use the double equal signs to compare the values in our conditions—this is how we do comparisons in JavaScript. If we were to use a single equal sign, it would treat the statement as an assignment operator, thereby resetting the value of browser. If the user is on a computer running the Macintosh platform, this first part of our test will return a value of true.

Now that our first test is finished, we move on to the second test, but first we need to tell the JavaScript engine how we want it to treat the next condition. By using the && operator, we tell it that not only does the first condition have to be true, but for it to move on and execute the code below, it needs the next condition to be `true` as well. In our second condition, we check the variable `browser` against a value of `Netscape`, so if the user is on a Macintosh and is using Netscape, our condition is thus far true.

For our final condition, we tell the JavaScript engine that our next condition must be `true` before it can move down and execute the following code. This condition uses the `<=` (less than or equal to) comparison operator to find out if the user is on a browser that is version 4 or lower. Notice that we didn't wrap the number 4 inside of either double or single quotes in this portion of our test. This is because only strings must be wrapped inside of quotes; you can simply use any number by itself.

If any of these three conditions come up as `false`, then the engine skips the statements that follow and execute the statements following the `else` portion of the code structure.

We now have a basic structure for our script, which will detect what platform, version, and browser are being used to view your page. The only remaining part is to insert the code that we want the browser to execute for each platform.

PRINTING OUT DYNAMIC HTML

As it is our goal to have one of two different CSS files to show up for the different user types, we need to have the JavaScript write out the `<link>` tag, which will let us link the proper external CSS file into the HTML Page dynamically. There are two statements you can use to write to an HTML document: `document.write()` and `document.writeln()`. Both will print out whatever falls between their parentheses; the difference is that `document.writeln()` will put a line break after it is finished printing. It usually will not matter which method you use, but for our script we use `document.writeln()` so that if you view the source of the HTML page once the code is printed out, it will be formatted for easier reading.

You can use these commands to print out several different types of information. You can print out any string you like simply by enclosing it within quotes. You could also have these commands print out the values held within variables by inserting the variable inside the parentheses without quotes. For our purposes, we just print out a string that contains the `<link>` tag. Let's insert the `document.writeln()` method into our `if` statements.

```
<!-- Begin JavaScript to embed the proper CSS file
     depending on platform -->


<script language="JavaScript1.2">
<!-- Code after this will be ignored by older browsers


     // Assign the user information to a Variable
     var platform = navigator.platform.substr(0,3);
     var browser  = navigator.appName;
     var version  = navigator.appVersion.substr(0,1);


     // An if statement used to print out the proper css
file
     if ((platform == 'Mac') && (browser == 'Netscape') &&
     (version <= 4)) {
          document.writeln("<link rel=\"stylesheet\"
type=\"text/css\" href=\"styles_mac_4x.css\">");
     } else {
          document.writeln("<link rel=\"stylesheet\"
type=\"text/css\" href=\"styles_default.css\">");
     }
// Stop hiding the code here -->
</script>
```

With that done, if the user is on a Macintosh using Netscape 4 or below, the `styles_mac_4x.css` file will be used, and if the user is on any other platform/browser combination, the `styles_default.css` will be used. You will notice in our `document.writeln` statement the addition of a backward slash in front of the quotes that surround the values of the REL, TYPE, and HREF attributes. The slashes tell the `document.writeln` statement to actually print out the quote instead of treating it as an end quote for the statement. This is known as *escaping a character*; you can use this to have JavaScript treat reserved characters at face value instead of evaluating them. If you are printing out a statement that has a lot of double quotes, it can get tiresome inserting a slash in front of every one. Another way to get around this issue is to use single quotes for the beginning and closing quotes of the `document.writeln()` statement. This way it won't see the double quotes as a closing quote.

Reviewing the Script

Congratulations—you are finished with your first script. We now have a script that delivers different content to users on different browsers. Let's take one last look at the entire script and quickly go over how we accomplished it.

```
<!-- Begin JavaScript to embed the proper CSS file
    depending on platform -->

<script language="JavaScript1.2">
<!-- Code after this will be ignored by older browsers

    // Assign the user information to a Variable
    var platform = navigator.platform.substr(0,3);
    var browser = navigator.appName;
    var version = navigator.appVersion.substr(0,1);

    // An if statement used to print out the proper css
file
    if ((platform == 'Mac') && (browser == 'Netscape') &&
    (version <= 4)) {
        document.writeln("<link rel=\"stylesheet\"
type=\"text/css\" href=\"styles_mac_4x.css\">");
    } else {
        document.writeln("<link rel=\"stylesheet\"
type=\"text/css\" href=\"styles_default.css\">");
    }
// Stop hiding the code here -->
</script>
```

Here are the steps we took to create this script:

1. We created our two different CSS files for use with our script.
2. We set up three variables to carry either the whole or a specific part of the value of several properties of the `navigator` object with the help of the `substr()` method.
3. We used the values of the `platform`, `browser`, and `version` variables as a test in an `if` statement to choose which statements we wanted our `if` statement to execute.
4. We used the `document.writeln()` method to dynamically print out the proper `<link>` tag.

Several new aspects of JavaScript were introduced in this first script, including

- Inserting scripts into HTML documents.
- Hiding scripts from non-JavaScript capable browsers.
- Inserting comments into JavaScript.
- An introduction to the JavaScript objects and their hierarchy.
- Creating a variable using an assignment operator to give it a value.
- A more detailed look at the `Navigator` object and three of its properties.
- The use of the `substr()` method.
- The syntax and use of an `if-else` statement.
- The `document.write` and `document.writeln` methods.
- Using the `\` to escape reserved characters.

◆ Project II: Dynamic Content Creation— Printing Out the Copyright Information and Last-Modified Date

Now that the boss knows that you can dynamically add content to a page, other possible uses have been brought up. One idea that he saw on a competitor's page was the addition of copyright information and the date a page was last modified to the bottom of each page on the site (Figure 1–4). The addition of the last-modified date will be especially helpful in the case of the Shelley Web site. Many people make changes to pages on the site, and it would be great if there were an easy way to tell if a file had been changed since you last edited it. Like most projects, even though 20 minutes ago the boss didn't know it could be done, it is now a high priority that must be done ASAP, so let's get started.

External JavaScript Files

In Project I we put our script directly into the HTML page itself, but for this project it will serve our purposes better to use an external file to hold our script. By using the external file, we can have a single location that the script is found in, as opposed to inserting our script into every page on the site, which would be quite a bit of work. In addition, if we ever want to change or add some-

FIGURE 1–4　Location of the last-modified date and copyright information.

thing to the script, we will only have to make the change in one place instead of all throughout the site.

The first thing we need to do is create a file that will hold our script. When creating a file to hold JavaScripts, use the file extension *.js*. So, open up your favorite HTML editor, create a new blank file, and save it as *jsFunctions.js*.

Great. Next we need to embed the external JavaScript file into the head of our HTML page.

```
<!-- Begin Embedding of js file -->

<script language="JavaScript" src="jsFunctions.js"></script>

<!-- end Embedding of js file -->
```

As always, we start by inserting an HTML comment that tells us what the following script does. Next, we insert our `<script>` tag; however, when embedding an external file, we need to take an extra step. We must specify the source property of the `<script>` tag and tell the JavaScript engine where the file we want to embed is located. In our case, we put it in the same directory as the rest of our HTML files, so we only need to insert the name of our script file, *jsFunctions.js*. Now we are ready to start writing our script.

Introduction of the Last-Modified Property

After a little research into the different properties of the DOCUMENT object, you come across a property that is going to make this project much easier. It looks as if we aren't the first people to think a last-modified date is a good idea. Those nice people who created JavaScript included the `lastModified` property to the DOCUMENT object. When a page is loaded and the JavaScript hierarchy is created, the engine goes to the HTTP header and gets the date of the last modification to the page and assigns it to the `lastModified` property. There is one drawback, however: Not all Web servers include this information in the header, so we have to use an `if` statement to make sure we only print it out if the value is given. But, hey, beggars can't be choosers, and an extra `if` statement will give us some more practice.

If the Web server doesn't provide a date, then the `lastModified` property will have a value of 0—we will use this value as our test in our `if` statement. The first step in our script is to create and assign a variable the value of the `lastModified` property. Let's put the first section of code into our external file.

```
// Assign the last modified date to the variable
lastmoddate
var lastmoddate = document.lastModified;
```

. . .

Notice above that we didn't insert a `<script>` tag into our external file. Because we are using the `<script>` tag to call the external file, the JavaScript engine already knows what follows is JavaScript. We also don't need to hide the script from an older browser in an HTML comment, because the source property of the `<script>` tag will be ignored by them and they will never call our external file.

You still want to use JavaScript comments to explain your code, though, so the first thing we did was insert one. On the next line, we create a variable called `lastmoddate` that will hold the value of the document object's `lastModified` property. Now let's set up an `if` statement to check if the `lastModified` property actually contains a date.

```
// Assign the last modified date to the variable
lastmoddate
var lastmoddate = document.lastModified;


// Create an if statement to test the value of lastmoddate
if(lastmoddate == 0) {
. . .
}
else {
. . .
}
```

The `if` statement in the preceding code is similar to the one that we used in our first script in this chapter; however, it is slightly less complicated in that it is testing only one condition. Therefore, if `lastmoddate` is equal to 0, the statements that follow will be executed, and if the value is anything else, then it will skip down to the statements that follow the `else`. Now that we have our `if` statement set up, let's look at what we want to print out as HTML.

In the previous script in this chapter, we used the `document.writeln()` method to print out a specified string as HTML. Because the script we are writing is in an external file and not placed where we want the data to print out, we must add another step to our script. We need to create a variable to temporarily hold the string data that we want to print onto the page. First, we insert the statement that will create and store the information we want to print out if there was no date found in the `lastModified` property. If this is the case, we want to print out two lines: The first is a line saying that the last-modified date is unknown, followed by an HTML line break and then the second line, which contains the copyright information.

```
// Assign the last modified date to the variable
lastmoddate
var lastmoddate = document.lastModified;


// Create an if statement to test the value of lastmoddate
if(lastmoddate == 0) {
```

```
var pageData = "Lastmodified: Unknown<BR>&copy;
2002 Copyright Shelley Biotech";
}
else {
. . .
}
```

In the above line of code we have created a variable called pageData and assigned a string that contains the fact that the last-modified date is unknown as well as the copyright information for the page. With that done, we now need to insert the code that will create and store the information needed if there was a date given in the lastModified property. To get the information we need for this section, we must combine the value held in the lastmoddate variable with the rest of the string we wish to print out and place it in the pageData variable. We accomplish this with the following line of code:

```
var pageData = "Lastmodified:" + lastmoddate +
"<BR>&copy; 2002 Copyright Shelley Biotech";
```

To combine the different types of data, we use the concatenation operator (+). This operator takes two or more strings and combines them to return a new string. Even though the variable lastmoddate isn't a string itself, the value that it holds is a string, so this method will work. Therefore, in this line we are first combining the string Lastmodified: with the value held within lastmoddate and then combining that new string with a string that contains an HTML line break and the copyright information. Let's see how this line of code looks in the rest of the script:

```
// Assign the last modified date to the variable
lastmoddate
var lastmoddate = document.lastModified;

// Create an if statement to test the value of lastmoddate
if(lastmoddate == 0) {
    var pageData = "Lastmodified:
Unknown<BR>&copy; 2002 Copyright Shelley Biotech";
}
else {
    var pageData = "Lastmodified:" + lastmoddate +
"<BR>&copy; 2002 Copyright Shelley Biotech";
}
```

Dynamically Printing Nonstring Data

That finishes up the code we need to put into our external file. Now we need to place a small script within the HTML page itself at the location where we want to print out the last-modified date and the copyright information. Since this information is not page-specific content that a typical user needs to read, we'll place it at the following point at the bottom of our HTML pages.

```
</table>
<script language="JavaScript1.2">
<!-- Code after this will be ignored by older browsers

.  .  .


// Stop hiding the code here -->
</script>
</body>
</html>
```

All we need to do in this script is print out the value that is held inside of our pageData variable. We use the document.writeln() method, as we did in our first project, but with a slight twist this time. Because we want the method to print out the value that pageData contains, and not the word pageData itself, we have to let it know that what is between the parentheses is a variable and not a string. To do this, we simply do not surround the contents of the parentheses with quotation marks; this tells the method that it needs to treat pageData as a variable and that it should print out its contents. With that said, let's add our last line of code.

```
</table>
<script language="JavaScript1.2">
<!-- Code after this will be ignored by older browsers

document.writeln(pageData);


// Stop hiding the code here -->
</script>
</body>
</html>
```

Reviewing the Script

We now have a script that dynamically prints out the last-modified date and the copyright information on all pages in which we place the script. As with all of our scripts in the book, we will take a look at the completed script, how we did it, and what new areas we covered in the process. Because there are three parts to this script, let's look at each piece one at a time.

```
<!-- Begin Embedding of js file -->

<script language="JavaScript"
src="jsFunctions.js"></script>

<!-- end Embedding of js file -->
```

First, we created our external JavaScript file, called *jsFunction.js*, and used the source property of the `<script>` tag to embed it into our HTML pages.

Next, we created our main script.

```
// Assign the last modified date to the variable
lastmoddate
var lastmoddate = document.lastModified;

// Create an if statement to test the value of lastmoddate
if(lastmoddate == 0) {
      var pageData = "Lastmodified:
Unknown<BR>&copy; 2002 Copyright Shelley Biotech";
}
else {
      var pageData = "Lastmodified:" + lastmoddate
+ "<BR>&copy; 2002 Copyright Shelley Biotech";
}
```

Here are the steps we took to create this script:

1. We assigned the value of the `document.lastModified` property to the variable `lastmoddate`.
2. We created an `if` statement to check if the Web server actually passed a last-modified date to the JavaScript engine.
3. We created a variable called `pageData` and assigned it a string value that says that the last-modified date is

unknown, and provides the copyright information if there was no date contained in the variable `lastmoddate`.

4. We created a variable called `pageData` and assigned it a string value that says the date contained in the `lastmoddate` variable and provides the copyright information if a last-modified date was given.

5. We inserted the script that will print out the value of variable `pageData` using the `document.writeln()` method.

```
<script language="JavaScript1.2">
<!-- Code after this will be ignored by older browsers

document.writeln(pageData);

// Stop hiding the code here -->
</script>
```

Let's look at the new concepts that we have used in this project.

-   We learned how to create and embed an external JavaScript file.
-   We were introduced to the `lastModified` property of the DOCUMENT object.
-   We learned how to combine strings and nonstring values with the use of the concatenation operator (+).
-   We learned how to have the `document.writeln()` method print out the value of a variable.

RECAP

We have gotten off to a great start with the Shelley Biotech Web site; in a relatively short time, we added two very useful new features to the site. As time passes and there are new browsers on the market that handle HTML a little differently, being able to get user information and customize your pages for them is becoming ever more important. The other area that we touched on in this chapter, dynamic creation of content, is an area of JavaScript that has major potential for making the upkeep and maintenance of a Web site more efficient. As we get further into this book, we will see many examples of what we can accomplish using these concepts.

ADVANCED PROJECTS

The first two scripts are fairly simple examples of what you can accomplish with platform/browser detection and dynamic HTML generation. Here are several other project ideas that use these techniques. You can implement them into your Web pages, which will give you a better understanding of the great stuff you can accomplish:

1. Use browser detection to dynamically create whole pages that are customized to work with specific browser versions.

2. Create a page that will gather all of the information contained in the NAVIGATOR object, and dynamically generate a table that will display that information to the user (this is very useful as a development tool).

2 Image Rollovers

IN THIS CHAPTER

- Project I: Image Rollover Script
- Project II: Multiple Image Rollover Script
- Project III: Random Banner Ad Rotator Script
- Recap
- Advanced Projects

You've gotten the ball rolling on the site and have shown that you've got what it takes to get the job done—now your boss wants you to wow him. He wants to make the site more dynamic and give it a little bit of "flash." He has checked out the competition's sites, and they all have image rollovers on theirs—JavaScript rollovers are used to swap an image with a different version of that image when the user moves the cursor over it. Conversely, when the user moves the cursor off of the image, the new image is replaced with the original. This technique is widely used on Web pages, and your boss feels this is just what your site needs to spruce it up.

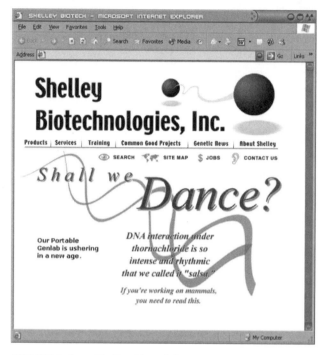

FIGURE 2–1　Shelley Biotech homepage.

The first thing to do is choose which graphics we want to be affected by the rollovers. The best place for image rollovers on most pages is on the main navigation images, and the Shelley Biotech site is no different (see Figure 2–1).

One of the designers has come up with a great graphic treatment for the rollovers (see Figure 2–2), and it's now up to you to implement them. There are three parts to creating an image rollover: Define the IMAGE objects, create the functions that will do the work, and insert the necessary JavaScript event handlers into your image and anchor tags. The first step in writing our script is the creation of the IMAGE objects.

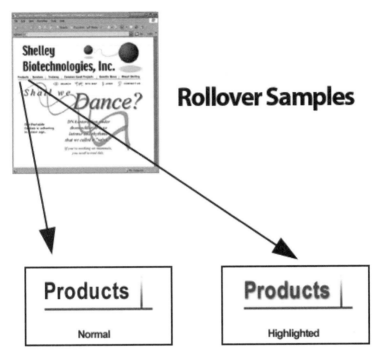

FIGURE 2-2   Image rollover sample.

◆ Project I: Image Rollover Script

Creating and Inserting the Image Objects

Before we get to the creation of the image objects themselves, we must decide where to put our script. Because the rollovers will be on every page of the site, it makes sense to place our script into an external JavaScript file. That way, we only need to place it in a single location instead of on each page. We have already created an external JavaScript file called *jsFunctions.js* for one of our previous projects, so we can simply add our new script to that file. The home page already has the call to the external file, so we can just copy that `<script>` tag to all of the other pages on the site.

The first step in our script is to cloak for older browsers that don't support the IMAGE object, which is necessary for our rollover script. In Chapter 1 we learned how to use JavaScript to gather the browser and platform information. We could use a variation of that method in which we set up a bunch of `if` statements that test for every browser that doesn't support the IMAGE object; however, this would be loads of work. Fortunately for us, there is a simpler way. We can test if the user's browser supports rollovers using only a single `if` statement, as shown in the following lines of code:

```
// Creation of the image objects
if (document.images) {
.  .  .
}
```

In the preceding lines of code we used

```
document.images
```

as the condition in our `if` statement. The condition returns a value of `true` if the browser supports the IMAGE object and a value of `false` if it does not. By inserting our code within this `if` statement, we are in effect cloaking our code from browsers that cannot handle the script.

When an HTML page is loaded and the browser creates the objects that make up the JavaScript hierarchy, every image laid out on the page is made into an object and put into an array called `images`. This is the first time we have come across arrays, so let's take a quick look at what an array is and, in particular, the `images` array and how we are going to use it.

You can think of an array as a filing cabinet. Let's say you have a page with four images on it. When the browser reads the HTML file, it goes down the page, and when it reaches the first image, it creates an IMAGE object for it and stores it in the first drawer of our filing cabinet. When it reaches the second image, it again creates a new IMAGE object, and then puts it into the second drawer of the filing cabinet, and so on until each of the images on the page has its own IMAGE object, which is stored in its own drawer.

When the browser needs to reference any of those images, it knows in which drawer to look for each of them. You, too, can reference the array and the IMAGE objects held therein—there are two ways to do this. The first is to reference the location in the array at which the IMAGE object resides. The problem with this method is that if you add an image somewhere on the page, the position of all of the images below it will change. This will cause you to go through your whole script and make sure an image you were calling isn't now in a different position. The second way, which we use in this script, takes care of this problem.

If you specify a NAME attribute in your <img> tags, you can then reference that graphic in the array by the name that you have assigned to it. With this method, even if you add other graphics to the page, you will still be able to reference the IMAGE object the same way, and your script won't be adversely affected.

There are six navigation images that will be affected by our rollover script, so for each of those images, we need to assign a NAME attribute in the <img> tags.

```
<a href="products.html"><img
src="images/products_off.gif" width=71 height=33
border=0 name="Products" alt="Products"></a>

<a href="services.html"><img
src="images/services_off.gif" width=67 height=33
border=0 name="Services" alt="Services"></a>

<a href="training.html"><img
src="images/training_off.gif" width=75 height=33
border=0 name="Training" alt="Training"></a>

<a href="common.html"><img
src="images/common_off.gif" width=157 height=33
border=0 name="Common" alt="Common Good"></a>

<a href="genetic.html"><img
src="images/news_off.gif" width=98 height=33
border=0 name="News" alt="Genetic News"></a>

<a href="about.html"><img
src="images/about_off.gif" width=106 height=33
border=0 name="About" alt="About Shelley"></a>
```

In the preceding lines of HTML, we added a NAME attribute to each of the six <img> tags. The name for each is the first word of the category that the graphic represents. JavaScript is case-sensitive, so take notice that the first letter of each name is capitalized. Now that we have the names of these images squared away, we can move on to the creation of some new IMAGE objects that we will need for our script.

Because the images that we want to come up when the user rolls over one of the six graphics aren't explicitly placed on the page with HTML, we need to create two new IMAGE objects for each image we want to roll over. This will add these images to the images array and allow us to access their properties. Let's start by creating the IMAGE objects for the Products image.

```
// Creation of the image objects
if (document.images) {
ProductsOn=new Image(71, 33);
. . .
}
```

In this first line, we initialize a new IMAGE object by using an image constructor, the syntax for which is

```
New Image(width, height);
```

By putting the image constructor on the right-hand side of the assignment operator, and the name that we wish the IMAGE object to have on the left, we have just created a new IMAGE object called ProductsOn.

The naming of these new objects is very important to the operation of the script. The first part of the name should be the same as the name of the image to which it corresponds that is already on the page. For example, in this first line, we created an object to hold the location of the rolled over version of the Products graphic, so the name starts with Products. Because this object holds the rolled over version of the graphic, the second part of the name is On. When combined, we have a new object with the name ProductsOn. For each of the six navigation images, we need not only an object to hold the rolled over version of the graphic but one to hold a regular version of the graphic as well. This second object's name for our Products image will also start with Products but will end with Off. Let's add this new IMAGE object after our first one.

```
// Creation of the image objects
if (document.images) {
```

```
ProductsOn=new Image(71, 33);
. . .
ProductsOff=new Image(71, 33);
. . .
}
```

If you deviate from this naming convention, the functions that we will be writing won't know which IMAGE object to use for replacement, and you will get errors. We now have the two new IMAGE objects that we will need for the Products rollover, but at the moment they are empty. We need to assign actual images to them. We do this by assigning the location (URL) of the image to the source property of the IMAGE object, as follows:

```
// Creation of the image objects
if (document.images) {
    ProductsOn=new Image(71, 33);
    ProductsOn.src="images/products_on.gif";

    ProductsOff=new Image(71, 33);
    ProductsOff.src="images/products_off.gif";
    . . .
}
```

We have completed On and Off objects for the Products rollover, but we now have to create objects for each of the other five image rollovers. We do this using the same naming conventions that we used for our first objects.

```
// Creation of the image objects
if (document.images) {
    ProductsOn=new Image(71, 33);
    ProductsOn.src="images/products_on.gif";

    ProductsOff=new Image(71, 33);
    ProductsOff.src="images/products_off.gif";


    ServicesOn=new Image(67, 33);
    ServicesOn.src="images/services_on.gif";

    ServicesOff=new Image(67, 33);
    ServicesOff.src="images/services_off.gif";


    TrainingOn=new Image(75, 33);
```

```
TrainingOn.src="images/training_on.gif";

TrainingOff=new Image(75, 33);
TrainingOff.src="images/training_off.gif";


CommonOn=new Image(157, 33);
CommonOn.src="images/common_on.gif";

CommonOff=new Image(157, 33);
CommonOff.src="images/common_off.gif";


NewsOn=new Image(98, 33);
NewsOn.src="images/news_on.gif";

NewsOff=new Image(98, 33);
NewsOff.src="images/news_off.gif";


AboutOn=new Image(106, 33);
AboutOn.src="images/about_on.gif";

AboutOff=new Image(106, 33);
AboutOff.src="images/about_off.gif";
}
    . . .
```

Creating the IMAGE objects in this manner also has another desired effect. When the browser creates the new IMAGE objects, it loads the images into its cache, thereby preloading it into memory. This preloading allows the image to display immediately upon rollover. It is important to keep this preloading in mind when creating your HTML pages—if you do not put Height, Width, and alt attributes into your <img> tags, some browsers will wait to display any of the page until all of the content and images are loaded into memory. You can run into some serious load times if you have a lot of IMAGE objects loading for rollovers in the background, so make sure you put all of the necessary tags into your HTML.

We have now created IMAGE objects for all of the graphics that we need to accomplish our rollovers. Our next step is the creation of the functions that will run our rollovers.

Image Rollover Functions

When the user rolls over one of our graphics, JavaScript event handlers call the functions we are going to write to actually perform the image replacements. Functions are an essential part of JavaScript; a function is a set of JavaScript statements that perform specific tasks. We cover both defining and calling functions in this example, but for now, let's concentrate on defining the functions we need for our rollovers. To define a function, you need four basic elements: the *function* keyword, a name for the function, a set of arguments that are separated with commas, and the statements that you want the function to execute.

We need to create two functions for our rollovers to work: one that switches to the `on` graphic when we roll onto an image and another to switch back to the `off` graphic when we roll off the image. Generally, you should define the functions for a page in the `<head>` of your HTML, so let's start our functions right after our `IMAGE` objects.

```
// function to turn on rolled over graphic
function on(pic) {
.  .  .
}
```

The first step in defining a function is to call the function keyword followed by the name of our function; in this case, we'll call it `on`. Following the name, within its set of parentheses, we need to put a list of variables separated by commas, one for each argument we want to pass into the function. These variables will let us pass values into our function from the event handlers that call the function. We need to pass only a single argument into our function; we'll use the variable `pic` to hold that argument.

Next, we need to insert the set of instructions that we want the function to execute—these statements are enclosed within curly brackets.

```
// function to turn on rolled over graphic
function on(pic) {
    if (document.images) {
       document.images[pic].src=eval(pic + "On.src");
    }
}
```

The first of the statements that we want the function to execute is an `if` statement that will check for older browsers. If the browser supports the IMAGE object, the next line will be executed. In this line, we tell the browser to replace the source of the image that is being rolled over with the source of the On version of the graphic. A lot is happening in this line, so let's break it down into smaller parts. First, let's look at the left-hand side of the assignment operator.

```
document.images[pic].src
```

We reference the source property of the image located at the position in the images array that has the value of the variable pic, so let's say the value of pic is Products. We would be referencing the source property of the Products IMAGE object and assigning it the value passed to it from the right-hand side of the assignment operator.

If we explicitly reference the images, like so:

```
document.product.src
```

we need separate functions for every image we wanted a rollover for—not the most efficient way to code. When scripting, you always should think about how you can most efficiently write your code. Any time you can use variables in this way, it will save you a lot of time and trouble. There are, however, occasions when you will want to call a specific image every time the function is called, and the preceding line of code is an example of how to do that.

On the right side of the operator, we use the eval() statement to combine the value of pic with a string to create a new value to assign as the source of the image being rolled over.

```
eval(pic + "On.src");
```

If the value of pic is Products, the eval() statement will return ProductsOn.src, and the value of the source of the ProductsOn IMAGE object will be assigned to the source of the Products IMAGE object. When this happens, the image on the page will change to the On image until the user rolls off.

When the user rolls off the image, another function will be called. This is the second function that we have to create—let's call this function off.

```
// function to turn off rolled over graphic

function off(pic) {
```

```
if(document.images) {
    document.images[pic].src= eval(pic + "Off.src");
    }
}
```

This function should look similar to your `on` function; in fact, the only difference is that the second half of what is being evaluated on the right-hand side of the assignment operator is `Off.src` instead of `On.src`. Therefore, when this line is evaluated, it will assign the source of the `ProductsOff` IMAGE object to be the source of the `Products` IMAGE object, thereby returning the image to its regular look.

Our functions are now complete and we are almost finished with the script. All that's left for us to do is to put the proper Java-Script event handlers into our HTML code.

Creating and Inserting the Event Handlers

You will find that most things in JavaScript are event-driven—events generally are the result of some action on the part of the user. If a user rolls over a link or changes the value of a text field, these would constitute events. To make use of these events with your JavaScript, you must define an event handler to react to these events. There are many predefined event handlers that you can use for this purpose; the two that we use for our rollovers are `onMouseOver` and `onMouseOut`. Let's first see what our existing HTML looks like without the event handlers.

```
<a href="products/index.html"><img
src="images/products_off.gif" width=71 height=33
border=0 name="Products" alt="Products"></a>
```

For our purposes, we must add the event handlers to the ANCHOR tag. First, we add the `onMouseOver` handler.

```
<a href="products/index.html"
onMouseOver="on('Products'); return true;">
```

When an event handler is called, it executes any JavaScript statements that follow the handler. We enclose these statements in quotes and separate them with semicolons. The first thing we want our event handler to do is call our `on` function. To call a function, you simply call its name and enclose any arguments you wish to pass along to the function in parentheses separated by commas.

```
on('Products');
```

The preceding statement calls the `on` function and passes it the value `Products`; again, we are passing it `Products` because that is the name of the image that we want our function to affect.

Another often seen addition to rollovers is the display of a relevant phrase in the browser's status bar. To do this, we add another statement to our event handler.

```
<a href="products/index.html" onMouseOver="on('Products');
window.status='Products'; return true;">
```

By calling on the `WINDOW` object's `status` property, we can display text in the browser's status bar by assigning it a new value. The last addition that we need to make to our event handler is the following statement:

```
return true;
```

This tells the JavaScript engine that this is the end of what needs to be executed in the event handler and it can go on with the rest of its business.

Well, one event handler down, and one more to go. Let's add our `onMouseOut` handler to take care of things when the user rolls off an image.

```
<a href="products/index.html" onMouseOver="on('Products');
window.status='Products'; return true; "
onMouseOut="off('Products'); window.status=' '; return
true;">
```

For our `onMouseOut` handler, we call the `off` function, again passing it the name of the graphic that we want to affect. To turn off the phrase that we put into the status bar, we now reset the `window.status` to a blank value and then leave the handler with the `return` statement.

Now that we have inserted the event handlers for the `Products` image, we need to put some in for the rest of the images we want to have rollovers for. The syntax will be the same, the only difference being that you have to change the value that you are passing to the functions to the name of the graphic that you want to be changed.

```
<a href="products/index.html" onMouseOver="on('Products');
window.status='Products'; return true; "
```

```
onMouseOut="off('Products'); window.status=' '; return
true;"><img src="images/products_off.gif" width=71
height=33 border=0 name="Products" alt="Products"></a>

<a href="services/index.html" onMouseOver="on('Services');
window.status='Services'; return true; "
onMouseOut="off('Services'); window.status=' '; return
true;"><img src="images/services_off.gif" width=67
height=33 border=0 name="Services" alt="Services"></a>

<a href="training/index.html" onMouseOver="on('Training');
window.status='Training'; return true; "
onMouseOut="off('Training'); window.status=' '; return
true;"><img src="images/training_off.gif" width=75
height=33 border=0 name="Training" alt="Training"></a>

<a href="common/index.html" onMouseOver="on('Common');
window.status='Common Good Projects'; return true; "
onMouseOut="off('Common'); window.status=' '; return
true;"><img src="images/common_off.gif" width=157 height=33
border=0 name="Common" alt="Common Good"></a>

<a href="genetic/index.html" onMouseOver="on('News');
window.status='Genetic News'; return true; "
onMouseOut="off('News'); window.status=' '; return
true;"><img src="images/news_off.gif" width=98 height=33
border=0 name="News" alt="Genetic News"></a>

<a href="about/index.html" onMouseOver="on('About');
window.status='About Shelly Biotechnologies'; return true;
" onMouseOut="off('About'); window.status=' '; return
true;"><img src="images/about_off.gif" width=106 height=33
border=0 name="About" alt="About Shelley"></a>
```

Reviewing the Script

We should now have all of the elements that we need to get our
Web site up and running with some great rollovers. Let's take a look
at the completed script and go over what we did in each section.

First, we created the IMAGE objects that we need in our script.

```
// Creation of the image objects
if (document.images) {
    ProductsOn=new Image(71, 33);
    ProductsOn.src="images/products_on.gif";

    ProductsOff=new Image(71, 33);
```

```
ProductsOff.src="images/products_off.gif";


ServicesOn=new Image(67, 33);
ServicesOn.src="images/services_on.gif";

ServicesOff=new Image(67, 33);
ServicesOff.src="images/services_off.gif";


TrainingOn=new Image(75, 33);
TrainingOn.src="images/training_on.gif";

TrainingOff=new Image(75, 33);
TrainingOff.src="images/training_off.gif";


CommonOn=new Image(157, 33);
CommonOn.src="images/common_on.gif";

CommonOff=new Image(157, 33);
CommonOff.src="images/common_off.gif";


NewsOn=new Image(98, 33);
NewsOn.src="images/news_on.gif";

NewsOff=new Image(98, 33);
NewsOff.src="images/news_off.gif";


AboutOn=new Image(106, 33);
AboutOn.src="images/about_on.gif";

AboutOff=new Image(106, 33);
AboutOff.src="images/about_off.gif";
}
```

Here are the steps we took in creating the needed IMAGE objects:

1. We set up cloaking for browsers that do not support IMAGE objects.
2. We added the NAME attribute to the six images that we want to put rollovers on.
3. We created a set of two new IMAGE objects for each of the six images that will be affected by our rollover script.

4. We assigned each of the IMAGE object's source property the location of the proper image file.

Next, we created the functions that run our rollovers.

```
// function to turn on rolled over graphic
function on(pic) {
    if (document.images) {
      document.images[pic].src=eval(pic + "On.src");
    }
}

// function to turn off rolled over graphic
function off(pic) {
      if(document.images) {
      document.images[pic].src= eval(pic + "Off.src");
    }
  }
```

Here are the steps we took in creating the rollover functions:

1. We first created a new function called on that changes the image the user is currently over to the rolled over version of that graphic.
2. We wrote a function called off that changed the graphic back to its default state when the user rolled off of it.

Finally, we made the necessary changes to the <a href> tags in the existing HTML.

```
<a href="products/index.html" onMouseOver="on('Products');
window.status='Products'; return true; "
onMouseOut="off('Products'); window.status=' '; return
true;"><img src="images/products_off.gif" width=71
height=33 border=0 name="Products" alt="Products"></a>

<a href="services/index.html" onMouseOver="on('Services');
window.status='Services'; return true; "
onMouseOut="off('Services'); window.status=' '; return
true;"><img src="images/services_off.gif" width=67
height=33 border=0 name="Services" alt="Services"></a>

<a href="training/index.html" onMouseOver="on('Training');
window.status='Training'; return true; "
onMouseOut="off('Training'); window.status=' '; return
true;"><img src="images/training_off.gif" width=75
height=33 border=0 name="Training" alt="Training"></a>
```

```
<a href="common/index.html" onMouseOver="on('Common');
window.status='Common Good Projects'; return true; "
onMouseOut="off('Common'); window.status=' '; return
true;"><img src="images/common_off.gif" width=157 height=33
border=0 name="Common" alt="Common Good"></a>

<a href="genetic/index.html" onMouseOver="on('News');
window.status='Genetic News'; return true; "
onMouseOut="off('News'); window.status=' '; return
true;"><img src="images/news_off.gif" width=98 height=33
border=0 name="News" alt="Genetic News"></a>

<a href="about/index.html" onMouseOver="on('About');
window.status='About Shelly Biotechnologies'; return true;"
onMouseOut="off('About'); window.status=' '; return
true;"><img src="images/about_off.gif" width=106 height=33
border=0 name="About" alt="About Shelley"></a>
```

Here are the steps we took to insert the event handlers into the HTML:

1. We added the `onMouseOver` event handlers to each of the six images' `<a href>` tags. Within that handler we called the `On` function, passing it the name of the graphic that we were rolling over, changed the status bar to display a new message, and added the `return` command to exit the handler.

2. We added the `onMouseOut` event handlers to each of the six images' `<a href>` tags. Within that handler we called the `Off` function, passing it the name of the graphic that we were rolling over, reset the status bar to nothing, and added the `return` command to exit the handler.

We introduced several new aspects of JavaScript in this first script, including

*   A new method of cloaking that looks for browsers that support specific objects that are needed in your script.
*   An introduction to arrays, specifically the `images` array.
*   How to create new IMAGE objects and how to change their source property.
*   How to create a function.
*   The concept of event handlers and how to use two of them: `onMouseOver` and `onMouseOut`.

- How to change the message being displayed in the status bar of the browser window.

◆ Project II: Multiple Image Rollover Script

It's that time of the year when the company puts out its annual report. This year the public relations department wants to make it available online. Most of it has already been posted, but there is one section that they could use a little help on. In the section of the report that deals with the sales figures, there is a set of graphs that compares sales over the last three years. The public relations department would like it if users could compare the charts for adjoining years. In other words, they want to be able to compare 1998 to 1999, and 1999 to 2000, and finally 2000 to 2001. After seeing the magic you've worked with the navigation rollovers, they wonder if you can set up this functionality with JavaScript rollovers instead of just laying out all of the graph comparisons in a huge page.

After some research and a little tinkering around with one of the designers, you think you have a way to give them what they are looking for, so you show them what you've worked out. Figure 2–3 shows what the page would look like before the user rolls over one of the year sets. Figure 2–4 shows what would happen if the user rolls over 2000–2001. They love the idea and tell you to get started on it.

First, let's look at the HTML for the section of the page that we are concerned with.

```
<tr>

    <td valign="top" align="left">
        <br><br><img
src="images/sales_comp_left_default.gif" alt=""
width="162" height="87" border="0"></td>

    <td valign="top" align="center">
        <font class="blkBldText">Year to Year Sales
Comparison</font><br>
        <br>
        <a href=" " class="blueLink">2000 - 2001</a><br>
        <br>
        <a href=" " class="blueLink">1999 - 2000</a><br>
```

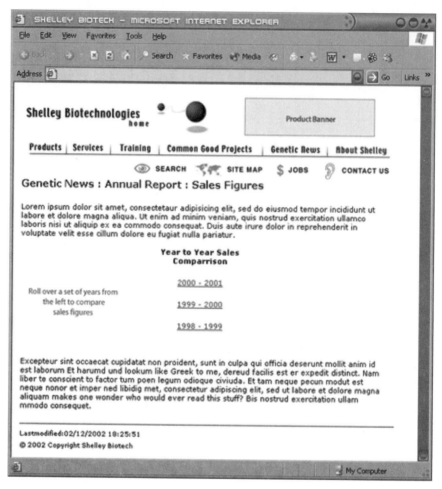

FIGURE 2–3   Shelley Biotech annual report page.

```
            <br>
            <a href=" " class="blueLink">1998 - 1999</a></td>
      <td vlaign="top" align="left">
            <br><br><img src="images/
sales_comp_right_default.gif" alt="" width="162"
height="87" border="0"></td>
      </tr>
```

The designer on the project has gone ahead and created some temporary images for us to use until they get the final chart graphics done. In the existing HTML, you will notice that there

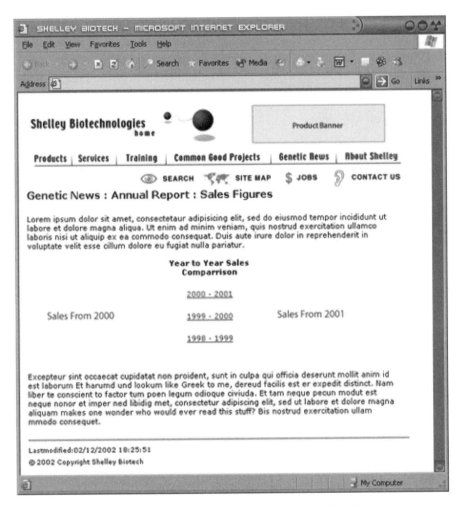

FIGURE 2–4   Annual report page—with a year set highlighted.

are two images that we will have to switch out when the user rolls over a set of years: `sales_comp_left_default.gif` and `sales_comp_right_default.gif`. At the moment, the image that goes on the left has instructions for the user, while the image on the right is a plain white image. When a user rolls over a set of years, the image on the left will change to a chart of the first year in the set, while the image on the right will change to a chart of the second year in the set. Luckily, this is fairly similar to what we did in the previous project, so we'll be able to use the functions we wrote for the navigation rollovers as a starting point for our functions here. But first we need to create the image objects we will need for the project.

Creating and Inserting the Image Objects

As stated above, the designer has created temporary chart graphics for each of the four years we need to use in our comparisons. They are called:

```
sales_1998.gif
sales_1999.gif
sales_2000.gif
sales_2001.gif
```

To use them in our script, we need to create an IMAGE object for each of them. Because this script will be used only on this page, there is no need to put our script into an external JavaScript file, so let's insert it into the <head> of the HTML page.

```
<head>
<script Language="JavaScript1.2">
<!-- Code after this will be ignored by older browsers

// Creating Image Objects for Rollovers
if (document.images) {
sales2001=new Image(162, 87);
sales2001.src="images/sales_2001.gif";

sales2000=new Image(162, 87);
sales2000.src="images/sales_2000.gif";

sales1999=new Image(162, 87);
sales1999.src="images/sales_1999.gif";

sales1998=new Image(162, 87);
sales1998.src="images/sales_1998.gif";
}


     . . .
// -->
</script>
```

Just as in our previous project, we've inserted the script tag, cloaked the script from older browsers, and created the IMAGE objects that we'll need for our script.

Now that we have all of the IMAGE objects that we will need, let's go on to the next step of our script—modifying the rollover functions.

Inserting the Rollover Functions

Let's take a look at the functions we are using for our navigation rollovers. First, the on function will replace the image of the category name that the user rolls over with a highlighted image. Then the off function changes the image back to the default version once the user rolls off of it. What's different in our current project is that we need the script to swap out not one but two images each time the on function is called; likewise, when the user rolls off of a set of years, the off function needs to turn both of the changed images back to the default versions that show up when the page is loaded. To get started, let's copy the on and off functions from the jsFunctions.js file and paste them underneath our new IMAGE objects.

```
<head>
<script Language="JavaScript1.2">
<!-- Code after this will be ignored by older browsers

// Creating Image Objects for Rollovers
if (document.images) {
sales2001=new Image(162, 87);
sales2001.src="images/sales_2001.gif";

sales2000=new Image(162, 87);
sales2000.src="images/sales_2000.gif";

sales1999=new Image(162, 87);
sales1999.src="images/sales_1999.gif";

sales1998=new Image(162, 87);
sales1998.src="images/sales_1998.gif";
}


// function to turn on rolled over graphic
function on(pic)  {
    if (document.images)  {
        document.images[pic].src=eval(pic + "On.src");
    }
}

// function to turn off rolled over graphic
```

```
function off(pic)  {
    if(document.images)  {
        document.images[pic].src= eval(pic + "Off.src");
    }
}
```

The first thing we need to do is change JavaScript comments and the names of the functions so that they don't conflict with the functions that control the navigation rollover functions. Let's call these new functions salesOn and salesOff.

```
// function to turn on sales comparison charts
function salesOn(pic)  {
    if (document.images)  {
        document.images[pic].src=eval(pic + "On.src");
    }
}

// function to turn off sales comparison charts
function salesOff(pic)  {
    if(document.images)  {
        document.images[pic].src= eval(pic + "Off.src");
    }
}
```

Now, let's make the changes to the salesOn function. Because we need this function to change two graphics, we need to create two variables to accept values passed in from the event handlers: one for the name of the image to be swapped out for the left-hand image and one for the name of the image that will show up on the right-hand side. Let's call these variables salesPic1 and salesPic2. These will replace the pic variable in our initial function declaration.

```
// function to turn on sales comparison charts
function salesOn(salesPic1, salesPic2)  {
    if (document.images)  {
        document.images[pic].src=eval(pic + ".src");
            . . .
    }
}
```

Next, we need to modify the line of code that will change out the image that will show up on the left-hand side. Now, because we are always going to be changing the same image on the left-hand side, we can specify exactly which image we want changed instead of using a variable as we did for the navigation images. So, where we had specified

```
document.image[pic].src
```

in the line that changes the navigation image, we will specify the image called `salesLeft` in our new line of code.

```
document.images['salesLeft'].src
```

On the right-hand side of the assignment operator, however, the image we want to show up will depend on which set of years the user has rolled over. We will use the `salesPic1` variable that is being passed into the function from the event handler to specify which year IMAGE object we want to use as the source for the image.

```
=eval(salesPic1 + ".src");
```

Let's see what our modified line of code looks like in the script.

```
// function to turn on sales comparison charts
function salesOn(salesPic1, salesPic2)  {
    if (document.images)  {

    document.images['salesLeft'].src=eval(salesPic1 +
".src");
        . . .

    }
}
```

This newly modified line will take care of turning on the proper year graphic for the left-hand side; now we need to add another line that will do the same for the right-hand side.

```
// function to turn on sales comparison charts
function salesOn(salesPic1, salesPic2)  {
    if (document.images)  {

    document.images['salesLeft'].src=eval(salesPic1 +
".src");
    document.images['salesRight'].src=eval(salesPic2 +
".src");
        }
}
```

This line is pretty much identical to the first line, except that we are specifying the `salesRight` image to change and for the script to use the year held in `salesPic2` as the new IMAGE object.

That will do it for the `On` function. Let's move on to the `off` function for the last step in our script functions. Here is the current `off` function.

```
// function to turn off sales comparison charts
function salesOff(pic)  {
    if(document.images)  {
        document.images[pic].src= eval(pic + "Off.src");
    }
}
```

Now let's add the two lines of code that will turn the chart graphics back to their default states once the user has rolled off the set of years.

```
function salesOff(pic) {
    if(document.images) {
        document.images['salesLeft].src= "images/
sales_comp_left_default.gif";
        document.images['salesRight'].src= "images/
sales_comp_right_default.gif";
    }
}
```

As in our `On` function, on the left-hand side of the assignment operator we are explicitly telling the JavaScript engine which images we want to change. On the right-hand side, though, we are doing something new: In the past we have always specified for the engine to look in the `source` property of another image object for the IMAGE we want to replace. However, because no matter which set of years the user has rolled over, we want to replace it with the original default images, when the user rolls off, we can explicitly tell the JavaScript engine the path to those images, which is what we have done above.

Well, that's it for the changes to the functions; we now simply have to add the event handlers to the right links and we'll be done.

Creating and Inserting the Event Handlers

We will not be swapping out an image that the user has rolled over, as we did in the previous project. Instead, we will swap out two other images when the user has rolled over a text link, so we will place the event handlers inside `<a href>` tags that are around the text instead of around an image. The event handlers don't really care what is used as the rollover focus, so we can put them in most any object on a page. In this case we're using the text links of the years that the sales charts compare.

```
<a href=" " class="blueLink">2000 - 2001</a><br>
<br>
<a href=" " class="blueLink">1999 - 2000</a><br>
<br>
<a href=" " class="blueLink">1998 - 1999</a>
```

Before we insert the handlers, we first need to add the name attribute to the left- and right-hand graphics that we are specifying in our functions.

```
<td valign="top" align="left">
    <br><br><img src="images/
sales_comp_left_default.gif" alt="" width="162"
height="87" border="0" name="salesLeft"></td>


<td valign="top" align="center">
    <font class="blkBldText">Year to Year Sales
Comparrison</font><br>
    <br>
    <a href=" " class="blueLink">2000 - 2001</a><br>
    <br>
    <a href=" " class="blueLink">1999 - 2000</a><br>
    <br>
    <a href=" " class="blueLink">1998 - 1999</a></td>
    <td valign="top" align="left">
    <br><br><img src="images/
sales_comp_right_default.gif" alt="" width="162"
height="87" border="0" name="salesRight"></td>
```

With that done, we can move on to inserting the handlers. The event handlers are going to be very similar to the handlers that we used in our navigation rollovers; there will be both an onMouseOver and onMouseOut. The difference is that we will be calling our new sales functions instead of the rollover functions. We will also not worry about changing the text that shows up in the status bar of the browser. Let's look at link for the years 2000–2001 with the new handlers inserted.

```
<a href=" " class="blueLink"
onMouseOver="salesOn('sales2000', 'sales2001'); return
true;" onMouseOut="salesOff(); return true;">2000 - 2001
</a>
```

In the onMouseOver handler, we are calling the salesOn() function and passing it the two years that we want to compare, first the year we want to show up on the left-hand side, then the year that shows up on the right-hand side. To pass multiple values into a function, you simply need to separate them with a comma. In the onMouseOut handler, we are calling the salesOff() function without passing any values into it. This is because we already know which images we need to change and what we need to change them back to. Let's add the handlers to the two other text links on the page.

```
<a href=" " class="blueLink"
onMouseOver="salesOn('sales2000', 'sales2001'); return
true;" onMouseOut="salesOff(); return true;">2000 - 2001
</a><br>
<br>
<a href=" " class="blueLink"
onMouseOver="salesOn('sales1999', 'sales2000'); return
true;" onMouseOut="salesOff(); return true;">1999 - 2000
</a><br>
<br>
<a href=" " class="blueLink"
onMouseOver="salesOn('sales1998', 'sales1999'); return
true;" onMouseOut="salesOff(); return true;">1998 - 1999
</a>
```

We now have handlers inserted for the other two sets of years that we want to compare, which wraps it up for this project. The public relations department will be thrilled with the results and no doubt will soon be looking for other ways we can enhance the annual report. Before they find anything else for us to do, let's go back over how we completed this script.

Reviewing the Script

While some of the functionality for our script was repurposed from our existing rollovers on the homepage, we made some changes and added some new functionality to our rollovers, which deserve to be gone over again. Let's review exactly what we did for this project.

First, we worked with the designer to come up with a new layout for the section and recoded the HTML to match the new layout.

```
<tr>

    <td valign="top" align="left">
```

```
        <br><br><img src="images/
sales_comp_left_default.gif" alt=""td>

    <td valign="top" align="center">
        <font class="blkBldText">Year to Year Sales
Comparison</font><br>
        <br>
        <a href=" " class="blueLink">2000 - 2001</a><br>
        <br>
        <a href=" " class="blueLink">1999 - 2000</a><br>
        <br>
        <a href=" " class="blueLink">1998 - 1999</a></td>
    <td valign="top" align="left">
        <br><br><img src="images/
sales_comp_right_default.gif" alt="" width="162"
height="87" border="0"></td>
</tr>
```

After redoing the HTML, we needed to create four new IMAGE objects to hold the years' sales chart graphics.

```
<script Language="JavaScript1.2">
<!-- Code after this will be ignored by older browsers

// Creating Image Objects for Rollovers
if (document.images) {
sales2001=new Image(162, 87);
sales2001.src="images/sales_2001.gif";

sales2000=new Image(162, 87);
sales2000.src="images/sales_2000.gif";

sales1999=new Image(162, 87);
sales1999.src="images/sales_1999.gif";

sales1998=new Image(162, 87);
sales1998.src="images/sales_1998.gif";
}
```

Here are the steps we took in creating the IMAGE objects:

1. We added a new image for each of the years that we needed a sales chart graphic.
2. We modified the functions that power the script.

```
// function to turn on rolled over graphic
function salesOn(salesPic1, salesPic2) {
    if (document.images) {
```

```
    document.images['salesLeft'].src=eval(salesPic1 +
".src");

    document.images['salesRight'].src=eval(salesPic2 +
".src");
    }
}


// function to turn off rolled over graphic
function salesOff()   {
    if(document.images)   {
        document.images['salesLeft'].src= "images/
sales_comp_left_default.gif";
        document.images['salesRight'].src= "images/
sales_comp_right_default.gif";
    }
}
// End cloaking from non JavaScript browsers -->
</script>
```

We had to do several things to get our functions to where they needed to be for this project:

1. We copied our on and off functions from our navigation rollovers and renamed them salesOn and salesOff.
2. We modified the function to accept two values instead of one to be passed into the function held in the variables salesPic1 and salesPic2.
3. We modified the statements within our salesOn function. In the first line, we changed the code to specify salesLeft as the image we would be swapping out and for it to use the IMAGE object specified in the salesPic1 variable. We then copied that line of code and changed it to change the salesRight image and use the value in the variable salesPic2 for the new IMAGE object.
4. We modified the salesOff function. First, we removed the pic variable from the function declaration, as we will not need to pass in any values for this function to work. Next, we modified the first line of code to specify the salesLeft as the image we would be swapping out, and for it to return to the image sales_comp_left_default.gif when the user triggered this function. We then copied that line of code and changed it to change the salesRight image and for it to return to the image sales_comp_right_default.gif again when the user triggered this function.

Finally, we inserted our event handlers into the HTML.

```
<td valign="top" align="left">
    <br><br>
    <img src="images/sales_comp_left_default.gif" alt=""
width="162" height="87" border="0" name="salesLeft"></td>

<td valign="top" align="center">
    <font class="blkBldText">Year to Year Sales
Comparison</font><br>
    <br>
    <a href=" " class="blueLink"
onMouseOver="salesOn('sales2000', 'sales2001'); return
true;" onMouseOut="salesOff(); return true;">2000 - 2001
</a><br>
    <br>
    <a href=" " class="blueLink"
onMouseOver="salesOn('sales1999', 'sales2000'); return
true;" onMouseOut="salesOff(); return true;">1999 - 2000
</a><br>
    <br>
    <a href=" " class="blueLink"
onMouseOver="salesOn('sales1998', 'sales1999'); return
true;" onMouseOut="salesOff(); return true;">1998 - 1999
</a></td>

<td valign="top" align="left">
    <br><br>
    <img src="images/sales_comp_right_default.gif" alt=""
name="salesRight" width="162" height="87" border="0"></td>
```

1. We added the name attributes salesLeft and salesRight to the left- and right-hand graphics, respectively.
2. We added the onMouseOver and onMouseOut event handlers to each of the three text links. In the onMouseOver handler, we inserted a call to the salesOn() function and passed it the two years of sales charts that we wanted to compare. In the onMouseOut handler, we inserted a call to the salesOff() function and passed in no values, as none are needed to return the graphics to their default state.

We have introduced several new aspects of JavaScript in this script, including

- Repurposing existing script elements for use with new scripts.
- Passing multiple values into a function.

- Explicitly specifying the name of the image we wish to change.
- Explicitly specifying the location of the image we want to use as the source for an image.

◆ Project III: Random Banner Ad Rotator Script

Word of your skills with JavaScript and images has spread to the marketing department, and they have tracked you down for a project that is near and dear to their hearts. Currently on the site, at the top of every secondary page, there is a little banner advertisement for one of the company's products that, if clicked, will take the user to the store section of the site (see Figure 2–5). The way it is set up now is that if they want to have different products showing up, they need to hardcode which product banner goes on a specific page. Because it's quite a hassle to keep track of multiple images and which page they show up on, up until now they have settled for having just a single product banner throughout the site. After seeing what you've done on the site, they're hoping that you can give them the ability to have multiple banners up on the site, so they can showcase a broader range of products. You've given it some thought and looked around on the Internet for similar functionality on other sites, and it looks as if you've come up with a good idea.

The plan is to set up a script that will not only randomly insert a different product banner on the page each time the page is loaded by a user, but rotate which banner is showing every 20 seconds while the user is on the page. So, if the marketing people want to showcase five different products, all they'll have to do is create the five graphics, drop them in a specified directory, and our script will randomly choose one of those five images to place on a given page. The first step is to find out the number of different banners the marketing department wants to have up on the site. After a quick call to marketing, you find out they indeed need five different product banners. Armed with that knowledge, it's time to get going on our script.

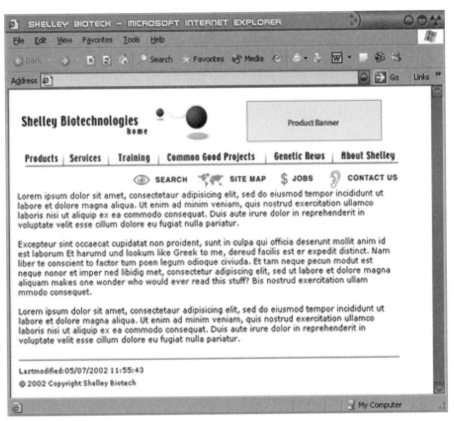

FIGURE 2-5   Secondary page with product banner.

Creating and Inserting the Image Objects

Because this is a script that is going to be used on all pages of the site except the home page, it makes sense to put it into our external JavaScript file, so that's where we will be working for the most part in this project. Now, as in the other scripts that we've done that have worked with image replacement, we need to create some IMAGE objects, one for each product banner that we want available to our script. Let's start by creating the five IMAGE objects that we'll need. Unlike in our previous scripts, we don't have the

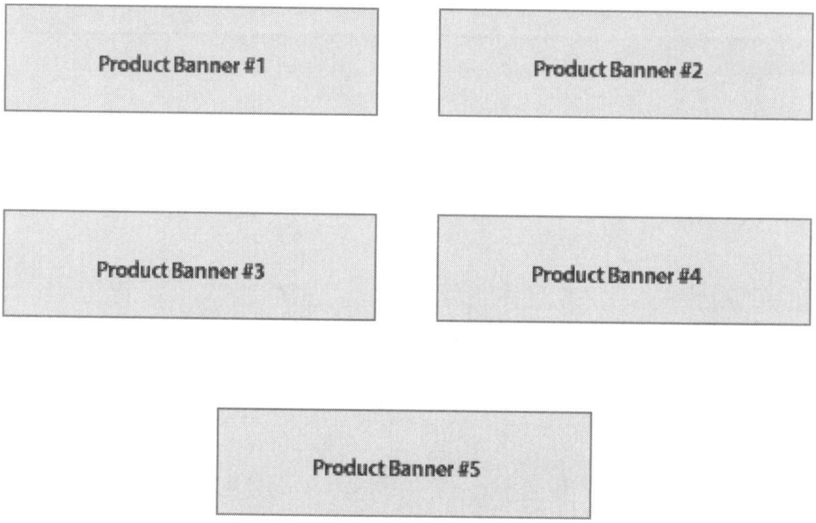

FIGURE 2-6   Temporary product banner images.

graphics that we'll be actually using up on the site yet—the marketing folks are still trying to figure out which products to highlight. We've had one of the designers create five temporary graphics that we can use for now (see Figure 2–6).

Because we don't know the names of the products that are going to be used and because marketing may want to occasionally change which products are showcased, we've named the graphics as follows:

```
product_banner_1.gif
product_banner_2.gif
product_banner_3.gif
product_banner_4.gif
product_banner_5.gif
```

This not only will make it easier to write our script, but it will make for less work later on when marketing wants to switch the products that they are showcasing. The reason for this will become clear when we get down to the function that will be running most of our script. But first, now that we have graphics to use in building our IMAGE objects, let's get that done. As we will be placing this script into our *jsFunctions.js* file, we'll place it right below our navigation rollover functions.

```
// Creating Image Objects for Product Banners
if (document.images) {
product1Banner=new Image(200, 56);
product1Banner.src="images/product_banners/
product_banner_1.gif";

product2Banner=new Image(200, 56);
product2Banner.src="images/product_banners/
product_banner_2.gif";

product3Banner=new Image(200, 56);
product3Banner.src="images/product_banners/
product_banner_3.gif";

product4Banner=new Image(200, 56);
product4Banner.src="images/product_banners/
product_banner_4.gif";

product5Banner=new Image(200, 56);
product5Banner.src="images/product_banners/
product_banner_5.gif";
}
. . .
```

We have created five IMAGE objects named in numeric order product1Banner through product5Banner, and we told the marketing department that the images they should use are in a subdirectory of the images directory called product_banners. This step should look pretty familiar, as we used it in the last two projects. Now that we have our IMAGE objects, let's move on the creation of the function that will run the script.

Random Image Generator Function

The first step we need to take in our script is to figure out which graphic will show up when the page first loads, because there are five images to choose from. We need to generate a random number between 1 and 5 that we can use to choose a graphic. Luckily for us, there is built-in functionality within JavaScript to do this. Let's get started on our first line.

THE MATH OBJECT

To achieve the first part of our script, we need to use the built-in Math object of JavaScript. This object contains methods and properties that supply mathematical functions and values. For our purposes, we need the two methods `Math.random()` and `Math.round()`. First, we use the random method.

```
// First Generate a Random number that will be used to
// choose the initial product banner displayed on the page

var prodStart = Math.random()*4+1;
. . .
```

Let's take a close look at what is going on here. On the left-hand side of the assignment operator, we have the by now familiar creation of a variable, which will hold the value of whatever is on the right-hand side of the operator. In this case, it's a variable name `prodStart`, which will end up holding a random number between 1 and 5. How we get the random number takes a little more explaining. The random method of the `Math` object returns a random number between 0 and 1, so what you end up with is a decimal between 0 and 1, like so:

```
0.5489732579249
```

You're probably wondering how we get from there to a number between 1 and 5, huh? Have no fear: Enter some of that math that you were sure you would never use once you got out of school. First, we multiply the decimal returned by the random method by 4; once this is done, we will have a decimal number somewhere between 0.0 and 4.0. Finally, we add a value of 1 to the current number so that we end up with a decimal number between 1.0 and 5.0, such as one of these:

```
1.2489732579249
3.4589378128
4.8628879248931138
```

For our purposes, however, we need a nice whole number, so we need to use another of the `Math` object's methods in the next line of our script.

```
// First Generate a Random number that will be used to
// choose the initial product banner displayed on the page

var prodStart = Math.random()*4+1;
prodStart = Math.round(prodStart);
. . .
```

This line uses the round method of the `Math` object; it will round off any number that is placed inside of its parentheses. In our case, we have inserted the `prodStart` variable, which carries the number we got from the random method on the line above. The round method then returns a whole number between 1 and 5, which will then be restored into the `prodStart` variable. We will use this variable later on in another part of our script, which actually prints out the initial product banner. First, however, we need to create the function that will be called to change the banner randomly every 20 seconds once the page is loaded. We call the function `bannerChanger()`. Let's add the framework for our function directly after the lines above.

```
// First Generate a Random number that will be used to
// choose the intitial product banner displayed on the page

var prodStart = Math.random()*4+1;
prodStart = Math.round(prodStart);

// Next Create the function which will change the images
// once the page is loaded

function bannerChanger ()   {
    . . .
}
```

The first thing we need to do when our function is called is to again generate a random number between 1 and 5, so this first portion of our function will be almost identical to the first two lines of code in our script, with only one small change.

```
// First Generate a Random number that will be used to
// choose the initial product banner displayed on the page

var prodStart = Math.random()*4+1;
prodStart = Math.round(prodStart);

// Next Create the function which will change the images
// once the page is loaded

function bannerChanger ()   {
    prodStart = Math.random()*4+1;
    prodStart = Math.round(prodStart);
    . . .
}
```

The only difference in these first two lines is that we took out the new variable declaration (`var`) from the first line. Because we have already created this variable, there is no reason to do so again. Once these first two lines execute, when the function is called, we now have a new random number to use to display a new graphic. All we need to do now is tell the JavaScript engine which graphic to display.

```
// First Generate a Random number that will be used to
// choose the initial product banner displayed on the page

var prodStart = Math.random()*4+1;
prodStart = Math.round(prodStart);

// Next Create the function which will change the images
// once the page is loaded

function bannerChanger ()  {
  prodStart = Math.random()*4+1;
  prodStart = Math.round(prodStart);
  document.images['addBanner'].src = eval("product" +
prodStart + "Banner.src");
     . . .
}
```

What we are doing in this new line of code should look pretty familiar. It's the same technique we've used in the first two projects in this chapter. We reset the source property of the image named prodBanner to one of the other five product banners, using the random number we have generated. The final step in creating our function is to make sure that this function will be called again in another 20 seconds to change the product banner once more. To do this, we use a built-in timer method called setTimeout(). The syntax of the setTimeout() method is as follows.

```
setTimeout(expression, msec)
```

Once called, setTimeout() waits the specified amount of time and then executes the expression that is given. In our case, we want it to wait 20 seconds and then call our bannerChanger() function again, so let's insert the setTimeout() method into our script.

```
// First Generate a Random number that will be used to
// choose the initial product banner displayed on the page

var prodStart = Math.random()*4+1;
prodStart = Math.round(prodStart);

// Next Create the function which will change the images
// once the page is loaded
```

```
function bannerChanger ()  {
    prodStart = Math.random()*4+1;
    prodStart = Math.round(prodStart);
    document.images['addBanner'].src = eval("product" +
prodStart + "Banner.src");
    setTimeout("bannerChanger()", 20000);
}
. . .
```

We are now finished with our `bannerChanger()` function. There is just one last piece we have to add to this section of our script, then we will move down to the section of HTML where we want to print out our product banner graphic. We set it up so that once the `bannerChanger()` function has been called, it will keep re-calling itself every 20 seconds. However, we need to set it up so that the function gets called in the first place, so we need to add another `setTimeout()` method which will be executed upon the loading of the page. It will be identical to our first `setTimeout()`, located outside of the `bannerChanger()` function, like so.

```
// First Generate a Random number that will be used to
// choose the intitial product banner displayed on the page

var prodStart = Math.random()*4+1;
prodStart = Math.round(prodStart);

// Next Create the function which will change the images
// once the page is loaded

function bannerChanger ()  {
    prodStart = Math.random()*4+1;
    prodStart = Math.round(prodStart);
    document.images['prodBanner'].src = eval("product" +
prodStart + "Banner.src");
    setTimeout("bannerChanger()", 20000);
}

// Set timer to call the bannerChanger() function for the
// first time

setTimeout("bannerChanger()", 20000);
```

There. We're done with this section of our script; let's move to where we want to have the product banner printed out on our page.

Dynamically Printing Out the Image

Here is the section of HTML where the existing product banner is.

```
<table cellspacing="0" cellpadding="0" width="590">
    <tr>
        <td>
            <img src="images/secondary_top.gif"
alt="Shelley Biotech" width="333" height="68" border="0"><a
href="store/index.html"><img src="images/product_banners/
product_banner.gif" alt="" width="204" height="68"
border="0"></a><br>
```

As you can see, it is currently just calling `product_banner.gif`. We need to add a script that will dynamically print out whichever product banner the initial random number generation specifies. We use a technique similar to the second project we did in Chapter 1. First, we take out the existing image and insert our `<script>` tags and our browser cloaking.

```
<table cellspacing="0" cellpadding="0" width="590">
    <tr>
        <td>
            <img src="images/secondary_top.gif"
alt="Shelley Biotech" width="333" height="68"
border="0"><a href="store/index.html">
<script language="JavaScript1.2">
<!-- cloak from non JavaScript capable browsers


. . .


// End cloaking from non JavaScript browsers -->
</script>
</a><br>
```

Next, we use the `document.write()` method to print out our random product banner graphic.

```
<table cellspacing="0" cellpadding="0" width="590">
    <tr>
        <td>
            <img src="images/secondary_top.gif"
alt="Shelley Biotech" width="333" height="68"
border="0"><a href="store/index.html">
<script language="JavaScript1.2">
<!-- cloak from non JavaScript capable browsers
```

```
document.write('<img src="images/product_banners/
product_banner_' + prodStart + '.gif" width="204"
height="68" alt="Buy Now" name="prodBanner">');

// End cloaking from non JavaScript browsers -->
</script>
</a><br>
```

Let's look at the `document.write()` line a little closer. We have it print out the first part of our image tag, specifying which directory to look in for our image as well as the first part of the image's name. Then we add to that the random number held in the `prodStart` variable, and finally finish the name of the graphic and the rest of its attributes, such as `width`, `height`, and `name`. So, if the variable `prodStart` is holding the value of 3, this is what will be printed out by the script:

```
<img src="images/product_banners/product_banner_3.gif"
width="204" height="68" alt="Buy Now" name="prodBanner">
```

That about wraps it up for this project. We now have a script that randomly prints out a product banner graphic and every 20 seconds refreshes it with another random product banner.

Reviewing the Script

We introduced several new concepts during the creation of the script, so let's take one more look at what we did to create this script. First, we created the IMAGE objects and the function.

```
// Creating Image Objects for Product Banners
if (document.images) {
product1Banner=new Image(200, 56);
product1Banner.src="images/product_banners/
product_banner_1.gif";

product2Banner=new Image(200, 56);
product2Banner.src="images/product_banners/
product_banner_2.gif";

product3Banner=new Image(200, 56);
product3Banner.src="images/product_banners/
product_banner_3.gif";

product4Banner=new Image(200, 56);
```

```
product4Banner.src="images/product_banners/
product_banner_4.gif";

product5Banner=new Image(200, 56);
product5Banner.src="images/product_banners/
product_banner_5.gif";
}
// Generate a Random number that will be used to choose the
// intitial product banner displayed on the page

var prodStart = Math.random()*4+1;
prodStart = Math.round(prodStart);

// Create the function which will change the images once
// the page is loaded

function bannerChanger () {
    prodStart = Math.random()*4+1;
    prodStart = Math.round(prodStart);
    document.images['prodBanner'].src = eval("product" +
prodStart + "Banner.src");
    setTimeout("bannerChanger()", 20000);
}

// Set timer to call the bannerChanger() function for the
// first time

setTimeout("bannerChanger()", 20000);
```

Here are the steps we took to create this portion of the script:

1. We created the five IMAGE objects that we needed for our product banners.
2. We created a variable name prodStart and assigned it a random number between 1.0 and 5.0.
3. We rounded off that number to a whole number between 1 and 5 and reassigned it to the variable prodStart. This variable holds the value of the graphic that will be displayed when the page is first loaded.
4. We created a function called bannerChanger(), which updates the product banner graphic every 20 seconds.
5. Inside of the function, we again generated a random number between 1 and 5 and assigned it to the prodStart variable.
6. We used that value to change the source property of the prodBanner image on the page.

7. We set a timer using the `setTimeout()` method to re-call the `bannerChanger()` function after 20 seconds.
8. Once finished with the `bannerChanger()` function, we added one more timer to call the `bannerChanger()` function when the page first loads.

Next we moved over to the spot in the HTML where we want the product banner to be located.

```
<table cellspacing="0" cellpadding="0" width="590">
    <tr>
        <td>
            <img src="images/secondary_top.gif"
alt="Shelley Biotech" width="333" height="68" border="0"><a
href="store/index.html">
<script language="JavaScript1.2">
<!-- cloak from non JavaScript capable browsers

document.write('<img src="images/product_banners/
product_banner_' + prodStart + '.gif" width="204"
height="68" alt="Buy Now" name="prodBanner">');

// End cloaking from non JavaScript browsers -->
</script>
</a><br>
```

1. We got rid of the existing product image `<img>` tag.
2. We inserted our script framework into the HTML and cloaked for non-JavaScript-capable browsers.
3. We used the `document.write()` method along with the value held in the `prodStart` variable to print out the random product banner graphic.

We have been introduced to several new aspects of JavaScript in this first script, including

- The `Math` object along with its random and round methods.
- The `setTimeout()` method.

RECAP

You will find that image rollovers are by far the most commonly used JavaScript implemented on Web sites today. Almost every site you go to these days makes use of them in one way or another, so a good knowledge of how they work and what their limitations are can be a great asset to a programmer. Once you have the basics down, use that knowledge to experiment with different rollover techniques. You will be surprised at some of the creative and exciting rollovers you can devise.

ADVANCED PROJECTS

1. Use the `onClick()` event handler to create navigation images that change not only upon rollover but when the user clicks on the image as well.
2. Create a page on which a random image replaces an existing image when the category images are rolled over.

3 JavaScript for Navigation

IN THIS CHAPTER

- Project I: JavaScript and Pull-Down Menus—Getting to Where You Want to Go!

- Project II: Using Multiple Pull-Down Menus for Navigation

- Project III: Using JavaScript on a Log-in Page

- Project IV: Using CSS/DHTML with JavaScript for Navigation

- Recap

- Advanced Projects

So far, you have done a great job adding some new functionality and pizzazz to Shelley Biotech's homepage. Now that your boss has seen how great JavaScript can be, another idea has popped into his head. The powers that be would love to be able to add a pull-down menu to the secondary navigation on the site that would let the user jump quickly to certain pages that are several levels down in the site with only a single click. Of course, like most of your projects, they need it done ASAP, so it's off we go on another "learn while you go" assignment.

FIGURE 3–1   Pull-down menu added to the secondary navigation.

After meeting with one of the designers, you feel that you have worked out a good place to put the pull-down menu on the homepage (see Figure 3–1). Now you just need to get the links that they want you to populate the pull-down with. An email to your boss takes care of that easily enough, and you're soon ready to go.

◆ Project I: JavaScript and Pull-Down Menus— Getting to Where You Want to Go!

The first thing we need to do is insert the HTML code into the secondary navigation that will give us our pull-down menu and Go button. Here is the code that we will use.

```
<select name="PullDown">
    <option value=" ">Get There Quick
    <option value=" ">What's New
    <option value=" ">Featured Product
    <option value=" ">Press Releases
    <option value=" ">Company Store
</select>
<input type="button" name="Go" value="Go">
```

Because we will be inserting the pull-down into a preexisting design, we will place the <FORM> tag, which will be named NavForm, at the beginning and end of the HTML body instead of directly around the form element to prevent any unwanted line breaks or spaces. You will also notice that the value properties of the options are left blank; we will fill those in later when we insert the event handler needed to run the script.

Creating the Navigation Function

As the pull-down navigation is going to be on every page in the site, we place the function that will run it in our external JavaScript file right below the Product Banner Randomizer functions, like so.

```
setTimeout("bannerChanger()", 20000);


// Pull-Down Menu Navigation Function
function PageChanger(page) {
    . . .
}
```

The function itself will be fairly simple and will consist of only two parts. Notice that we pass a value into the function that is assigned to the variable page. This value will be the location of the page that the user has selected from the pull-down menu. In the first line, we use that value to change the location property of the DOCUMENT object; this reloads the browser window with the new Web page.

```
 // Pull-Down Menu Navigation Function
function PageChanger(page) {
    document.location= page;
    . . .
}
```

Next, we add a line that serves a housekeeping function more than anything else. When the function is run, this line resets the pull-down menu to the first choice in the menu. This is helpful if the user uses the Back button to return to this page. If we didn't put this line in, on some browsers the last selection the user made in the pull-down would still be visible.

```
// Pull-Down Menu Navigation Function
function PageChanger(page) {
    document.location= page;
    document.NavForm.PullDown.options[0].selected=true;
}
```

Inserting the Event Handler

Now that we have created our function, we need to insert the event handler into our HTML to call the function. Before we do that, let's insert the value properties into the pull-down menu's options. As stated earlier, the value that we pass into our function is the URL for the page we want to send the user to. This value comes from the VALUE attribute of our menu options. Therefore, for the value of each option, we need to put the location of the page for that selection.

```
<select name="PullDown">
    <option value="">Get There Quick
    <option value="whatsnew.html">What's New
    <option value="featured_product.html">Featured Product
    <option value="press.html">Press Releases
    <option value="store.html">Company Store
</select>
```

For the first menu option, which is just a title put there for aesthetic purposes, we don't put in a value because we don't want that option to send the user anywhere. Once the user selects the desired menu option, he or she needs to click on the Go button to get there. To trigger this, we need to insert an onClick handler into the HTML for the Go button.

```
<select name="PullDown">
    <option value="">Get There Quick
    <option value="whatsnew.html">What's New
    <option value="featured_product.html">Featured Product
    <option value="press.html">Press Releases
    <option value="store.html">Company Store
```

```
</select>

<input type="button" name="Go" value="Go"
onClick="PageChanger(document.NavForm.PullDown.options
[NavForm.PullDown.selectedIndex].value)">
```

We do two things in the event handler: We call the `PageChanger()` function and we pass a value to it. The value that we pass is the value of the option that the user has chosen from the pull-down menu. In the functions we have created so far, the value that we have passed into the function has been a simple string. In this event handler, we are trying something new: We are referencing the pull-down menu object that has been selected and accessing its value. This value is then passed into the function and used to send the user to the page he or she wants.

Our script is now functional and ready to go. However, because of the Go button we added to the page, the categories to the right of the pull-down menu have been forced to take up two lines (Figure 3–2), which unfortunately isn't acceptable, so we need to find another way to do it. Luckily for us, there is another way we can power our script that will not only take care of this problem, but will make navigating with the pull-down menu even faster.

Using onChange for Instant Gratification

To get the page layout back to its original state, we need to get rid of the Go button; however, at the moment, it contains the event handler that triggers our script. What we need is a handler that we can put into the pull-down menu itself to run our script for us. Fortunately, just such a handler exists, the onChange event handler. This handler looks for a change in the state of the object that it is contained within, and when it finds one, it triggers.

By inserting it in our pull-down menu, we can have it activate our function when the user changes the menu option from the default option that is loaded with the page. Let's see how this changes our HTML code.

```
<select name="PullDown"
onChange="PageChanger(this.options[this.selectedIndex]
.value)">
        <option value=" ">Get There Quick
        <option value="whatsnew.html">What's New
        <option value="featured_product.html">Featured Product
```

FIGURE 3–2   Page with pull-down menu and Go button.

```
      <option value="press.html">Press Releases
      <option value="store.html">Company Store
</select>
```

First, notice that we have removed the Go button, as it is no longer needed. Second, the `onChange` event handler has been added to the pull-down menu. The value we pass to the function is the same: the value of the option the user has selected. However, we call that value differently than the way we called it before. Because the event handler is in the form element that we wish to get the value from, we can use the following method.

```
this.options[this.selectedIndex].value
```

Instead of calling the specific form element by name, we tell it to "grab the requested information from the form element that contains this handler." Both methods work equally well, and it's always good to be exposed to multiple ways of accomplishing a task.

With the insertion of the new event handler, our script is finished and ready to work. With the onChange handler, the page now changes as soon as the user makes a choice from the menu, without having to press a button.

Reviewing the Script

Let's look at what we did to create this script. We first created a function that accepts a value from a form element and uses it to send the user to another HTML page. We also went over two different event handlers that can be used to drive the scripts.

First, let's look at the function.

```
// Pull-Down Menu Navigation Function
function PageChanger(page) {
        document.location= page;
        document.NavForm.PullDown.options[0].selected=true;
}
```

1. We created the function PageChanger().
2. We set the location property of the DOCUMENT object to the value contained within the variable page. This value is the URL that is being passed into the function from the pull-down menu.
3. We reset the option that shows in the pull-down menu to the first option.

Now let's look at the HTML needed for use with the onClick handler.

```
<select name="PullDown">
    <option value="">Get There Quick
    <option value="whatsnew.html">What's New
    <option value="featured_product.html">Featured Product
    <option value="press.html">Press Releases
    <option value="store.html">Company Store
</select>

<input type="button" name="Go" value="Go"
onClick="PageChanger(document.NavForm.PullDown.options
[NavForm.PullDown.selectedIndex].value)">
```

1. Our function is called when the user clicks on the Go button. We inserted the `onClick` event handler into the button form element.
2. Within the event handler, we call our `PageChanger()` function and pass into it the value held by the menu option that has been chosen from the pull-down menu.
3. Once we decided to take the Go button off the page because of design issues, we used the `onChange` event handler instead.

```
<select name="PullDown"
onChange="PageChanger(this.options[this.selectedIndex]
.value)">
    <option value=" ">Get There Quick
    <option value="whatsnew.html">What's New
    <option value="featured_product.html">Featured Product
    <option value="press.html">Press Releases
    <option value="store.html">Company Store
</select>
```

4. We inserted the `onChange` event handler into our pull-down menu. Again within this event handler, we call our `PageChanger()` function and pass into it the URL of the selected menu option.

Let's take a look at the new concepts that we have covered during this project.

- We learned how to access and change the location property of the DOCUMENT object.
- We learned how to access the values of pull-down menu options and how to change which option is currently selected within a pull-down menu.
- We were introduced to two new event handlers, `onClick` and `onChange`.

As Web sites become more and more important to the success of companies, the amount of content contained in them grows by leaps and bounds. Finding quick and efficient methods to navigate the information is now more important than ever. The two methods just discussed are definitely useful.

◆ Project II: Using Multiple Pull-Down Menus for Navigation

With the success of our pull-down navigation script, the boss has thought of another area of the company's Web site that could benefit from pull-down menu navigation. This time it is in the company store section of the site. At the moment, navigating among the various product groups and products is cumbersome and not very intuitive for the user. A new wave of products is about to be launched, and this would be a perfect opportunity to give the section a face lift (see Figure 3–3). It would be great if we could use pull-down menus and JavaScript to increase efficiency and usability.

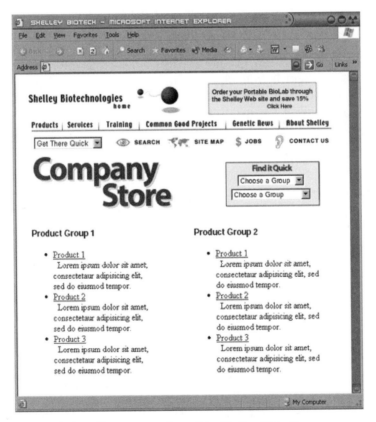

FIGURE 3–3   The store section of the Shelley Web site.

The boss's idea is to have two pull-down menus, one that contains a list of the different product groups and another that dynamically populates itself with the products of the group that is chosen from the first pull-down menu. The user would then be sent to the page that corresponds to the product chosen from the second menu.

This may sound like a daunting task at the moment, but we have already learned much of what we need to accomplish it in the previous chapters. This project will be broken into four sections: creating the arrays that will hold the product information needed for each product group, creating the function that dynamically populates the second menu, creating the function that handles navigation, and inserting the proper event handlers into the HTML code.

Creating the Arrays

Because the new products haven't been released, the marketing department is not sure which product groups and products they want to include in the navigation. They do know, however, that there will be at least four product groups containing a minimum of five products each. Using this information, we will create a navigation menu system using placeholders that can be substituted for the real thing at a later date. Let's get started.

We had a brief introduction to the concept of arrays in the first two chapters. We learned to access the arrays that are created by the JavaScript engine as a page is loaded and how to add objects to some of those arrays. Now, however, we need to create some arrays of our own and populate them with the product information we need to complete the job.

To create an array, use the following syntax.

```
arrayObjectName = new Array(arrayLength)
```

In this statement, `arrayObjectName` is a placeholder for the name you wish to call the array and `arrayLength` is an optional placeholder for the number of entries your array will have.

We need two different values for each product in order to dynamically insert a choice for it in the second pull-down menu. The first is the product's name and the second is the location of the HTML page to which it corresponds. To store this data, we create two arrays for each product group, one that stores the product names and another that holds the locations of the pages. As we don't know the names of the product groups, we use `group1` through `group4` to identify them. Because this script will only be on the main store page, we place the script into the `<head>` of the page.

```
// Arrays for Products

       //Define the arrays

group1_names = new Array(5);
group1_locations = new Array(5);

group2_names = new Array(5);
group2_locations = new Array(5);

group3_names = new Array(5);
group3_locations = new Array(5);

group4_names = new Array(5);
group4_locations = new Array(5);

.  .  .
```

Let's look at the code that defines the first set of arrays.

```
group1_names = new Array(5);
group1_locations = new Array(5);
```

The first line defines a new array, `group1_names`, and assigns it a length of 5, which is the number of products we expect for each group—this array will hold the names of the products from `group1`. The second line defines a new array, `group1_locations`, and assigns it a length of 5 as well—this array will hold the locations of the pages for the products in `group1`. After defining the arrays for product `group1`, we create the arrays for the other three groups.

Now that the arrays have been defined, we need to populate them with the information about the products. First, let's take a quick look at the syntax for adding an entry to an array.

```
arrayName[arrayPosition] = "arrayValue"
```

`arrayName` is the name of the array that you wish to add an entry to, `arrayPosition` is the position in the array that you want to store the value in, and `arrayValue` is the actual value that you wish to store in the array.

Let's populate `group1`'s arrays with its product information.

```
// Populate Group1's Arrays

group1_names[0] = 'Group1_product one';
group1_locations[0] = 'group1/prod_1.html';

group1_names[1] = 'Group1_product two';
group1_locations[1] = 'group1/prod_2.html';

group1_names[2] = 'Group1_product three';
group1_locations[2] = 'group1/prod_3.html';

group1_names[3] = 'Group1_product four';
group1_locations[3] = 'group1/prod_4.html';

group1_names[4] = 'Group1_product five';
group1_locations[4] = 'group1/prod_5.html';

var group1_length = group1_names.length;
```

We assigned a product name and a product page location to the two different arrays at the same position in each array. In other words, after the first two lines,

```
group1_names[0] = 'Group1_product one';
group1_locations[0] = 'group1/prod_1.html';
```

we assigned the value `product one` to the first position in the `group1_names` array and the value `group1/prod_1.html` to the first position in the `group1_locations` array. The rest of this code continues on and puts the information for the remaining products into the two arrays at positions corresponding to their numbers. As in the naming of the groups, we use placeholders for the product names and their page locations.

There will be many times when you are working on a project and you may not have the finalized content that will exist in your pages. Using placeholder content is a great way to let you finish up your coding so that when the finalized content is sent along, all you have to do is drop it in. The trick is to use placeholder values that are clear and easily decipherable, just in case you are not the person inserting the final content.

The last line in our code for populating the `group1` arrays is as follows.

```
var group1_length = group1_names.length;
```

This line assigns the length of the group1 arrays to the variable group1_length; we do this by accessing the length property of the ARRAY object. We will use this variable later in the function that will populate the second menu.

Here is the rest of the code that will populate the arrays for the other product groups. It shares the same structure as that of the first group.

```
// Populate Group2's Arrays

group2_names[0] = 'Group2_product one';
group2_locations[0] = 'group2/prod_1.html';

group2_names[1] = 'Group2_product two';
group2_locations[1] = 'group2/prod_2.html';

group2_names[2] = 'Group2_product three';
group2_locations[2] = 'group2/prod_3.html';

group2_names[3] = 'Group2_product four';
group2_locations[3] = 'group2/prod_4.html';

group2_names[4] = 'Group2_product five';
group2_locations[4] = 'group2/prod_5.html';

var group2_length = group2_names.length;


    // Populate Group3's Arrays

group3_names[0] = 'Group3_product one';
group3_locations[0] = 'group3/prod_1.html';

group3_names[1] = 'Group3_product two';
group3_locations[1] = 'group3/prod_2.html';

group3_names[2] = 'Group3_product three';
group3_locations[2] = 'group3/prod_3.html';

group3_names[3] = 'Group3_product four';
group3_locations[3] = 'group3/prod_4.html';

group3_names[4] = 'Group3_product five';
group3_locations[4] = 'group3/prod_5.html';
```

```
var group3_length = group3_names.length;



    // Populate Group4's Arrays

group4_names[0] = 'Group4_product one';
group4_locations[0] = 'group4/prod_1.html';

group4_names[1] = 'Group4_product two';
group4_locations[1] = 'group4/prod_2.html';

group4_names[2] = 'Group4_product three';
group4_locations[2] = 'group4/prod_3.html';

group4_names[3] = 'Group4_product four';
group4_locations[3] = 'group4/prod_4.html';

group4_names[4] = 'Group4_product five';
group4_locations[4] = 'group4/prod_5.html';

var group4_length = group4_names.length;
```

Now we have two arrays for each product group populated with the data for all of the products within those groups. We also have four variables that contain the lengths of each array. With this done, it is time to move on to the next step, creating the function that will populate our second pull-down menu.

Creating the Drill-Down Menu Function

Before we begin writing the function, we must find the value that we will need inside the function. When the user selects a product group from the first menu, the script has to clear out any values that are currently occupying the second menu before it puts the new products in. This is important because the new product group the user picks could have fewer products than the one that was previously chosen. If this was the case, the new group's products may not overwrite all of the products from the previous group. To make sure we clear all of the possible products from the menu, we need the length of the largest set of arrays. We accomplish this with the following code:

```
// Find the length of the largest set of arrays
```

```
var maxLength = group1_length;

if (group2_length > maxLength) {
    maxlength = group2_length;
}
if (group3_length > maxLength) {
    maxlength = group3_length;
}
if (group4_length > maxLength) {
    maxlength = group4_length;
}
```

This code first assigns the value of the length of the first set of arrays to the variable maxLength. It then uses if statements to check if the lengths of any of the other array groups are longer than maxLength, and if so, it assigns that new value to the variable. In the end, maxLength is left holding the value of the longest array group.

With that done, we can move on to our function. The first thing we need to do is use our maxLength variable to clear the contents of the second menu.

```
// Creating the drill down menu function

function MenuFiller(choice)  {

    // Clear out second menu
    var currentPosition = 0;
    while (currentPosition < maxLength) {
        . . .
            ++currentPosition;
    }
    . . .

}
```

The first line of code creates a variable currentPosition and assigns it a value of 0. Next, we have a structure called a while loop. We haven't used a while loop yet, so a quick look at its syntax is in order.

We have already used if statements in our scripts—they execute a chunk of code if a specific condition is true. While loops work in a similar fashion; however, in their case, for as long as the condition evaluates true, the while loop will continue to execute the code chunk within it until the condition is no longer true. The syntax for a while loop is as follows.

```
while (condition) {
    statements
}
```

While loops are very useful when you want to access or change many properties in the same way. Loops can be tricky, though; if you create a loop where the condition will always be true and never false, you will find yourself in something called an *infinite* loop. In other words, your script will be stuck running forever, and it will never be able to finish, which in effect renders your script useless and more often than not will crash the browser.

Now, how do you change the condition you are testing for to false if you can't leave the loop until it changes? I'm glad you asked. The most common way is to change the condition from within the loop.

The while loop in the preceding code will keep cycling through for as long as the variable currentPosition is less than the value of maxLength. Each time the loop cycles, we will have it first clear out the menu option whose position corresponds with the value of currentPosition, and then at the end, have it add 1 to the value of currentPosition. This way, currentPosition will eventually equal maxLength and we will exit the loop. In the preceding code, this is also the first time we have seen the ++ increment operator. It adds 1 to the value of its operand (in this case, currentPosition), so the line

```
++currentPosition;
```

is responsible for incrementing our variable.

The loop will cycle until the value of currentPosition is equal to the length of the longest array. This way, we will be sure to clear out all of the possible options from the menu. We accomplish the actual clearing of the menu by putting the following code into the while loop. The form that holds the two pull-down menus is named ProductPicker. This way, we know how to get access to the pull-down menus in the JavaScript hierarchy.

```
// Creating the drill down menu function

function MenuFiller(choice)   {

    // Clear out second menu
    var currentPosition = 0;
    while (currentPosition < maxLength) {
```

```
        document.ProductPicker.Products.options
   [currentPosition].text = ' ' ;

        document.ProductPicker.Products.options
   [currentPosition].value = ' ' ;

        ++ currentPosition;
   }
      . . .

}
```

The first line of code in the loop sets the text of the menu option corresponding to the present value of the variable currentPosition to be blank. The second line does the same with the value of that menu option. Once the loop has run through all of its cycles, we are left with a blank pull-down menu ready to accept the values of the new product group.

Now that we have cleared out the Products menu, it is time to populate it with the products of the new product group that was chosen. Before we can know what products to put there, we have to find out which product the user chose. As in our previous projects, we have the event handler pass a value into the function that we can use to check which option has been chosen. For this function, the value is stored in the variable choice. The next chunk of code that we add is a set of if statements to test which group was chosen.

```
// Creating the drill down menu function

function MenuFiller(choice)   {

    // Clear out second menu
    var currentPosition = 0;
    while (currentPosition < maxLength)
    {
document.ProductPicker.Products.options[currentPosition]
.text = ' ' ;
document.ProductPicker.Products.options[currentPosition]
.value = ' ' ;
            ++ currentPosition;
    }

    // Select which Product Group was chosen
    if (choice == 0) {
            . . .
    }
    else if (choice == 1) {
```

```
    . . .
}
else if (choice == 2)  {
    . . .
}
else if (choice == 3)  {
    . . .
}
else if (choice == 4)  {
    . . .
}
    . . .
}
```

If you look at the HTML code for our pull-down menus, you will see that the values we have given to the product groups are the numbers 1 through 4, with each number corresponding to the number of the group.

```
<select name="ProductGroup">
    <option value="0">Choose a Group
    <option value="1">Group One
    <option value="2">Group Two
    <option value="3">Group Three
    <option value="4">Group Four
</select>
```

Because it is possible that someone will choose the default menu entry Choose a Group, we also have assigned a value to that choice, the number 0. When the event handler is put into action, it passes the chosen value into the function, assigns it to the variable choice, and the if statements we just added execute the commands that follow the test that proves true.

So, let's put in the commands that we want executed after each if statement. These commands need to accomplish two things: First, they must assign the length of the chosen group's PRODUCTS array to a variable, and second, assign the name of the chosen group to a variable as well.

```
// Creating the drill down menu function

function MenuFiller(choice)  {

  // Clear out second menu
    var currentPosition = 0;
    while (currentPosition < maxLength)
    {
```

```
document.ProductPicker.Products.options[currentPosition].
text = ' ' ;

document.ProductPicker.Products.options[test].value = ' ' ;
        ++ currentPosition;
    }


// Select which Product Group was chosen
  if (choice == 0) {
        . . .
    }
    else if (choice == 1) {
            OutputListSize = group1_length;
            arrayName = "group1";
    }
    else if (choice == 2)  {
            OutputListSize = group2_length;
            arrayName = "group2";
    }
    else if (choice == 3)  {
            OutputListSize = group3_length;
            arrayName = "group3";
    }
    else if (choice == 4)  {
            OutputListSize = group4_length;
            arrayName = "group4";
    }
        . . .
}
```

We found out the lengths of the individual arrays earlier in this script and assigned them to different variables, such as group1_length, group2_length, and so forth. Using these values later in our function will require having a single variable that will hold the array length of just the group that was chosen. So, in the preceding lines of code, we assign the array length of the chosen group to the variable OutputListSize.

The second line that we added to each if statement assigns the name of the group, if it was chosen, to the variable arrayName. This variable will be used later to help call information from the proper array.

So far, we have taken care of the code for all of the if statements except for the first one, which will be true if the user has chosen the default Choose a Group menu option. Because this option doesn't correspond to any product group, there are no

PRODUCT arrays to refill the second menu, so we don't need to worry about finding an array length or the name of a product group. There is something that we want to do if this option is chosen; because the second menu is automatically wiped clean when the function is run, we need to repopulate the default option of the menu with the text of Choose a Group. To accomplish this, we add the following commands. The first will assign the default message to the text property of the first option of the second menu. The second line will then reset that option's value to 0. Finally, we add a last command, which will select the first option of the menu.

```javascript
// Creating the drill down menu function

function MenuFiller(choice)  {

        // Clear out second menu
    var currentPosition = 0;
    while (currentPosition < maxLength)
    {

document.ProductPicker.Products.options[currentPosition].
text = ' ';

document.ProductPicker.Products.options[currentPosition].
value = ' ';
        ++currentPosition;
    }


        // Choose which Product Group was chosen
    if (choice == 0) {

document.ProductPicker.Products.options[0].text = 'Choose a
Group    ';
document.ProductPicker.Products.options[0].value = 0;


document.ProductPicker.Products.options[0].selected=true;
    }
    else if (choice == 1) {
        OutputListSize = group1_length;
        arrayName = "group1";
    }
    else if (choice == 2)  {
        OutputListSize = group2_length;
        arrayName = "group2";
    }
```

```
else if (choice == 3)  {
    OutputListSize = group3_length;
    arrayName = "group3";
}
else if (choice == 4)  {
    OutputListSize = group4_length;
    arrayName = "group4";
}
```

We now have all of the information we need to repopulate the second menu with the products from the chosen group, so let's move on to the final section of our function, which will actually do the repopulating. The first thing we need to do is reset the value of the variable currentPosition to 0 and make sure that the default Choose a Group option wasn't selected. If it was, we won't want to repopulate the menu, so we will use an if statement to make sure that choice is greater than 0.

```
// Creating the drill down menu function

function MenuFiller(choice)  {

        // Clear out second menu
    var currentPosition = 0;
    while (currentPosition < maxLength)
    {

document.ProductPicker.Products.options[currentPosition].
text = ' ';

document.ProductPicker.Products.options[currentPosition].
value = ' ';
        ++currentPosition;
    }

        // Choose which Product Group was chosen
    if (choice == 0) {
document.ProductPicker.Products.options[0].text = 'Choose a
Group       ';
document.ProductPicker.Products.options[0].value = 0;


    document.ProductPicker.Products.options[0].selected=true;
    }
    else if (choice == 1) {
        OutputListSize = group1_length;
        arrayName = "group1";
    }
```

```
else if (choice == 2) {
    OutputListSize = group2_length;
    arrayName = "group2";
}
else if (choice == 3) {
    OutputListSize = group3_length;
    arrayName = "group3";
}
else if (choice == 4) {
    OutputListSize = group4_length;
    arrayName = "group4";
}


var currentPosition = 0;

if (choice > 0) {
    . . .
}
}
```

Now that we know that a new product group has actually been chosen, we can start repopulating the second menu. To do this, we use a while loop similar to the one that we have clearing the menu at the beginning of the function. It will test the value of currentPosition against the variable OutputListSize, which contains the length of the chosen PRODUCT arrays.

```
var currentPosition = 0;
    if (choice > 0) {
        while (currentPosition < OutputListSize)
        {
            . . .
            ++currentPosition;
        }
        . . .
    }
}
```

The statements on the inside of the loop of course will be different. To repopulate both the text and value properties of each menu option, we need to put in two lines of code for the while loop to execute.

```
var currentPosition = 0;
    if (choice > 0) {
        while (currentPosition < OutputListSize)
```

```
                {

document.ProductPicker.Products.options[currentPosition]
.text = eval(arrayName + '_names[currentPosition]');

document.ProductPicker.Products.options[currentPosition]
.value = eval(arrayName + '_locations[currentPosition]');
                ++currentPosition;
                }
        }
}
```

There is a lot going on in those lines, so let's take a closer look at them. In the first half of the first line, we call the text property of the menu option that currently matches the value of the variable currentPosition.

```
document.ProductPicker.Products.options[currenPosition]
.text
```

Each time the while loop cycles through, this property is assigned the value of what it finds in the second half of our line.

```
= eval(arrayName + '_names[currentPosition]');
```

This part of the line is similar to one that we used in Chapter 2 when dealing with image rollovers. Here we are using the eval() method to combine the value of the variable arrayName, which holds the name of the group that was chosen with a string that, when combined, will call on the proper PRODUCT array and retrieve the entry at the position that corresponds to the current value of currentPosition.

While the first line takes care of repopulating the text property of the option in the pull-down menu, the second does the same thing with the value property of each menu option.

The last command that we need to add to our function is to make sure that the first position on the repopulated second menu is the one that is selected by default.

```
var currentPosition = 0;
        if (choice > 0) {
            while (currentPosition < OutputListSize)
                {

document.ProductPicker.Products.options[currentPosition].
text = eval(arrayName + '_names[currentPosition]');
```

```
document.ProductPicker.Products.options[currentPosition].
value = eval(arrayName + '_locations[currentPosition]');
                ++currentPosition;
        }

document.ProductPicker.Products.options[0].selected=true;
    }
}
```

Congratulations. We have now finished our function. This is definitely an advanced piece of code, so be proud of yourself. Only two more steps to go, and we will be finished with the project. We now must add the navigation function that will take the user to the page of the product that he or she chooses, and then insert the event handlers that will call our function.

Creating the Navigation Function

Okay, what we need now is a function that will send the user to a different page depending upon which item he or she chooses from the Products pull-down menu. Wait, does this sound familiar to anyone else? Well, it should; we created just such a function at the beginning of this chapter. With a little modification, we can use a copy of that existing function for our Products pull-down menu.

Here is a look at the existing function, just to refresh your memory.

```
// Pull-Down Menu Navigation Function

function PageChanger(page) {
    document.location= page;

document.NavForm.PullDown.options[0].selected=true;

    }
```

The first thing we need to do is make a copy of the existing function and rename it. We will call our new function `ProductPageChanger()`.

```
// Pull-Down Menu Navigation Function

function ProductPageChanger(page) {
    document.location= page;
```

```
document.NavForm.PullDown.options[0].selected=true;

}
```

The next thing we need to do is change which form and form element are being accessed by our functions. In this case, we want to access the Products pull-down menu of the `Product-Picker` form.

```
// Pull-Down Menu Navigation Function

function ProductPageChanger(page) {
     document.location= page;
     document.ProductPicker.Products.options[0].
     selected=true;

}
```

Now that we have the new function and it's accessing the proper form element, we need to add one more thing for our function to be complete.When the page is first loaded and the user has not yet chosen a product group, the Products pull-down menu is empty and will stay that way until a group is chosen. The addition we need to make to the function is a test that will make sure that if an option from the Products pull-down menu is chosen, it is populated with data. If it's not, we don't want the `Navigation` function to try sending the person off to some nonexistent page.

We can use the value of the menu option, which is being passed into the function to make our test. We will insert an `if` statement that says as long as the value of variable `page` is not equal to (`!=` is the symbol for not equal to) a blank entry, then execute the rest of the function.

```
// Pull-Down Menu Navigation Function

 function ProductPageChanger(page) {
     if (page != ' ')  {
          document.location= page;
          document.ProductPicker.Products.options[0].
     selected=true;
     }

}
```

With the addition of one simple `if` statement, we can repurpose an existing function to work for more than one purpose. Keep this trick in mind when you are coding; there is no reason to always reinvent the wheel.

Now that we have a function sending the user where he or she wants to go, all that is left for us to do is put in the event handlers.

Inserting the Event Handlers

There are two event handlers that we need to insert, one for each of our pull-down menus. The Product Group pull-down will call our `MenuFiller()` function, while the Products pull-down will call the `PageChanger()` function. Let's look at the Product Group pull-down first:

```
<select name="ProductGroup"
onChange="MenuFiller(this.options[this.selectedIndex].value
)">
    <option value="0">Choose a Group
    <option value="1">Group One
    <option value="2">Group Two
    <option value="3">Group Three
    <option value="4">Group Four
</select>
```

The event handler should look familiar; it is for the most part the same as the handler that we used for our Navigation pull-down at the beginning of the chapter. The only difference is that we are calling a different function.

For our Products pull-down, since we are using the same function as our Navigation pull-down, we use the same event handler.

```
<select name="Products"
onChange="ProductPageChanger(this.options[this.selected
Index].value)">
    <option value=" ">Choose a
Group      
    <option value=" "> 
    <option value=" "> 
    <option value=" "> 
    <option value=" "> 
    <option value=" "> 
</select>
```

Believe it or not, that's it. We are now finished. This is one of the longest scripts we have worked on so far, so let's review it one last time as a whole so we can see see exactly what we have accomplished.

Reviewing the Script

The first thing we did in this script was define the arrays that would hold all of the information for the products of each product group.

```
// Arrays for Products

    //Define the arrays

group1_names = new Array(5);
group1_locations = new Array(5);

group2_names = new Array(5);
group2_locations = new Array(5);

group3_names = new Array(5);
group3_locations = new Array(5);

group4_names = new Array(5);
group4_locations = new Array(5);
```

1. We created two arrays for each product group. One set of arrays holds the product names for each group, and the other holds the URLs that correspond to each product.
2. Once the arrays were created, we populated all of the arrays with the information.

```
// Populate Group1's Arrays

group1_names[0] = 'Group1_product one';
group1_locations[0] = 'group1/prod_1.html';

group1_names[1] = 'Group1_product two';
group1_locations[1] = 'group1/prod_2.html';

group1_names[2] = 'Group1_product three';
group1_locations[2] = 'group1/prod_3.html';
```

```
group1_names[3] = 'Group1_product four';
group1_locations[3] = 'group1/prod_4.html';

group1_names[4] = 'Group1_product five';
group1_locations[4] = 'group1/prod_5.html';

var group1_length = group1_names.length;


    // Populate Group2's Arrays

group2_names[0] = 'Group2_product one';
group2_locations[0] = 'group2/prod_1.html';

group2_names[1] = 'Group2_product two';
group2_locations[1] = 'group2/prod_2.html';

group2_names[2] = 'Group2_product three';
group2_locations[2] = 'group2/prod_3.html';

group2_names[3] = 'Group2_product four';
group2_locations[3] = 'group2/prod_4.html';

group2_names[4] = 'Group2_product five';
group2_locations[4] = 'group2/prod_5.html';

var group2_length = group2_names.length;


    // Populate Group3's Arrays

group3_names[0] = 'Group3_product one';
group3_locations[0] = 'group3/prod_1.html';

group3_names[1] = 'Group3_product two';
group3_locations[1] = 'group3/prod_2.html';

group3_names[2] = 'Group3_product three';
group3_locations[2] = 'group3/prod_3.html';

group3_names[3] = 'Group3_product four';
group3_locations[3] = 'group3/prod_4.html';

group3_names[4] = 'Group3_product five';
group3_locations[4] = 'group3/prod_5.html';

var group3_length = group3_names.length;
```

```
// Populate Group4's Arrays

group4_names[0] = 'Group4_product one';
group4_locations[0] = 'group4/prod_1.html';

group4_names[1] = 'Group4_product two';
group4_locations[1] = 'group4/prod_2.html';

group4_names[2] = 'Group4_product three';
group4_locations[2] = 'group4/prod_3.html';

group4_names[3] = 'Group4_product four';
group4_locations[3] = 'group4/prod_4.html';

group4_names[4] = 'Group4_product five';
group4_locations[4] = 'group4/prod_5.html';

var group4_length = group4_names.length;
```

3. With all of the arrays populated, we created a variable for each group that would hold the length of each group's arrays.

```
// Find the length of the largest set of arrays

var maxLength = group1_length;

if (group2_length > maxLength) {
    maxlength = group2_length;
}
if (group3_length > maxLength) {
    maxlength = group3_length;
}
if (group4_length > maxLength) {
    maxlength = group4_length;
}
```

4. Once we had the lengths of all of the arrays stored in the variables, we set up a series of if statements to find the longest of the groups and assigned that length to the variable maxLength.

Next, we created the function MenuFiller() that will populate the pull-down menus.

```
// Creating the drill down menu function

function MenuFiller(choice)  {

        // Clear out second menu
    var currentPosition = 0;
    while (currentPosition < maxLength)
    {

document.ProductPicker.Products.options[currentPosition].
text = ' ' ;

document.ProductPicker.Products.options[currentPosition].
value = ' ' ;
        ++currentPosition;
    }

        // Choose which Product Group was chosen
    if (choice == 0) {

document.ProductPicker.Products.options[0].text = 'Choose a
Group    ';

document.ProductPicker.Products.options[0].value = ' ';

document.ProductPicker.Products.options[0].selected=true;
    }
    else if (choice == 1) {
        OutputListSize = group1_length;
        arrayName = "group1";
    }
    else if (choice == 2)  {
        OutputListSize = group2_length;
        arrayName = "group2";
    }
    else if (choice == 3)  {
        OutputListSize = group3_length;
        arrayName = "group3";
    }
    else if (choice == 4)  {
        OutputListSize = group4_length;
        arrayName = "group4";
    }


    var currentPosition = 0;
    if (choice > 0) {
        while (currentPosition < OutputListSize)
        {
```

```
document.ProductPicker.Products.options[currentPosition].
text = eval(arrayName + '_names[currentPosition]');

document.ProductPicker.Products.options[currentPosition].
value = eval(arrayName + '_locations[currentPosition]');
            ++currentPosition;
    }

document.ProductPicker.Products.options[0].selected=true;
    }
}
```

1. We have our function clear out any data from the Products pull-down menu.
2. The function takes the variable passed into it from the event handler and decides which Product group the user has chosen.
3. Our function repopulates the Products pull-down with the information from the proper array.

With that function complete, we made a quick adjustment to the existing Navigation function.

```
// Pull-Down Menu Navigation Function

function ProductPageChanger(page) {
    if (page != ' ')  {
        document.location= page;
        document.ProductPicker.Products.options[0].
    selected=true;
    }

}
```

1. We made a copy of our original navigation function and renamed it ProductPageChanger().
2. We redefined which form and form element the function was accessing.
3. We added an if statement to our PageChanger() function that will make sure that the option chosen from the pull-down menu is valid.

Finally, we added event handlers to our two Product pull-downs.

```
<select name="ProductGroup"
onChange="MenuFiller(this.options[this.selectedIndex].value
)">
    <option value="0">Choose a Group
    <option value="1">Group One
    <option value="2">Group Two
    <option value="3">Group Three
    <option value="4">Group Four
</select>


<select name="Products"
onChange="ProductPageChanger(this.options[this.selected
Index].value)">
    <option value=" ">Choose a
Group      
    <option value=" "> 
    <option value=" "> 
    <option value=" "> 
    <option value=" "> 
    <option value=" "> 
</select>
```

We inserted an `onChange` event handler into our two pull-down menus.

- The event handler in the Product Group pull-down menu will call our `MenuFiller()` function.
- The event handler in the Products pull-down menu will call the `PageChanger()` function.

Let's look at the new concepts we have covered in this project.

- We learned how to create and populate user-defined arrays.
- We used a `while` loop for the first time.
- We were introduced to the `!=` logical operator.
- We furthered our knowledge of accessing the information and properties contained in arrays.
- We built on lessons learned in previous chapters in regard to accessing and changing the values and properties of form elements.

Now that we are finished, it's time to hand the work over to the boss so he can lavish you with much deserved praise. You're becoming a downright JavaScript guru. Of course, now that you have finished with this project, the boss has found another one for you to work on. Geez! Our work is never done.

◆ Project III: Using JavaScript on a Log-in Page

The company is about to add a new Partners section to the site. Part of this new section will not be accessible by the general public; only existing partners will be allowed entry. One of the Perl programmers has created a log-in page (see Figure 3–4), written the script, and is going to maintain the database with the usernames and passwords. So what is there for you to do, you ask?

Well, the powers that be saw a log-in page where once you entered your password, all you had to do was press Enter or hit the Tab key and the log-in script was called. The log-in page that the Perl guys came up with requires the user to manually press a log-in button to call the script. Our job is to take the page they created and modify it with JavaScript so that it will work when either the Enter or Tab key is pressed.

FIGURE 3–4   Partners log-in page.

After our last script, this will seem like a walk in the park. We won't even need to write a function; all we need is to insert the proper event handler in the HTML, and we will be off and running.

Inserting the Event Handler

In our last two scripts in this chapter, we used the onChange() event handler on form pull-down menus to call the functions needed to run the scripts. For this script, we use onChange() again; however, this time we will see how it works on a form text field.

When the onChange() handler is used within a text field, it triggers when the value in the box has been changed and the field loses focus by the user either pressing Tab or the Enter key or clicking outside the field. So, in this script we will put the onChange() handler on the password field. The user will come to the page, enter a username, and then move to the password field. The user will enter a password, thereby changing the value of the field, and then either press Enter or click on the Log-in button, which will in turn cause the password field to lose focus and trigger the event. The event we have triggered is the calling of the SUBMIT property of the form that holds our log-in text fields.

Let's look at the code after we have inserted the event handler.

```
<input type="password" name="_User_Pass"
onChange="document.login.submit();">
```

Reviewing the Script

We inserted the onChange() event handler into the password form element. That's all there is to it. This is a great example of a very short script that can be really useful. Not all scripts have to be as long or as complex as the second one in this chapter. In fact, it is best to always look for the most efficient way to create a script.

◆ Project IV: Using CSS/DHTML with JavaScript for Navigation

It's a good thing the last project was nice and easy, because the next idea the boss has come up with is going to not only use pretty much all of the techniques that we've acquired, but push us into new and exciting territory. Up until now, we've only used

CSS/DHTML to specify the font attributes for our site. Well, that's about to change. The boss was recently at an industry meeting and was talking to one of our competitors about Web sites; the competitor was all aglow with the new navigation menus that had been added to their site. So, needless to say, the boss ran home and checked them out and of course now wants you to implement them on the Shelley site.

How the menus work is that when the user rolls over a main navigation image, a small menu pops up that lists the secondary level categories available for that section. After a little bit of research, you've figured out that they are using CSS/DHTML to achieve this feat. Before we can go much further, however, we need a little deeper understanding of CSS/DHTML.

Introduction to CSS/DHTML

We've had a little exposure to some CSS/DHTML in some of our previous scripts, but what exactly is it? CSS stands for Cascading Style Sheets, which is a language specification that was created to enhance standard HTML. Through the use of CSS, you can have very specific control over the layout of the page by specifying document attributes, font attributes, and the positioning of content. In the first project in the book, we used a CSS class to specify the font attributes for the text on the homepage. This is just the tip of the iceberg of what you can do with CSS; imagine having pixel-perfect control over the positioning of a table or image on a page or being able to layer text over an image. CSS makes this all possible.

DHTML is simply using both CSS and JavaScript together to create more dynamic Web pages. When using CSS on a page, you are opening up new attributes to the object model of JavaScript. When we used the CSS class in the first chapter to create a font style for the homepage text, we also created a new object that we could then go in and modify with JavaScript. So, just like when we specified a new source property for our IMAGE objects for our rollover scripts, we could use JavaScript to specify a new font or color for the homepage text when the user rolls over it. If we were to create a block of content and use a CSS selector to specify where it was located on the page, we could animate that block of content by changing the selectors' top and left properties. Both of these are examples of DHTML. For a much more in-depth look at CSS and DHTML check out Dan Livingston's *Essential CSS and DHTML for Web Professionals*, Second Edition, which is another book in this series. Now that we have a broad idea of what these two concepts are, we're going to move on to the project at hand. We will go into more detail on the specific CSS/DHTML features that come up in our script.

After a little more research into how people are creating these menus, it becomes clear that most of these menus are just HTML tables with a list of the subcategories inside of them. These tables are then assigned to a specific CSS selector which specifies where on the page they should be positioned, whether the table is visible or not, and that they should be displayed in front of the main content of the page. Then, using a set of functions much like our image rollover scripts, they are able to turn the menus off and on as the user rolls over the main navigation graphic. Because we already have image rollovers on the site, we already have some of the code that we'll need to get our new script up and running. The main thing we will be able to salvage from our previous script is the IMAGE object definitions, which preload our navigation images. We will leave those in our external JavaScript file for use in our script and simply replace the On and Off functions with the new ones we write. Before we get to our functions, however, we must first create the menus that will be displayed upon rollover of a navigation image.

Creating the Menu Layers

The first step is building the menus themselves, so we sat down with one of the designers and figured out what we want these menus to look like. Figure 3–5 shows a sample of what we need the menu to look like.

The designer has created a look that should be easy to duplicate just using HTML tables, so you went ahead and created the HTML for the Products menu.

```
<table border="1" cellpadding="0" cellspacing="0"
bordercolor="#CAD142">
    <tr>
        <td valign="top" align="left" bgcolor="#F3FB82">
        <img src="images/clear.gif" width="10"
height="18" border="0" alt="" align="absmiddle"><a href=" "
class="menuLink">Product Group 1</a><img src="images/
clear.gif" width="10" height="18" border="0" alt=""
align="absmiddle"></td>
    </tr>
    <tr>
```

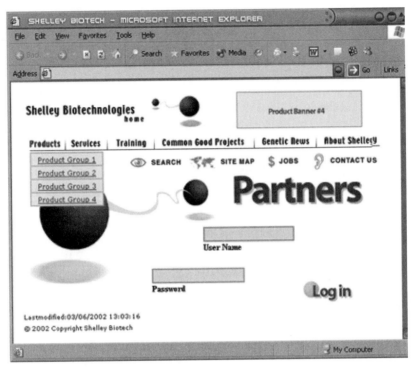

FIGURE 3–5   Navigation menus.

```
        <td valign="top" align="left" bgcolor="#F3FB82">
        <img src="images/clear.gif" width="10"
height="18" border="0" alt="" align="absmiddle"><a href=" "
class="menuLink">Product Group 2</a><img src="images/
clear.gif" width="10" height="18" border="0" alt=""
align="absmiddle"></td>
    </tr>
    <tr>
        <td valign="top" align="left" bgcolor="#F3FB82">
        <img src="images/clear.gif" width="10"
height="18" border="0" alt="" align="absmiddle"><a href=" "
class="menuLink">Product Group 3</a><img src="images/
clear.gif" width="10" height="18" border="0" alt=""
align="absmiddle"></td>
    </tr>
    <tr>
        <td valign="top" align="left" bgcolor="#F3FB82">
        <img src="images/clear.gif" width="10"
height="18" border="0" alt="" align="absmiddle"><a href=" "
```

```
class="menuLink">Product Group 4</a><img src="images/
clear.gif" width="10" height="18" border="0" alt=""
align="absmiddle"></td>
    </tr>
</table>
```

The table that creates the menu is straightforward; there is nothing in it that we haven't dealt with before. It's basically a simple table with a new row for each item that we want in our menu. The only piece that isn't straight HTML is that we are assigning a *class* to each link so that we can control their look through CSS. If we were to just place this table into our page's HTML, it would show up wherever we inserted it into our page and would not be useful to us at all, so the next step is to let the browser know that we want to treat this section of HTML differently from the rest of the code on the page. We do that by first wrapping our table in a `<div>` tag, and then assigning a CSS selector to the `<div>`. This way, we can tell the browser where on the page we want the menu to show up and that when the page is first loaded, we want the menu invisible. Let's take the first step of putting our table into a `<div>` tag.

```
<div>
<table border="1" cellpadding="0" cellspacing="0"
bordercolor="#CAD142">
    <tr>
        <td valign="top" align="left" bgcolor="#F3FB82">
        <img src="images/clear.gif" width="10"
height="18" border="0" alt="" align="absmiddle"><a href=" "
class="menuLink">Product Group 1</a><img src="images/
clear.gif" width="10" height="18" border="0" alt=""
align="absmiddle"></td>
    </tr>
    <tr>
        <td valign="top" align="left" bgcolor="#F3FB82">
        <img src="images/clear.gif" width="10"
height="18" border="0" alt="" align="absmiddle"><a href=" "
class="menuLink">Product Group 2</a><img src="images/
clear.gif" width="10" height="18" border="0" alt=""
align="absmiddle"></td>
    </tr>
    <tr>
        <td valign="top" align="left" bgcolor="#F3FB82">
        <img src="images/clear.gif" width="10"
height="18" border="0" alt="" align="absmiddle"><a href=" "
class="menuLink">Product Group 3</a><img src="images/
```

```
clear.gif" width="10" height="18" border="0" alt=""
align="absmiddle"></td>
      </tr>
      <tr>
            <td valign="top" align="left" bgcolor="#F3FB82">
            <img src="images/clear.gif" width="10"
height="18" border="0" alt="" align="absmiddle"><a href=" "
class="menuLink">Product Group 4</a><img src="images/
clear.gif" width="10" height="18" border="0" alt=""
align="absmiddle"></td>
      </tr>
</table></div>
```

Now that we have our table inside a <div>, we need to specify
a name by which we can reference this menu from CSS as well as
our JavaScript. To do this we use the id attribute of the <div> tag,
like so.

```
<div id="ProductsMenu">
<table border="1" cellpadding="0" cellspacing="0"
bordercolor="#CAD142">
      <tr>
            <td valign="top" align="left" bgcolor="#F3FB82">
            <img src="images/clear.gif" width="10"
height="18" border="0" alt="" align="absmiddle"><a href=" "
class="menuLink">Product Group 1</a><img src="images/
clear.gif" width="10" height="18" border="0" alt=""
align="absmiddle"></td>
      </tr>
      <tr>
            <td valign="top" align="left" bgcolor="#F3FB82">
            <img src="images/clear.gif" width="10"
height="18" border="0" alt="" align="absmiddle"><a href=" "
class="menuLink">Product Group 2</a><img src="images/
clear.gif" width="10" height="18" border="0" alt=""
align="absmiddle"></td>
      </tr>
      <tr>
            <td valign="top" align="left" bgcolor="#F3FB82">
            <img src="images/clear.gif" width="10"
height="18" border="0" alt="" align="absmiddle"><a href=" "
class="menuLink">Product Group 3</a><img src="images/
clear.gif" width="10" height="18" border="0" alt=""
align="absmiddle"></td>
      </tr>
      <tr>
            <td valign="top" align="left" bgcolor="#F3FB82">
```

```
          <img src="images/clear.gif" width="10"
height="18" border="0" alt="" align="absmiddle"><a href="  "
class="menuLink">Product Group 4</a><img src="images/
clear.gif" width="10" height="18" border="0" alt=""
align="absmiddle"></td>
     </tr>
</table></div>
```

INSERTING THE MENU LAYERS INTO YOUR HTML

We now have the basics of our menu finished; next, we need to
place our menu `<div>` into our existing HTML page. Because we
are going to be controlling the location of our menu with CSS, it
doesn't really matter where inside the `<body>` of our HTML we
place our `<div>`. However, to make it easier for us and others to
read our source, let's place our menus directly after the `<body>` tag
in our HTML, right before the code that creates the main portion
of our page.

```
<body bgcolor="#FFFFFF">
<div id="ProductsMenu">
<table border="1" cellpadding="0" cellspacing="0"
bordercolor="#CAD142">
     <tr>
          <td valign="top" align="left" bgcolor="#F3FB82">
          <img src="images/clear.gif" width="10"
height="18" border="0" alt="" align="absmiddle"><a href="  "
class="menuLink">Product Group 1</a><img src="images/
clear.gif" width="10" height="18" border="0" alt=""
align="absmiddle"></td>
     </tr>
     <tr>
          <td valign="top" align="left" bgcolor="#F3FB82">
          <img src="images/clear.gif" width="10"
height="18" border="0" alt="" align="absmiddle"><a href="  "
class="menuLink">Product Group 2</a><img src="images/
clear.gif" width="10" height="18" border="0" alt=""
align="absmiddle"></td>
     </tr>
     <tr>
          <td valign="top" align="left" bgcolor="#F3FB82">
          <img src="images/clear.gif" width="10"
height="18" border="0" alt="" align="absmiddle"><a href="  "
class="menuLink">Product Group 3</a><img src="images/
clear.gif" width="10" height="18" border="0" alt=""
align="absmiddle"></td>
     </tr>
```

```
<tr>
        <td valign="top" align="left" bgcolor="#F3FB82">
        <img src="images/clear.gif" width="10"
height="18" border="0" alt="" align="absmiddle"><a href=" "
class="menuLink">Product Group 4</a><img src="images/
clear.gif" width="10" height="18" border="0" alt=""
align="absmiddle"></td>
        </tr>
</table>
</div>


. . .

<table cellspacing="0" cellpadding="0" width="590">
    <tr>
        <td>
            <img src="images/secondary_top.gif"
alt="Shelley Biotech" width="333" height="68" border="0">
```

Now that we know how to create our menus and where to
insert them into our HTML, let's create the menu `<div>`s for the
rest of the main categories.

```
<body bgcolor="#FFFFFF">
<div id="ProductsMenu">
<table border="1" cellpadding="0" cellspacing="0"
bordercolor="#CAD142">
    <tr>
        <td valign="top" align="left" bgcolor="#F3FB82">
        <img src="images/clear.gif" width="10"
height="18" border="0" alt="" align="absmiddle"><a href=" "
class="menuLink">Product Group 1</a><img src="images/
clear.gif" width="10" height="18" border="0" alt=""
align="absmiddle"></td>
        </tr>
        <tr>
        <td valign="top" align="left" bgcolor="#F3FB82">
        <img src="images/clear.gif" width="10"
height="18" border="0" alt="" align="absmiddle"><a href=" "
class="menuLink">Product Group 2</a><img src="images/
clear.gif" width="10" height="18" border="0" alt=""
align="absmiddle"></td>
        </tr>
        <tr>
        <td valign="top" align="left" bgcolor="#F3FB82">
        <img src="images/clear.gif" width="10"
height="18" border="0" alt="" align="absmiddle"><a href=" "
class="menuLink">Product Group 3</a><img src="images/
```

```
clear.gif" width="10" height="18" border="0" alt=""
align="absmiddle"></td>
    </tr>
    <tr>
        <td valign="top" align="left" bgcolor="#F3FB82">
        <img src="images/clear.gif" width="10"
height="18" border="0" alt="" align="absmiddle"><a href=" "
class="menuLink">Product Group 4</a><img src="images/
clear.gif" width="10" height="18" border="0" alt=""
align="absmiddle"></td>
    </tr>
</table>
</div>


<div id="ServicesMenu">
<table border="1" cellpadding="0" cellspacing="0"
bordercolor="#CAD142">
    <tr>
        <td valign="top" align="left" bgcolor="#F3FB82">
        <img src="images/clear.gif" width="10"
height="18" border="0" alt="" align="absmiddle"><a href=" "
class="menuLink">Service 1</a><img src="images/clear.gif"
width="10" height="18" border="0" alt=""
align="absmiddle"></td>
    </tr>
    <tr>
        <td valign="top" align="left" bgcolor="#F3FB82">
        <img src="images/clear.gif" width="10"
height="18" border="0" alt="" align="absmiddle"><a href=" "
class="menuLink">Services 2</a><img src="images/clear.gif"
width="10" height="18" border="0" alt=""
align="absmiddle"></td>
    </tr>
    <tr>
        <td valign="top" align="left" bgcolor="#F3FB82">
        <img src="images/clear.gif" width="10"
height="18" border="0" alt="" align="absmiddle"><a href=" "
class="menuLink">Services 3</a><img src="images/clear.gif"
width="10" height="18" border="0" alt=""
align="absmiddle"></td>
    </tr>
</table>
</div>


<div id="TrainingMenu">
<table border="1" cellpadding="0" cellspacing="0"
bordercolor="#CAD142">
    <tr>
```

```
            <td valign="top" align="left" bgcolor="#F3FB82">
            <img src="images/clear.gif" width="10"
height="18" border="0" alt="" align="absmiddle"><a href=" "
class="menuLink">Class Descriptions</a><img src="images/
clear.gif" width="10" height="18" border=0 alt=""
align="absmiddle"></td>
        </tr>
        <tr>
            <td valign="top" align="left" bgcolor="#F3FB82">
            <img src="images/clear.gif" width="10"
height="18" border="0" alt="" align="absmiddle"><a href=" "
class="menuLink">Current Schedule</a><img src="images/
clear.gif" width="10" height="18" border=0 alt=""
align="absmiddle"></td>
        </tr>
</table>
</div>

<div id="CommonMenu">
<table border="1" cellpadding="0" cellspacing="0"
bordercolor="#CAD142">
        <tr>
            <td valign="top" align="left" bgcolor="#F3FB82">
            <img src="images/clear.gif" width="10"
height="18" border="0" alt="" align="absmiddle"><a href=" "
class="menuLink">Project 1</a><img src="images/clear.gif"
width="10" height="18" border=0 alt=""
align="absmiddle"></td>
        </tr>
        <tr>
            <td valign="top" align="left" bgcolor="#F3FB82">
            <img src="images/clear.gif" width="10"
height="18" border="0" alt="" align="absmiddle"><a href=" "
class="menuLink">Project 2</a><img src="images/clear.gif"
width="10" height="18" border=0 alt=""
align="absmiddle"></td>
        </tr>
        <tr>
            <td valign="top" align="left" bgcolor="#F3FB82">
            <img src="images/clear.gif" width="10"
height="18" border="0" alt="" align="absmiddle"><a href=" "
class="menuLink">Project 3</a><img src="images/clear.gif"
width="10" height="18" border=0 alt=""
align="absmiddle"></td>
        </tr>
</table>
</div>
```

```
<div id="NewsMenu">
<table border="1" cellpadding="0" cellspacing="0"
bordercolor="#CAD142">
    <tr>
        <td valign="top" align="left" bgcolor="#F3FB82">
        <img src="images/clear.gif" width="10"
height="18" border="0" alt="" align="absmiddle"><a href=" "
class="menuLink">News Articles</a><img src="images/
clear.gif" width="10" height="18" border="0" alt=""
align="absmiddle"></td>
    </tr>
    <tr>
        <td valign="top" align="left" bgcolor="#F3FB82">
        <img src="images/clear.gif" width="10"
height="18" border="0" alt="" align="absmiddle"><a href=" "
class="menuLink">Press Releases</a><img src="images/
clear.gif" width="10" height="18" border="0" alt=""
align="absmiddle"></td>
    </tr>
</table>
</div>

<div id="AboutMenu">
<table border="1" cellpadding="0" cellspacing="0"
bordercolor="#CAD142">
    <tr>
        <td valign="top" align="left" bgcolor="#F3FB82">
        <img src="images/clear.gif" width="10"
height="18" border="0" alt="" align="absmiddle"><a href=" "
class="menuLink">Coporate Information</a><img src="images/
clear.gif" width="10" height="18" border="0" alt=""
align="absmiddle"></td>
    </tr>
    <tr>
        <td valign="top" align="left" bgcolor="#F3FB82">
        <img src="images/clear.gif" width="10"
height="18" border="0" alt="" align="absmiddle"><a href=" "
class="menuLink">History</a><img src="images/clear.gif"
width="10" height="18" border="0" alt=""
align="absmiddle"></td>
    </tr>
    <tr>
        <td valign="top" align="left" bgcolor="#F3FB82">
        <img src="images/clear.gif" width="10"
height="18" border="0" alt="" align="absmiddle"><a href=" "
class="menuLink">Mission</a><img src="images/clear.gif"
width="10" height="18" border="0" alt=""
align="absmiddle"></td>
    </tr>
```

```
    </tr>
    <tr>
        <td valign="top" align="left" bgcolor="#F3FB82">
        <img src="images/clear.gif" width="10"
height="18" border="0" alt="" align="absmiddle"><a href=" "
class="menuLink">Contact Us</a><img src="images/clear.gif"
width="10" height="18" border="0" alt=""
align="absmiddle"></td>
    </tr>
</table>
</div>
<table cellspacing="0" cellpadding="0" width="590">
    <tr>
        <td>
            <img src="images/secondary_top.gif"
alt="Shelley Biotech" width="333" height="68" border="0">
```

If you were to load the page right now, you would notice that our menus still just display one after another at the top of our page. To make sure that they are positioned correctly and are not visible upon page load, we need to create CSS selectors that will control these properties of the menus.

CREATING THE CSS SELECTORS

To create our CSS selectors, we open up our *.css* file. We will create a selector for each menu that we have created. Creating a selector is almost identical to creating a class, which we have already done in previous projects, so it should be easy to pick up. Let's start with the selector for the Products menu. We have already assigned a name to this menu, ProductsMenu, so our selector will need to have the same name. Let's insert our new selector at the top of the CSS file styles_default.css, which already holds our font styles.

```
#ProductsMenu  {

    .  .  .

}
```

This should look very similar to the way in which we have created classes in the past, the only difference being that we are starting our definition with the pound (#) symbol as opposed to a period (.). This tells the browser that the definition that follows will be for a selector as opposed to a class. Now that we've got the framework for our definition, let's add the properties that will control the layout and appearance of the menu.

```
#ProductsMenu   {
      z-index : 2;
      position : absolute;
      top : 115px;
      left : 22px;
      visibility : hidden;
}
```

Okay, we've added five properties to our selector definitions: z-index, position, top, left, and visibility. Let's go over each property as well as the value we have assigned to each.

First we have the z-index property; this is the property that controls how items overlap each other. If you think of a grid with x and y coordinates, x would be the lines going left to right, while y would be the lines going top to bottom. Now imagine an axis that is coming towards and going away from you—this would be the z axis. So, the higher we make the value of the z-index, the closer the selector would be to you. For example, if you have two menus that are positioned to overlap each other, the one with the higher z-index would be in front of the one with the lower z-index.

For our purposes, we will assign all of our menus the value of 2 for their z-index. This will make them display in front of the main HTML of the page, which by default has a z-index value of 1. But, you ask, won't the menus overlap each other if they all have the same z-index? The answer is no. Only one of our menus will be visible at a time, so we don't have to worry about them overlapping; all we care about is that they show up in front of the main HTML of the page. If we were working on a project that had multiple menus visible at the same time, then we would want to make sure that the z-index values were different.

Next, we have the position property; this property is always set to either absolute or relative. If it's set to absolute, the selector will be positioned from the top left corner of the page, no matter where the <div> that holds our menu is located within the HTML. If it is set to relative, the position we set the menu to will be applied from the location of the parent of the <div> or, if there is no style defined for its parent, it will be positioned from the location where the <div> is within the HTML. In our project, we want to explicitly position our menus so we won't have to worry about their positions within the HTML, so we will choose absolute for the position property.

Now that we know how we're going to position our menu, it's time to actually tell the browser where we want the menu to be located. To do this, we use the top and left properties. For the Products menu, we set the top to 115 pixels from the top of the page, and we set left to 22 pixels from the left side of the page.

Finally, we need to tell the browser that we initially want the menu to be hidden when the page is first loaded. To do this, we specify a value of hidden for the visibility property.

That's it for our ProductsMenu selector. Let's create the selectors for the rest of our menus.

```
#ProductsMenu {
        z-index : 2;
        position : absolute;
        top : 115px;
        left : 22px;
        visibility : hidden;
}

#ServicesMenu {
        z-index : 2;
        position : absolute;
        top : 115px;
        left : 87px;
        visibility : hidden;
}

#TrainingMenu {
        z-index : 2;
        position : absolute;
        top : 115px;
        left : 160px;
        visibility : hidden;
}

#CommonMenu {
        z-index : 2;
        position : absolute;
        top : 115px;
        left : 234px;
        visibility : hidden;
}

#NewsMenu {
        z-index : 2;
```

```
        position : absolute;
        top : 115px;
        left : 390px;
        isibility : hidden;
    }

#AboutMenu   {
        z-index : 2;
        position : absolute;
        top : 115px;
        left : 487px;
        visibility : hidden;
    }
```

That does it for our menu selectors; you'll notice that if you reload your page, the menus are now hidden, and you'll have to take my word for it that they are positioned right until we get our functions built and our event handlers in place. Now that the selectors are defined in our styles_default.css file, we need to copy them into our styles_mac_4x.css file as well. Don't forget that these are the files that are being linked to our HTML pages and that define all of our styles for the site. Let's close up our CSS files and move on to our JavaScript file and the functions that will run our script.

Creating the Navigation Function

Again, because this script will be located on all of the pages in the site, we place it in our external JavaScript file. Our new script will not only be showing and hiding the navigation menus, but will also take care of the image rollovers of the navigation images, so we are going to get rid of our existing image rollover functions. We'll insert our new functions right below the existing IMAGE objects for the navigation rollovers. Before we get to our navigation function, though, we need to define some variables that will be used in our script.

```
var over = 'no';
var lastMenu = ' ';
var styleSheetElement;
var oldElement;
```

Let's take a quick look at the variables that we've added to our script. First, we declared a variable called over; we will use this variable to let us know if the user is currently over a navigation image or menu. We assign it a default value of no. Next, we have the variable `lastMenu`, which holds the name of the menu that was displayed by our script. The next two variables, `styleSheetElement` and `oldElement`, are used to gather the name of the menu if the user is browsing with Internet Explorer 5 or above or Netscape 6x browsers. We'll get into a deeper explanation for these two when we reach that part of the script. With our variables defined, let's create our functions.

The first function we create is called when a navigation image is rolled over and we want to display a menu; it is called `menuOn`. The first thing we want to do when this function is called is set the value of our `over` variable to yes. This tells us that the user currently is over either the navigation image or its menu.

```
function menuOn(currentMenu) {
over = 'yes';
. . .
}
```

As in our image rollover functions that we did in a previous project, different browser and versions of browsers have different methods for accessing and modifying the objects and properties that we need to work with. So, we are going to have to create some `if` statements that will let us treat different browsers and versions differently. For our script, we must treat Netscape 4.x one way and Internet Explorer and Netscape 6.x another way. Let's set up our `if` statements to allow us to do that. We have already created variables inside our external JavaScript file to hold the various details of the user's browser. We will use these to help us decide which method we will use to gather and modify the necessary information.

```
function menuOn(currentMenu) {
    over = 'yes';
    if ((browser == 'Netscape') && (version < 5)) {
        . . .
    }
    else {
        . . .
    }
}
```

We now have an `if` statement that will execute one section of code if the user is on Netscape with a version below 5, and execute another section of code for all other browsers. As in our image rollovers functions, we do the same things in both sections of code, but we go about it in slightly different ways. The first thing we want our function to do is check if there is currently a navigation menu being displayed. If there is, we want to turn that menu and the navigation image it corresponds to off before we display the new menu that the user wants.

```
function menuOn(currentMenu) {
     over = 'yes';
     if ((browser == 'Netscape') && (version < 5)) {
          if (lastMenu != ' ')  {
                    . . .
          }
             . . .
     }
     else {
             . . .
     }
}
```

What we've done is set up another if statement, this time checking to see if the variable lastMenu has a value. You will remember that we initially assigned it a blank value. So, if the user has just loaded the page and no menu is yet showing, this next section of code will not be executed and our function will move down to the part that turns on the new menu. However, if lastMenu does hold the name of a menu, that means there's a good chance that another menu is currently being displayed. If that is the case, the engine needs to turn off whichever menu is visible.

```
function menuOn(currentMenu) {
     over = 'yes';
     if ((browser == 'Netscape') && (version < 5)) {
          if (lastMenu != ' ')  {
                    document.images[lastMenu].src =
               eval(lastMenu + 'Off.src');
                    eval('document.' + lastMenu +
'Menu.visibility = "hidden"');
          }
             . . .
      }
     else {
             . . .
     }
}
```

The first of these two new lines should look somewhat familiar. Not only do we need to turn off any currently showing menu, we also need to unhighlight the navigation image that corresponds to that menu. That's what we do in this first line, using the same technique that we used in our normal image rollover functions. Because `lastMenu` holds the name of the menu, which shares the same name as the navigation image that corresponds to it, we can use the `lastMenu` variable to turn off both the navigation image and the menu. In the second line, we turn off the menu. By creating a selector and assigning it to our menu `<div>`, we also created a JavaScript object through which we can modify and access the selector/menu's properties. This is the object we access in the second line of code. We are telling the engine to turn the visibility property of that menu to the value of hidden, which will in effect hide the menu. Now that we've turned off any menu that was already being displayed, it's time to turn on the new image and navigation menu.

```
function menuOn(currentMenu) {
     over = 'yes';
     if ((browser == 'Netscape') && (version < 5)) {
          if (lastMenu != ' ')  {
               document.images[lastMenu].src =
          eval(lastMenu + 'Off.src');
               eval('document.' + lastMenu +
'Menu.visibility = "hidden"');
          }
          document.images[currentMenu].src =
eval(currentMenu + 'On.src');
          eval('document.' + currentMenu + 'Menu.visibility
= "visible"');
          . . .
     }
     else {
          . . .
     }
}
```

The next two lines are pretty much duplicates of the ones we used to turn off the image and menu in the previous section of code. However, there are two important differences. First, instead of using the value of the `lastMenu` variable, we are now using the value of the `currentMenu` variable, which is being passed into our function from the event handler. This means we will be accessing the properties of the objects for the image and menu that the user has rolled over. Second, we are now specifying the `On` image object as well as changing the `visibility` property of the menu to visible. This will actually do the work of turning on the new image and menu. There is one last step before we move on to taking care of users on Internet Explorer or Netscape 6.x. We must set the `lastMenu` variable to hold the name of the menu currently held in the `currentMenu` variable.

```
function menuOn(currentMenu) {
    over = 'yes';
    if ((browser == 'Netscape') && (version < 5)) {
        if (lastMenu != ' ')  {
            document.images[lastMenu].src =
        eval(lastMenu + 'Off.src');
            eval('document.' + lastMenu +
    'Menu.visibility = "hidden"');
        }
        document.images[currentMenu].src =
    eval(currentMenu + 'On.src');
        eval('document.' + currentMenu + 'Menu.visibility
    = "visible"');
        lastMenu = currentMenu;
    }
    else {
        . . .
    }
}
```

This is done so that when the function is called the next time, the function knows which image and menu to turn off before turning on the new image and menu. So, if the user first comes to the page and rolls over the products images, the function will first check to see if there is anything held in the `lastMenu` variable. If there is not, it will turn on the products image and menu, and then store Products in the `lastMenu` variable. Then, if the user rolls over the services image, the function will see that the `lastMenu` variable has a value and turn off the products image and menu before turning on the services image and menu.

All right, we've finished up the Netscape 4.x portion of the function. Let's move on to the section that deals with those users on Internet Explorer or Netscape 6.x.

As in the code for the older versions of Netscape, the first thing we need to do is turn off any menu and image that is currently being displayed, so let's start with the if statement to do that.

```
function menuOn(currentMenu) {
    over = 'yes';
    if ((browser == 'Netscape') && (version < 5)) {
```

```
        if (lastMenu != ' ')  {
            document.images[lastMenu].src =
        eval(lastMenu + 'Off.src');
            eval('document.' + lastMenu +
'Menu.visibility = "hidden"');
        }
        document.images[currentMenu].src =
eval(currentMenu + 'On.src');
        eval('document.' + currentMenu + 'Menu.visibility
= "visible"');
        lastMenu = currentMenu;
    }
    else {
        if (lastMenu != ' ') {
        . . .
        }
        . . .
    }
}
```

Next, we add the line to turn off the currently highlighted
navigation image.

```
function menuOn(currentMenu) {
    over = 'yes';
    if ((browser == 'Netscape') && (version < 5)) {
        if (lastMenu != ' ')  {
            document.images[lastMenu].src =
        eval(lastMenu + 'Off.src');
            eval('document.' + lastMenu +
'Menu.visibility = "hidden"');
        }
        document.images[currentMenu].src =
eval(currentMenu + 'On.src');
        eval('document.' + currentMenu + 'Menu.visibility
= "visible"');
        lastMenu = currentMenu;
    }
    else {
        if (lastMenu != ' ') {
            eval('document.images[lastMenu].src =
' + lastMenu + 'Off.src');
            . . .
        }
        . . .
    }
}
```

You'll notice that again this is the same code that we used to turn off the images in our old image rollover function. Let's move on to the code that will turn off the currently displayed menu. As was stated previously, the manner in which we access the `menu` object in Internet Explorer and Netscape 6.x varies from the method that we used above. Both of these browsers strictly follow the World Wide Web Consortium (W3C) standards for CSS, and because the menu object is created with a CSS selector, we must follow these standards to access and modify their properties.

```
function menuOn(currentMenu) {
      over = 'yes';
      if ((browser == 'Netscape') && (version < 5)) {
            if (lastMenu != ' ')  {
                  document.images[lastMenu].src =
            eval(lastMenu + 'Off.src');
                  eval('document.' + lastMenu +
'Menu.visibility = "hidden"');
            }
            document.images[currentMenu].src =
eval(currentMenu + 'On.src');
            eval('document.' + currentMenu + 'Menu.visibility
= "visible"');
            lastMenu = currentMenu;
      }
      else {
            if (lastMenu != ' ') {
                  eval('document.images[lastMenu].src = ' +
lastMenu + 'Off.src');
lastMenu = lastMenu + 'Menu';
                  oldElement =
document.getElementById(lastMenu);
                  oldElement.style.visibility = "hidden";}
            . . .
      }
}
```

Let's go over the three lines of code that perform this section of our script. First, we need to combine the value of the `lastMenu` variable with the word `Menu` to create the full name of the navigation menu; we then store this back into the `lastMenu` variable.

```
lastMenu = lastMenu + 'Menu';
```

We then use this value to go into the document object model (DOM) and retrieve the internal name of our menu by its ID, which is now held in the variable `lastMenu`. Once we have that name, we store it in the variable `oldElement`.

```
oldElement = document.getElementById(lastMenu);
```

We call the variable `oldElement` because this holds the ID of the menu that is already showing, not the one that the user has most recently rolled over. The final line in this section is the line that actually turns the previously displayed menu invisible.

```
oldElement.style.visibility = "hidden";
```

Now that we know the ID of this object, we simply have to call on its `visibility` property and give it a value of `hidden`. These lines will take care of turning off any menu/image that is already being displayed, so let's move on to the next step: turning on the new menu/image.

To do this, we again follow the same method that we used to turn off the old menu/image, only making calls to the new image and menu, the names of which are being passed into the function from the event handler. First, we turn on the new navigation image.

```
function menuOn(currentMenu) {
    over = 'yes';
    if ((browser == 'Netscape') && (version < 5)) {
        if (lastMenu != ' ') {
            document.images[lastMenu].src =
        eval(lastMenu + 'Off.src');
                eval('document.' + lastMenu +
'Menu.visibility = "hidden"');
        }
        document.images[currentMenu].src =
eval(currentMenu + 'On.src');
        eval('document.' + currentMenu + 'Menu.visibility
= "visible"');
            lastMenu = currentMenu;
    }
    else {
        if (lastMenu != ' ') {
            eval('document.images[lastMenu].src = ' +
lastMenu + 'Off.src');
lastMenu = lastMenu + 'Menu';
            oldElement =
document.getElementById(lastMenu);
            oldElement.style.visibility = "hidden";}
```

```
        eval('document.images[currentMenu].src = ' +
currentMenu + 'On.src');
            . . .
    }
}
```

Next, we find the internal ID of the new menu and assign its visibility property to visible.

```
function menuOn(currentMenu) {
    over = 'yes';
    if ((browser == 'Netscape') && (version < 5)) {
        if (lastMenu != ' ') {
            document.images[lastMenu].src =
        eval(lastMenu + 'Off.src');
            eval('document.' + lastMenu +
'Menu.visibility = "hidden"');
        }
        document.images[currentMenu].src =
eval(currentMenu + 'On.src');
        eval('document.' + currentMenu + 'Menu.visibility
= "visible"');
    lastMenu = currentMenu;
    }
    else {
        if (lastMenu != ' ') {
            eval('document.images[lastMenu].src = ' +
lastMenu + 'Off.src');
    lastMenu = lastMenu + 'Menu';
            oldElement =
document.getElementById(lastMenu);
            oldElement.style.visibility = "hidden";}
        eval('document.images[currentMenu].src = ' +
currentMenu + 'On.src');
        var layerName = currentMenu + 'Menu';
        styleSheetElement =
    document.getElementById(layerName);
        styleSheetElement.style.visibility = "visible";
            . . .
    }
}
```

As in the section of code where we turn off the old menu, the first thing we do is create the full name of the menu and store it in a variable called layerName. Next, we use that name to get the ID of the menu, and then use that ID to turn on the new menu. The last thing we need to do is update the lastMenu variable to hold the name of the new menu.

```
function menuOn(currentMenu) {
    over = 'yes';
    if ((browser == 'Netscape') && (version < 5)) {
        if (lastMenu != ' ')  {
document.images[lastMenu].src = eval(lastMenu + 'Off.src');
            eval('document.' + lastMenu +
'Menu.visibility = "hidden"');
        }
        document.images[currentMenu].src =
eval(currentMenu + 'On.src');
        eval('document.' + currentMenu + 'Menu.visibility
= "visible"');
lastMenu = currentMenu;
    }
    else {
        if (lastMenu != ' ') {
            eval('document.images[lastMenu].src = ' +
lastMenu + 'Off.src');
lastMenu = lastMenu + 'Menu';
            oldElement =
document.getElementById(lastMenu);
            oldElement.style.visibility = "hidden";
        }
        eval('document.images[currentMenu].src = ' +
currentMenu + 'On.src');
        var layerName = currentMenu + 'Menu';
        styleSheetElement =
document.getElementById(layerName);
        styleSheetElement.style.visibility = "visible";
        lastMenu = currentMenu;
    }
}
```

We are now done with the menuOn function, which is by far
the most complicated of the three that we need to create to run
this script.

"Three?" you ask. "We only used two in our image rollover
script." This is true, but we have an extra element in this script
that we didn't have in the standard rollover script. In the standard rollover script, it was fairly straightforward; the user would
roll over an image and the image would highlight. When the
user rolled off the image, it would return to normal. Now, even if
the user rolled directly from one image to another, the script
would turn off the old one before highlighting the new one. In
our new script, however, we're not only dealing with images, but
we have thrown CSS menus in to boot. If we were to call the off
function the minute the user rolled off of the navigation image,

the menu would disappear before the user had a chance to get to the menu and select any of its options. This wouldn't work at all. What we need to do in our script is insert a slight delay into this process, giving the user time to get over the menu, which would stay visible once the user was over it. To accomplish this, we need the third function that was mentioned above. The purpose of this function is to tell the script that the user has rolled off of the navigation image or menu and to set a timer, which will call the menuOff() function after a short delay. This gives the user time to get over the navigation menu, and if the user were truly rolling off of the image, then the menuOff() function would be called and it would turn off the navigation image/menu. Let's get started on our timer function. We'll call it overChecker() and place it right below our menuOn() function.

```
function overChecker(currentMenu) {
    . . .
}
```

We now have our overChecker() function defined, and we pass in the name of the menu the user is currently over and store it in the variable currentMenu. Next, we set a couple of variables that we will need later on in the script.

```
function overChecker(currentMenu) {
    over = 'no';
    lastMenu = currentMenu;
    . . .
}
```

First, we set the over variable to the value of no to let our script know that the user is currently not over either a navigation image or menu. Next, we again set the lastMenu variable to the value of currentMenu to let the script know which menu or image was most recently rolled off of.

Next, we use the setTimeOut() function to create a timer that will call the menuOff function after a short delay.

```
function overChecker(currentMenu) {
    over = 'no';
    lastMenu = currentMenu;
    setTimeout("menuOff()", 300);
}
```

With the addition of our timer, when the overChecker() function is called, there will be a delay of 300 milliseconds, then the `menuOff()` function will be called. This delay should give the user plenty of time to get to the navigation menu if that is his or her intent. Now, let's move on to the final function, the `menuOff()` function. As always, we start by defining our function.

```
function menuOff() {
    . . .
}
```

The first thing we need to do in this function is find out if the user truly has rolled off of both the navigation image and the menu. When the user rolled off of either the image or the menu, the `overChecker()` function was called and the variable `over` was set to `no`. If the user hasn't rolled back over an image or menu, then `over` should still contain that value. So, we set up an `if` statement to check the value of the variable `over`.

```
function menuOff() {
    if (over == 'no')   {
        . . .
    }
}
```

If `over` is still equal to `no`, then we need to have code that will turn off the navigation image and menu. If the user has rolled back over an image or menu, then the rest of the code will be ignored and we'll leave the function. The next step is to insert the code that will execute if the `over` variable is still equal to `no`. As with our `menuOn()` function, we need to have two sections of code to handle this: one for Netscape 4.x browsers and one to handle the browsers that follow the W3C CSS standard.

```
function menuOff() {
    if (over == 'no')   {
        if ((browser == 'Netscape') && (version < 5)) {
            . . .
        }
        else {
            . . .
        }
    }
}
```

Again, we added an `if` statement to funnel the right browser to the right version of the code. Let's put in the code that will turn off the menu/image for Netscape 4.x browsers.

```
function menuOff() {
    if (over == 'no')  {
        if ((browser == 'Netscape') && (version < 5)) {
            document.images[lastMenu].src =
eval(lastMenu + 'Off.src');
            eval('document.' + lastMenu +
'Menu.visibility = "hidden"');
        }
        else {
            . . .
        }
    }
}
```

These two lines of code are identical to the ones we used in the menuOn() function to turn off any previously displayed menu and image. In the first line, we turn off the currently displayed image, and then in the second line, we turn the corresponding menu invisible. With that done, let's add the code we need for the W3C-compliant browsers.

```
function menuOff() {
    if (over == 'no')  {
        if ((browser == 'Netscape') && (version < 5)) {
            document.images[lastMenu].src =
eval(lastMenu + 'Off.src');
            eval('document.' + lastMenu +
'Menu.visibility = "hidden"');
        }
        else {
            eval('document.images[lastMenu].src = ' +
lastMenu + 'Off.src');
            styleSheetElement.style.visibility =
"hidden";
        }
    }
}
```

Again, we use nearly the same code that we inserted to turn off the menu and image in the menuOn() function. We first turn off the navigation image, and then we move on to the navigation menu. You will notice that unlike in the menuOn() function, we use only a single line to turn off the menu. This is because the variable sytleSheetElement still holds the ID of the menu that we need to turn off, so all we need to do in this function is set the visibility property to hidden.

That finishes off the functions that we need for our script. Let's move on to the event handlers that we need to insert into the HTML.

Creating and Inserting the Event Handlers

As with our regular image rollover script, we will use the `onMouseOver` and `onMouseOut` event handlers. However, for this project we need to use them in more than just the anchor tags for the navigation images. We also need to put them in the menu `<div>`s themselves. This is so the script will know to keep the menus visible when the user is over them or turn them invisible when the user rolls off. Let's start with the event handlers for the navigation image anchor tags. We'll first insert the handlers for the product's image.

```
<a href="index.html" onMouseOver="menuOn('Products');
window.status='Products'; return true;"
onMouseOut="overChecker('Products'); window.status=' ';
return true;">
```

In the `onMouseOver` handler, we call the `menuOn()` function and pass it the value `Products`. We also set the window status to `Products`. In the `onMouseOut` handler, we call the `overChecker()` function and pass it the value `Products` as well. We then reset the window status to be blank. We now insert the handlers into the rest of the navigation image anchors with the proper values being sent to the functions.

```
<a href="index.html" onMouseOver="menuOn('Products');
window.status='Products'; return true;"
onMouseOut="overChecker('Products'); window.status=' ';
return true;"><img src="images/products_off.gif" width=71
height=33 border=0 name="Products" alt="Products"></a>

<a href="services/index.html"
onMouseOver="menuOn('Services'); window.status='Services';
return true;" onMouseOut="overChecker('Services');
window.status=' '; return true;"><img src="images/
services_off.gif" width=67 height=33 border=0
name="Services" alt="Services"></a>

<a href="training/index.html"
onMouseOver="menuOn('Training'); window.status='Training';
return true;" onMouseOut="overChecker('Training');
window.status=' '; return true;"><img src="images/
```

```
training_off.gif" width=75 height=33 border=0
name="Training" alt="Training"></a>

<a href="common/index.html" onMouseOver="menuOn('Common');
window.status='Common Good Projects'; return true;"
onMouseOut="overChecker('Common'); window.status=' ';
return true;"><img src="images/common_off.gif" width=157
height=33 border=0 name="Common" alt="Common Good"></a>

<a href="genetic/index.html" onMouseOver="menuOn('News');
window.status='Genetic News'; return true;"
onMouseOut="overChecker('News'); window.status=' ';
return true;"><img src="images/news_off.gif" width=98
height=33 border=0 name="News" alt="Genetic News"></a>

<a href="about/index.html" onMouseOver="menuOn('About');
window.status='About Us'; return true;"
onMouseOut="overChecker('About'); window.status=' ';
return true;"><img src="images/about_off.gif" width=106
height=33 border=0 name="About" alt="About Shelley"></a>
```

Now that we have all of the event handlers in the anchor tags, we must insert event handlers into the individual menus. Again, we use the onMouseOver and onMouseOut handlers, but we do slightly different things inside the menus: Once the user has rolled from the navigation image to the menu, we want to stop the menuOff() function from running. You will remember that once the user has rolled off the navigation image, the overChecker() function sets the variable over equal to no and then waits 300 milliseconds and calls the menuOff() function. If we don't stop the menuOff() function, then even though the user is now over the menu, it will disappear. To stop that from happening, we have the onMouseOver handler set the value of over to yes. This stops the menuOff() function from turning off the navigation image and menu.

The onMouseOut() handler will be the same as the handlers in the anchors of the images; it will call the overChecker() function. Let's insert these two handlers into the Products menu. We place them inside the <div> tag, like so.

```
<div id="ProductsMenu" onMouseOver="over = 'yes';"
onMouseOut="overChecker('Products');">
. . .
```

In a perfect world, we would be done with this menu; however, just as in the functions, we have to code for the different browsers in these event handlers. This time, however, it means extra coding for Netscape 4.x instead of the W3C-compliant browsers. Because Netscape 4.x doesn't follow all of the CSS standards, it has problems seeing the built-in event handlers when they are being called from inside an object that is controlled by a CSS selector. So, we need to insert a little script into the menu `<div>` that will re-create these two functions: `onMouseOver()` and `onMouseOut`. These functions will then be called when the handlers in the `<div>` tag are triggered. Let's insert these functions into our Products menu.

```
<div id="ProductsMenu" onMouseOver="over = 'yes';"
onMouseOut="overChecker('Products');">
<script language="JavaScript1.2" >
    function onMouseOver() {over = 'yes';}
    function onMouseOut() {overChecker('Products');}
</script>
```

Inside the script, we first define a new `onMouseOver` function and make it set `over` equal to `yes` when it is called. Next, we define the `onMouseOut` function and have it call the `overChecker()` function and pass into it the value `Products`. This will take care of the problems that we would have run into with Netscape 4.x. Let's add the event handlers to the rest of the menus.

```
<div id="ProductsMenu" onMouseOver="over = 'yes';"
onMouseOut="overChecker('Products');">
<script language="JavaScript" type="text/javascript">
    function onMouseOver() {over = 'yes';}
    function onMouseOut() {overChecker('Products');}
</script>
<table border="1" cellpadding="0" cellspacing="0"
bordercolor="#CAD142">
    <tr>
        <td valign="top" align="left" bgcolor="#F3FB82">
        <img src="images/clear.gif" width="10"
height="18" border="0" alt="" align="absmiddle"><a href=" "
class="menuLink">Product Group 1</a><img src="images/
clear.gif" width="10" height="18" border="0" alt=""
align="absmiddle"></td>
    </tr>
    <tr>
        <td valign="top" align="left" bgcolor="#F3FB82">
        <img src="images/clear.gif" width="10"
height="18" border="0" alt="" align="absmiddle"><a href=" "
class="menuLink">Product Group 2</a><img src="images/
```

```
clear.gif" width="10" height="18" border="0" alt=""
align="absmiddle"></td>
    </tr>
    <tr>
        <td valign="top" align="left" bgcolor="#F3FB82">
        <img src="images/clear.gif" width="10"
height="18" border="0" alt="" align="absmiddle"><a href=" "
class="menuLink">Product Group 3</a><img src="images/
clear.gif" width="10" height="18" border="0" alt=""
align="absmiddle"></td>
    </tr>
    <tr>
        <td valign="top" align="left" bgcolor="#F3FB82">
        <img src="images/clear.gif" width="10"
height="18" border="0" alt="" align="absmiddle"><a href=" "
class="menuLink">Product Group 4</a><img src="images/
clear.gif" width="10" height="18" border="0" alt=""
align="absmiddle"></td>
    </tr>
</table>
</div>

<div id="ServicesMenu" onMouseOver="over = 'yes';"
onMouseOut="overChecker('Services');">
<script language="JavaScript" type="text/javascript">
    function onMouseOver() {over = 'yes';}
    function onMouseOut() {overChecker('Services');}
</script>
<table border="1" cellpadding="0" cellspacing="0"
bordercolor="#CAD142">
    <tr>
        <td valign="top" align="left" bgcolor="#F3FB82">
        <img src="images/clear.gif" width="10"
height="18" border="0" alt="" align="absmiddle"><a href=" "
class="menuLink">Service 1</a><img src="images/clear.gif"
width="10" height="18" border="0" alt=""
align="absmiddle"></td>
    </tr>
    <tr>
        <td valign="top" align="left" bgcolor="#F3FB82">
        <img src="images/clear.gif" width="10"
height="18" border="0" alt="" align="absmiddle"><a href=" "
class="menuLink">Services 2</a><img src="images/clear.gif"
width="10" height="18" border="0" alt=""
align="absmiddle"></td>
    </tr>
    <tr>
        <td valign="top" align="left" bgcolor="#F3FB82">
```

```
            <img src="images/clear.gif" width="10"
height="18" border="0" alt="" align="absmiddle"><a href=" "
class="menuLink">Services 3</a><img src="images/clear.gif"
width="10" height="18" border="0" alt=""
align="absmiddle"></td>
        </tr>
</table>
</div>

<div id="TrainingMenu" onMouseOver="over = 'yes';"
onMouseOut="overChecker('Training');">
<script language="JavaScript" type="text/javascript">
        function onMouseOver() {over = 'yes';}
        function onMouseOut() {overChecker('Training');}
</script>
<table border="1" cellpadding="0" cellspacing="0"
bordercolor="#CAD142">
        <tr>
            <td valign="top" align="left" bgcolor="#F3FB82">
            <img src="images/clear.gif" width="10"
height="18" border="0" alt="" align="absmiddle"><a href=" "
class="menuLink">Class Descriptions</a><img src="images/
clear.gif" width="10" height="18" border="0" alt=""
align="absmiddle"></td>
        </tr>
        <tr>
            <td valign="top" align="left" bgcolor="#F3FB82">
            <img src="images/clear.gif" width="10"
height="18" border="0" alt="" align="absmiddle"><a href=" "
class="menuLink">Current Schedule</a><img src="images/
clear.gif" width="10" height="18" border="0" alt=""
align="absmiddle"></td>
        </tr>
</table>
</div>

<div id="CommonMenu" onMouseOver="over = 'yes';"
onMouseOut="overChecker('Common');">
<script language="JavaScript" type="text/javascript">
        function onMouseOver() {over = 'yes';}
        function onMouseOut() {overChecker('Common');}
</script>
<table border="1" cellpadding="0" cellspacing="0"
bordercolor="#CAD142">
        <tr>
            <td valign="top" align="left" bgcolor="#F3FB82">
            <img src="images/clear.gif" width="10"
height="18" border="0" alt="" align="absmiddle"><a href=" "
class="menuLink">Project 1</a><img src="images/clear.gif"
```

```
width="10" height="18" border="0" alt=""
align="absmiddle"></td>
     </tr>
     <tr>
         <td valign="top" align="left" bgcolor="#F3FB82">
         <img src="images/clear.gif" width="10"
height="18" border="0" alt="" align="absmiddle"><a href=" "
class="menuLink">Project 2</a><img src="images/clear.gif"
width="10" height="18" border="0" alt=""
align="absmiddle"></td>
     </tr>
     <tr>
         <td valign="top" align="left" bgcolor="#F3FB82">
         <img src="images/clear.gif" width="10"
height="18" border="0" alt="" align="absmiddle"><a href=" "
class="menuLink">Project 3</a><img src="images/clear.gif"
width="10" height="18" border="0" alt=""
align="absmiddle"></td>
     </tr>
</table>
</div>

<div id="NewsMenu" onMouseOver="over = 'yes';"
onMouseOut="overChecker('News');">
<script language="JavaScript" type="text/javascript">
     function onMouseOver() {over = 'yes';}
     function onMouseOut() {overChecker('News');}
</script>
<table border="1" cellpadding="0" cellspacing="0"
bordercolor="#CAD142">
     <tr>
         <td valign="top" align="left" bgcolor="#F3FB82">
         <img src="images/clear.gif" width="10"
height="18" border="0" alt="" align="absmiddle"><a href=" "
class="menuLink">News Articles</a><img src="images/
clear.gif" width="10" height="18" border="0" alt=""
align="absmiddle"></td>
     </tr>
     <tr>
         <td valign="top" align="left" bgcolor="#F3FB82">
         <img src="images/clear.gif" width="10"
height="18" border="0" alt="" align="absmiddle"><a href=" "
class="menuLink">Press Releases</a><img src="images/
clear.gif" width="10" height="18" border="0" alt=""
align="absmiddle"></td>
     </tr>
</table>
</div>
```

```html
<div id="AboutMenu" onMouseOver="over = 'yes';"
onMouseOut="overChecker('About');">
<script language="JavaScript" type="text/javascript">
     function onMouseOver() {over = 'yes';}
     function onMouseOut() {overChecker('About');}
</script>
<table border="1" cellpadding="0" cellspacing="0"
bordercolor="#CAD142">
     <tr>
          <td valign="top" align="left" bgcolor="#F3FB82">
          <img src="images/clear.gif" width="10"
height="18" border="0" alt="" align="absmiddle"><a href=" "
class="menuLink">Coporate Information</a><img src="images/
clear.gif" width="10" height="18" border="0" alt=""
align="absmiddle"></td>
     </tr>
     <tr>
          <td valign="top" align="left" bgcolor="#F3FB82">
          <img src="images/clear.gif" width="10"
height="18" border="0" alt="" align="absmiddle"><a href=" "
class="menuLink">History</a><img src="images/clear.gif"
width="10" height="18" border="0" alt=""
align="absmiddle"></td>
     </tr>
     <tr>
          <td valign="top" align="left" bgcolor="#F3FB82">
          <img src="images/clear.gif" width="10"
height="18" border="0" alt="" align="absmiddle"><a href=" "
class="menuLink">Mission</a><img src="images/clear.gif"
width="10" height="18" border="0" alt=""
align="absmiddle"></td>
     </tr>
     <tr>
          <td valign="top" align="left" bgcolor="#F3FB82">
          <img src="images/clear.gif" width="10"
height="18" border="0" alt="" align="absmiddle"><a href=" "
class="menuLink">Contact Us</a><img src="images/clear.gif"
width="10" height="18" border="0" alt=""
align="absmiddle"></td>
     </tr>
</table>
</div>
```

Believe it or not, that's it. We're done with our script. Reload your page and give it a shot. This was a fairly complex project, so let's go over the steps we took in creating it.

Reviewing the Script

First, we had a brief intoduction to the workings of CSS and DHTML. Then, we moved on to creating our navigation menus.

```
<div id="ProductsMenu">
<table border="1" cellpadding="0" cellspacing="0"
bordercolor="#CAD142">
    <tr>
        <td valign="top" align="left" bgcolor="#F3FB82">
        <img src="images/clear.gif" width="10"
height="18" border="0" alt="" align="absmiddle"><a href=" "
class="menuLink">Product Group 1</a><img src="images/
clear.gif" width="10" height="18" border="0" alt=""
align="absmiddle"></td>
    </tr>
    <tr>
        <td valign="top" align="left" bgcolor="#F3FB82">
        <img src="images/clear.gif" width="10"
height="18" border="0" alt="" align="absmiddle"><a href=" "
class="menuLink">Product Group 2</a><img src="images/
clear.gif" width="10" height="18" border="0" alt=""
align="absmiddle"></td>
    </tr>
    <tr>
        <td valign="top" align="left" bgcolor="#F3FB82">
        <img src="images/clear.gif" width="10"
height="18" border="0" alt="" align="absmiddle"><a href=" "
class="menuLink">Product Group 3</a><img src="images/
clear.gif" width="10" height="18" border="0" alt=""
align="absmiddle"></td>
    </tr>
    <tr>
        <td valign="top" align="left" bgcolor="#F3FB82">
        <img src="images/clear.gif" width="10"
height="18" border="0" alt="" align="absmiddle"><a href=" "
class="menuLink">Product Group 4</a><img src="images/
clear.gif" width="10" height="18" border="0" alt=""
align="absmiddle"></td>
    </tr>
</table>
</div>

<div id="ServicesMenu">
<table border="1" cellpadding="0" cellspacing="0"
bordercolor="#CAD142">
    <tr>
```

```
            <td valign="top" align="left" bgcolor="#F3FB82">
            <img src="images/clear.gif" width="10"
height="18" border="0" alt="" align="absmiddle"><a href=" "
class="menuLink">Service 1</a><img src="images/clear.gif"
width="10" height="18" border="0" alt=""
align="absmiddle"></td>
      </tr>
      <tr>
            <td valign="top" align="left" bgcolor="#F3FB82">
            <img src="images/clear.gif" width="10"
height="18" border="0" alt="" align="absmiddle"><a href=" "
class="menuLink">Services 2</a><img src="images/clear.gif"
width="10" height="18" border="0" alt=""
align="absmiddle"></td>
      </tr>
      <tr>
            <td valign="top" align="left" bgcolor="#F3FB82">
            <img src="images/clear.gif" width="10"
height="18" border="0" alt="" align="absmiddle"><a href=" "
class="menuLink">Services 3</a><img src="images/clear.gif"
width="10" height="18" border="0" alt=""
align="absmiddle"></td>
      </tr>
</table>
</div>

<div id="TrainingMenu">
<table border="1" cellpadding="0" cellspacing="0"
bordercolor="#CAD142">
      <tr>
            <td valign="top" align="left" bgcolor="#F3FB82">
            <img src="images/clear.gif" width="10"
height="18" border="0" alt="" align="absmiddle"><a href=" "
class="menuLink">Class Descriptions</a><img src="images/
clear.gif" width="10" height="18" border="0" alt=""
align="absmiddle"></td>
      </tr>
      <tr>
            <td valign="top" align="left" bgcolor="#F3FB82">
            <img src="images/clear.gif" width="10"
height="18" border="0" alt="" align="absmiddle"><a href=" "
class="menuLink">Current Schedule</a><img src="images/
clear.gif" width="10" height="18" border="0" alt=""
align="absmiddle"></td>
      </tr>
</table>
</div>
```

```html
<div id="CommonMenu">
<table border="1" cellpadding="0" cellspacing="0"
bordercolor="#CAD142">
    <tr>
        <td valign="top" align="left" bgcolor="#F3FB82">
        <img src="images/clear.gif" width="10"
height="18" border="0" alt="" align="absmiddle"><a href=" "
class="menuLink">Project 1</a><img src="images/clear.gif"
width="10" height="18" border="0" alt=""
align="absmiddle"></td>
    </tr>
    <tr>
        <td valign="top" align="left" bgcolor="#F3FB82">
        <img src="images/clear.gif" width="10"
height="18" border="0" alt="" align="absmiddle"><a href=" "
class="menuLink">Project 2</a><img src="images/clear.gif"
width="10" height="18" border="0" alt=""
align="absmiddle"></td>
    </tr>
    <tr>
        <td valign="top" align="left" bgcolor="#F3FB82">
        <img src="images/clear.gif" width="10"
height="18" border="0" alt="" align="absmiddle"><a href=" "
class="menuLink">Project 3</a><img src="images/clear.gif"
width="10" height="18" border="0" alt=""
align="absmiddle"></td>
    </tr>
</table>
</div>

<div id="NewsMenu">
<table border="1" cellpadding="0" cellspacing="0"
bordercolor="#CAD142">
    <tr>
        <td valign="top" align="left" bgcolor="#F3FB82">
        <img src="images/clear.gif" width="10"
height="18" border="0" alt="" align="absmiddle"><a href=" "
class="menuLink">News Articles</a><img src="images/
clear.gif" width="10" height="18" border="0" alt=""
align="absmiddle"></td>
    </tr>
    <tr>
        <td valign="top" align="left" bgcolor="#F3FB82">
        <img src="images/clear.gif" width="10"
height="18" border="0" alt="" align="absmiddle"><a href=" "
class="menuLink">Press Releases</a><img src="images/
clear.gif" width="10" height="18" border="0" alt=""
align="absmiddle"></td>
```

```
        </tr>
</table>
</div>

<div id="AboutMenu">
<table border="1" cellpadding="0" cellspacing="0"
bordercolor="#CAD142">
    <tr>
        <td valign="top" align="left" bgcolor="#F3FB82">
        <img src="images/clear.gif" width="10"
height="18" border="0" alt="" align="absmiddle"><a href=" "
class="menuLink">Coporate Information</a><img src="images/
clear.gif" width="10" height="18" border="0" alt=""
align="absmiddle"></td>
        </tr>
        <tr>
        <td valign="top" align="left" bgcolor="#F3FB82">
        <img src="images/clear.gif" width="10"
height="18" border="0" alt="" align="absmiddle"><a href=" "
class="menuLink">History</a><img src="images/clear.gif"
width="10" height="18" border="0" alt=""
align="absmiddle"></td>
        </tr>
        <tr>
        <td valign="top" align="left" bgcolor="#F3FB82">
        <img src="images/clear.gif" width="10"
height="18" border="0" alt="" align="absmiddle"><a href=" "
class="menuLink">Mission</a><img src="images/clear.gif"
width="10" height="18" border="0" alt=""
align="absmiddle"></td>
        </tr>
        <tr>
        <td valign="top" align="left" bgcolor="#F3FB82">
        <img src="images/clear.gif" width="10"
height="18" border="0" alt="" align="absmiddle"><a href=" "
class="menuLink">Contact Us</a><img src="images/clear.gif"
width="10" height="18" border="0" alt=""
align="absmiddle"></td>
        </tr>
</table>
</div>
```

1. We met with one of the designers who came up with a layout for the menus.
2. Once we had a look and feel for the menus, we created the tables that would make up the menus.

3. We wrapped our menu tables in `<div>` tags and gave each of them a name using the `id` attribute of the `<div>` tag.

Next, we created the CSS selectors to define our menu `<div>`s.

```
#ProductsMenu   {
        z-index : 2;
        position : absolute;
        top : 115px;
        left : 22px;
        visibility : hidden;
}

#ServicesMenu   {
        z-index : 2;
        position : absolute;
        top : 115px;
        left : 87px;
        visibility : hidden;
}

#TrainingMenu   {
        z-index : 2;
        position : absolute;
        top : 115px;
        left : 160px;
        visibility : hidden;
}

#CommonMenu   {
        z-index : 2;
        position : absolute;
        top : 115px;
        left : 234px;
        visibility : hidden;
}

#NewsMenu   {
        z-index : 2;
        position : absolute;
        top : 115px;
        left : 390px;
        visibility : hidden;
}

#AboutMenu   {
        z-index : 2;
        position : absolute;
        top : 115px;
```

```
left : 487px;
visibility : hidden;
}
```

1. We created a CSS selector for each menu.
2. We assigned each selector values for five different properties.
   - `z-index`
   - `position`
   - `top`
   - `left`
   - `visibility`

With the menu `<div>`s built and assigned to a CSS selector, it was then time to create the three functions that would run our script. We started by defining some variables that we need in the functions.

```
var over = 'no';
var lastMenu = ' ';
var styleSheetElement;
var oldElement;
```

1. We defined the `over` variable, which tells us if the user is currently over a navigation image or menu.
2. We defined a variable called `lastMenu` to hold the name of the menu that was most recently displayed.
3. We defined the variables `styleSheetElement` and `oldElement` to hold the IDs of the menus for use with the W3C CSS-compliant browsers.

Next, we got started with the `menuOn()` function.

```
function menuOn(currentMenu) {
    over = 'yes';
        if ((browser == 'Netscape') && (version < 5)) {
        if (lastMenu != ' ') {
            document.images[lastMenu].src =
eval(lastMenu + 'Off.src');
                eval('document.' + lastMenu +
'Menu.visibility = "hidden"');
        }
        document.images[currentMenu].src =
eval(currentMenu + 'On.src');
        eval('document.' + currentMenu + 'Menu.visibility
= "visible"');
        lastMenu = currentMenu;
```

```
     }
     else {
         if (lastMenu != ' ') {
             eval('document.images[lastMenu].src = ' +
lastMenu + 'Off.src');
             lastMenu = lastMenu + 'Menu';
             oldElement =
document.getElementById(lastMenu);
             oldElement.style.visibility = "hidden";
         }
         eval('document.images[currentMenu].src = ' +
currentMenu + 'On.src');
         var layerName = currentMenu + 'Menu';
         styleSheetElement =
document.getElementById(layerName);
         styleSheetElement.style.visibility = "visible";
         lastMenu = currentMenu;
     }

}
```

1. We set the variable over equal to yes so the script will know that the user is currently over a navigation image or menu.

2. We inserted a chunk of code to turn off a navigation menu or image if one was currently displayed before turning the new set on.

   • We had two sections to this part of the code: one that took care of Netscape 4.x browsers and another to take care of the W3C-compliant Internet Explorer and Netscape 6.x browsers. We used an if statement to separate the two sections of code.

   • For Netscape 4.x browsers, we turned the IMAGE object referenced in the lastMenu variable to its off state, and we set the visibility property of the corresponding menu to hidden.

   • For the W3C-compliant browsers, we first set the IMAGE object of the visible image to its off state. Next, we gathered the ID of the object that holds the currently displayed menu and set its visibility property to hidden.

3. Once we turned off any previously displayed menu and image, it was time to insert the code to turn on the new navigation image and menu. Again, we broke this into two sections: one for Netscape 4.x and one for the rest of

the browsers. We followed the same methods we used to turn off the previously displayed menu and image to turn on the new ones.

With the completion of the `menuOn()` function, we moved along to create the `overChecker()` function.

```
function overChecker(currentMenu) {
    over = 'no';
    lastMenu = currentMenu;
    setTimeout("menuOff()", 300);
}
```

1. We set the value of the variable `over` equal to `no` to let our script know that the user had rolled off the navigation image or menu.
2. We reassigned the value of `lastMenu` to hold the name of the menu that was most recently displayed.
3. We inserted a `setTimeout()` function to call the `menuOff()` function after a delay of 300 milliseconds.

Once we finished up with the `overChecker()` function, we moved on to the `menuOff()` function.

```
function menuOff()
{
    if (over == 'no')  {
            if ((browser == 'Netscape') &&
(version < 5)) {
                    document.images[lastMenu].src =
eval(lastMenu + 'Off.src');
                    eval('document.' + lastMenu +
'Menu.visibility = "hidden"');
            }
            else {
            eval('document.images[lastMenu].src = ' +
lastMenu + 'Off.src');
                    styleSheetElement.style.visibility =
"hidden";

        }
    }
}
```

1. We set up an `if` statement to check the value of the variable `over`. If the user still is not rolling over a navigation image or menu and the value of `over` is equal to `no`, then

the function turns off the currently displayed navigation image and menu.

2. We inserted the code needed to actually turn off the currently displayed navigation image and menu for both Netscape 4.x and the W3C standardized browsers. We again use the same methods that we used in the menuOn() function.

The last step in our script was to insert the event handlers into the anchor tags of the navigation images as well as the navigation menus themselves. First, we inserted them into the anchors of the images.

```
<a href="index.html" onMouseOver="menuOn('Products');
window.status='Products'; return true;"
onMouseOut="overChecker('Products'); window.status=' ';
return true;"><img src="images/products_off.gif" width=71
height=33 border=0 name="Products" alt="Products"></a>

<a href="services/index.html"
onMouseOver="menuOn('Services'); window.status='Services';
return true;"  onMouseOut="overChecker('Services');
window.status=' '; return true;"><img src="images/
services_off.gif" width=67 height=33 border=0
name="Services" alt="Services"></a>

<a href="training/index.html"
onMouseOver="menuOn('Training'); window.status='Training';
return true;"  onMouseOut="overChecker('Training');
window.status=' '; return true;"><img src="images/
training_off.gif" width=75 height=33 border=0
name="Training" alt="Training"></a>

<a href="common/index.html" onMouseOver="menuOn('Common');
window.status='Common Good Projects'; return true;"
onMouseOut="overChecker('Common'); window.status=' ';
return true;"><img src="images/common_off.gif" width=157
height=33 border=0 name="Common" alt="Common Good"></a>

<a href="genetic/index.html" onMouseOver="menuOn('News');
window.status='Genetic News'; return true;"
onMouseOut="overChecker('News'); window.status=' '; return
true;"><img src="images/news_off.gif" width=98 height=33
border=0 name="News" alt="Genetic News"></a>

<a href="about/index.html" onMouseOver="menuOn('About');
window.status='About Us'; return true;"
onMouseOut="overChecker('About'); window.status=' '; return
```

```
true;"><img src="images/about_off.gif" width=106 height=33
border=0 name="About" alt="About Shelley"></a>
```

1. We inserted two handlers into each anchor tag: first, the `onMouseOver` handler, which we set to call the `menuOn()` function and pass it the name of the current image or menu. We also set it to change the window status of the browser to display the name of the section.

2. The second handler we inserted was the `onMouseOut` handler, which we set to call the `overChecker()` function, passing it the name of the current menu or image as well as resetting the window status of the browser.

The last step was to insert the necessary handlers into the menu `<div>`s themselves.

```
<div id="ProductsMenu" onMouseOver="over = 'yes';"
onMouseOut="overChecker('Products');">
<script language="JavaScript" type="text/javascript">
    function onMouseOver() {over = 'yes';}
    function onMouseOut() {overChecker('Products');}
</script>
<table border="1" cellpadding="0" cellspacing="0"
bordercolor="#CAD142">
    <tr>
        <td valign="top" align="left" bgcolor="#F3FB82">
        <img src="images/clear.gif" width="10"
height="18" border="0" alt="" align="absmiddle"><a href=" "
class="menuLink">Product Group 1</a><img src="images/
clear.gif" width="10" height="18" border="0" alt=""
align="absmiddle"></td>
    </tr>
    <tr>
        <td valign="top" align="left" bgcolor="#F3FB82">
        <img src="images/clear.gif" width="10"
height="18" border="0" alt="" align="absmiddle"><a href=" "
class="menuLink">Product Group 2</a><img src="images/
clear.gif" width="10" height="18" border="0" alt=""
align="absmiddle"></td>
    </tr>
    <tr>
        <td valign="top" align="left" bgcolor="#F3FB82">
        <img src="images/clear.gif" width="10"
height="18" border="0" alt="" align="absmiddle"><a href=" "
class="menuLink">Product Group 3</a><img src="images/
clear.gif" width="10" height="18" border="0" alt=""
align="absmiddle"></td>
    </tr>
```

```
    <tr>
        <td valign="top" align="left" bgcolor="#F3FB82">
        <img src="images/clear.gif" width="10"
height="18" border="0" alt="" align="absmiddle"><a href=" "
class="menuLink">Product Group 4</a><img src="images/
clear.gif" width="10" height="18" border="0" alt=""
align="absmiddle"></td>
    </tr>
</table>
</div>

<div id="ServicesMenu" onMouseOver="over = 'yes';"
onMouseOut="overChecker('Services');">
<script language="JavaScript" type="text/javascript">
    function onMouseOver() {over = 'yes';}
    function onMouseOut() {overChecker('Services');}
</script>
<table border="1" cellpadding="0" cellspacing="0"
bordercolor="#CAD142">
    <tr>
        <td valign="top" align="left" bgcolor="#F3FB82">
        <img src="images/clear.gif" width="10"
height="18" border="0" alt="" align="absmiddle"><a href=" "
class="menuLink">Service 1</a><img src="images/clear.gif"
width="10" height="18" border="0" alt=""
align="absmiddle"></td>
    </tr>
    <tr>
        <td valign="top" align="left" bgcolor="#F3FB82">
        <img src="images/clear.gif" width="10"
height="18" border="0" alt="" align="absmiddle"><a href=" "
class="menuLink">Services 2</a><img src="images/clear.gif"
width="10" height="18" border="0" alt=""
align="absmiddle"></td>
    </tr>
    <tr>
        <td valign="top" align="left" bgcolor="#F3FB82">
        <img src="images/clear.gif" width="10"
height="18" border="0" alt="" align="absmiddle"><a href=" "
class="menuLink">Services 3</a><img src="images/clear.gif"
width="10" height="18" border="0" alt=""
align="absmiddle"></td>
    </tr>
</table>
</div>
<div id="TrainingMenu" onMouseOver="over = 'yes';"
onMouseOut="overChecker('Training');">
<script language="JavaScript" type="text/javascript">
```

```
        function onMouseOver() {over = 'yes';}
        function onMouseOut() {overChecker('Training');}
</script>
<table border="1" cellpadding="0" cellspacing="0"
bordercolor="#CAD142">
     <tr>
          <td valign="top" align="left" bgcolor="#F3FB82">
          <img src="images/clear.gif" width="10"
height="18" border="0" alt="" align="absmiddle"><a href=" "
class="menuLink">Class Descriptions</a><img src="images/
clear.gif" width="10" height="18" border="0" alt=""
align="absmiddle"></td>
     </tr>
     <tr>
          <td valign="top" align="left" bgcolor="#F3FB82">
          <img src="images/clear.gif" width="10"
height="18" border="0" alt="" align="absmiddle"><a href=" "
class="menuLink">Current Schedule</a><img src="images/
clear.gif" width="10" height="18" border="0" alt=""
align="absmiddle"></td>
     </tr>
</table>
</div>

<div id="CommonMenu" onMouseOver="over = 'yes';"
onMouseOut="overChecker('Common');">
<script language="JavaScript" type="text/javascript">
     function onMouseOver() {over = 'yes';}
     function onMouseOut() {overChecker('Common');}
</script>
<table border="1" cellpadding="0" cellspacing="0"
bordercolor="#CAD142">
     <tr>
          <td valign="top" align="left" bgcolor="#F3FB82">
          <img src="images/clear.gif" width="10"
height="18" border="0" alt="" align="absmiddle"><a href=" "
class="menuLink">Project 1</a><img src="images/clear.gif"
width="10" height="18" border="0" alt=""
align="absmiddle"></td>
     </tr>
     <tr>
          <td valign="top" align="left" bgcolor="#F3FB82">
          <img src="images/clear.gif" width="10"
height="18" border="0" alt="" align="absmiddle"><a href=" "
class="menuLink">Project 2</a><img src="images/clear.gif"
width="10" height="18" border="0" alt=""
align="absmiddle"></td>
     </tr>
```

```
        <tr>
            <td valign="top" align="left" bgcolor="#F3FB82">
            <img src="images/clear.gif" width="10"
height="18" border="0" alt="" align="absmiddle"><a href=" "
class="menuLink">Project 3</a><img src="images/clear.gif"
width="10" height="18" border="0" alt=""
align="absmiddle"></td>
        </tr>
    </table>
    </div>


    <div id="NewsMenu" onMouseOver="over = 'yes';"
    onMouseOut="overChecker('News');">
    <script language="JavaScript" type="text/javascript">
        function onMouseOver() {over = 'yes';}
        function onMouseOut() {overChecker('News');}
    </script>
    <table border="1" cellpadding="0" cellspacing="0"
    bordercolor="#CAD142">
        <tr>
            <td valign="top" align="left" bgcolor="#F3FB82">
            <img src="images/clear.gif" width="10" height="18"
border="0" alt="" align="absmiddle"><a href=" "
class="menuLink">News Articles</a><img src="images/
clear.gif" width="10" height="18" border="0" alt=""
align="absmiddle"></td>
        </tr>
        <tr>
            <td valign="top" align="left" bgcolor="#F3FB82">
            <img src="images/clear.gif" width="10"
height="18" border="0" alt="" align="absmiddle"><a href=" "
class="menuLink">Press Releases</a><img src="images/
clear.gif" width="10" height="18" border="0" alt=""
align="absmiddle"></td>
        </tr>
    </table>
    </div>


    <div id="AboutMenu" onMouseOver="over = 'yes';"
    onMouseOut="overChecker('About');">
    <script language="JavaScript" type="text/javascript">
        function onMouseOver() {over = 'yes';}
        function onMouseOut() {overChecker('About');}
    </script>
    <table border="1" cellpadding="0" cellspacing="0"
    bordercolor="#CAD142">
        <tr>
            <td valign="top" align="left" bgcolor="#F3FB82">
```

```
            <img src="images/clear.gif" width="10"
height="18" border="0" alt="" align="absmiddle"><a href=" "
class="menuLink">Coporate Information</a><img src="images/
clear.gif" width="10" height="18" border="0" alt=""
align="absmiddle"></td>
        </tr>
        <tr>
            <td valign="top" align="left" bgcolor="#F3FB82">
            <img src="images/clear.gif" width="10"
height="18" border="0" alt="" align="absmiddle"><a href=" "
class="menuLink">History</a><img src="images/clear.gif"
width="10" height="18" border="0" alt=""
align="absmiddle"></td>
        </tr>
        <tr>
            <td valign="top" align="left" bgcolor="#F3FB82">
            <img src="images/clear.gif" width="10"
height="18" border="0" alt="" align="absmiddle"><a href=" "
class="menuLink">Mission</a><img src="images/clear.gif"
width="10" height="18" border="0" alt=""
align="absmiddle"></td>
        </tr>
        <tr>
            <td valign="top" align="left" bgcolor="#F3FB82">
            <img src="images/clear.gif" width="10"
height="18" border="0" alt="" align="absmiddle"><a href=" "
class="menuLink">Contact Us</a><img src="images/clear.gif"
width="10" height="18" border="0" alt=""
align="absmiddle"></td>
        </tr>
    </table>
</div>
```

1. We inserted both the `onMouseOver` and `onMouseOut` handlers into each menu. The `onMouseOver` was set to reset the value of the variable `over` to yes. This let our functions know that even though the user rolls off of the navigation image, it still needs to display the menu.

2. The `onMouseOut` handler was set to call the `overChecker()` function, just as in the anchor tags.

3. We took one extra step in inserting the handlers into the menus. Netscape 4.x browsers have a problem finding the predefined event handlers when they are called from within a CSS-defined object. Therefore, we had to insert a small script into each menu that defined two functions with the names of the event handlers that are called.

Wow, if that project wasn't a big chunk of code, then I don't know what is. We covered quite a bit of ground and introduced several new concepts.

- We were given a general introduction to CSS/DHTML.
- We learned how to use the `<div>` tag to specify blocks of content.
- We were introduced to CSS selectors, some of their properties, and how to assign a selector to a block of content.
- We learned how to access and modify CSS elements in browsers that are fully W3C-compliant in their implementation of CSS.
- We figured out how to get around a limitation in the implementation of CSS in Netscape 4.x browsers by redefining event handlers inside of each layer you want to access them in.

RECAP

You should now have a sound base of knowledge of not only JavaScript-based navigation and how to use JavaScript in forms for enhanced interactivity and efficiency, but of some of the exciting ways you can combine CSS and JavaScript to add advanced functionality to your Web pages. We have also broadened our knowledge of arrays, learning how to create them and access information that we have stored in them. In Chapter 4, we will leave the Shelley Biotech site and start working on *Stitch Magazine*'s site. We will build on what we have learned of JavaScript and forms, and learn how to handle error checking with JavaScript.

ADVANCED PROJECTS

1. Create a system of three pull-down menus, where the second menu populates based on the choice made from the first menu, and the third menu then populates based on the choice made from the second menu.

2. Create a system of CSS navigation menus that have multiple levels so that if a navigation choice on the top level has more choices below it, when it is rolled over, it will display a second menu that holds the choices specific to the selection.

4 Error Handling in Forms

IN THIS CHAPTER

- Project I: Dynamically Selecting Multiple Form Fields
- Project II: Error Handling of Forms
- Project III: Letting the User Know What's Wrong
- Recap
- Advanced Projects

For the rest of the book we will be working on the Web site of Stitch Magazine. Stitch *is a fictional online fashion magazine. It's racy, visually interesting, and its reporters are remarkably good at spotting trends, reclusive designers, and embarrassing gossip. However, it's now beginning to grow up and needs more interactivity to enhance its Web site content. In the next three chapters, we'll implement some truly advanced JavaScript for a rare user experience. In* this *chapter, we'll learn how to check your forms for user-entered errors.*

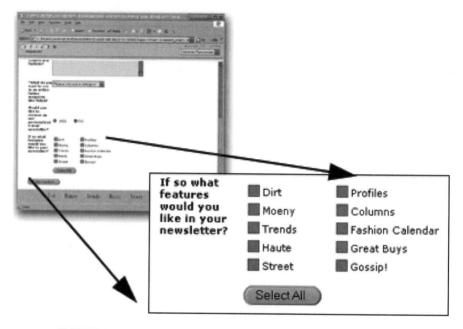

FIGURE 4–1   New checkboxes on promotion form.

The marketing folks at *Stitch* are running a promotion to generate some leads. To enter the promotion, Web surfers must come to the *Stitch* Web site and enter some information about themselves in a form (for example, their name, email address, and what they want to know about fashion).

The marketing department has dusted off a form that was used for a previous contest, but it needs to be updated for the new promotion. *Stitch* also has a new email newsletter that the powers that be want to get the subscriber numbers up for, so we'll be adding the ability to sign up for it. The newsletter is personalized for each subscriber, so not only will we need a form field where users can subscribe, but also fields that let them customize the content they want to receive in the newsletter. One of the other Web engineers has already made the addition of the new fields to the form page (see Figure 4–1). It has a set of radio buttons that lets the user subscribe or not to the newsletter, as well as a series of checkboxes with the different subject matter that the user can add to his or her personalized content.

The marketing people like what they see so far, but are curious if there is a way that we could add a button that would automatically check all of the checkboxes if the user wished to add all of the content options. This would save the user the time of having to check off each box. The other engineer doesn't really know any JavaScript, so it's now our project to run with.

◆ Project I: Dynamically Selecting Multiple Form Fields

Here is the portion of the HTML page that contains the form named *promotion*, which holds the newsletter questions. It contains 10 checkboxes named `content1` through `content10` as well as a button that the user will click on to select all of the checkboxes.

```
<td class="blkText">
    <table border="0" cellpadding="5" cellspacing="0">
        <tr>
        <td valign="top" align="left"
    class="blkText">
            <input type="checkbox"  name="content1"
        value="trends">Dirt<br>
            <input type="checkbox"  name="content2"
        value="models">Moeny<br>
            <input type="checkbox"  name="content3"
        value="designers">Trends<br>
            <input type="checkbox"  name="content4"
        value="rage">Haute<br>
            <input type="checkbox"  name="content5"
        value="gossip">Street<br><br>
            <input type="button" value="Select
        All"><br><br></td>
        <td valign="top" align="left"
    class="blkText">
            <input type="checkbox"  name="content6"
        value="trends">Profiles<br>
            <input type="checkbox"  name="content7"
        value="models">Columns<br>
            <input type="checkbox"  name="content8"
         value="designers">Fashion Calendar<br>
            <input type="checkbox"  name="content9"
        value="rage">Great Buys<br>
            <input type="checkbox"  name="content10"
        value="gossip">Gossip!</td>
        </tr>
    </table></td>
```

There are two parts to this project: first, we need to create a function that will select all of the checkboxes that are part of the content question, and second, we need to insert the proper event handler into the HTML.

Creating the Change Checkbox State Function

Let's get started on our function. Because this script is only going to be located on this page, we'll just put it into the <head> of the HTML instead of into an external file.

```
<script language="JavaScript1.2">
<!-- Code after this will be ignored by older browsers

function boxSelector() {

. . .

}

// -->
</script>
```

Above, we inserted our script tags and started a new function called boxSelector(). This is the function that selects all of the content checkboxes. Because we know the names of the checkboxes that we need to have our function select, there is no need to pass a variable into the function. Let's now move on to the first part of our function.

```
<script language="JavaScript1.2">
<!-- Code after this will be ignored by older browsers

function boxSelector() {
    var counter = 1;
    while(counter < 11) {
        . . .
    }
}

// -->
</script>
```

There are 10 different types of content that the users can choose from for their newsletter. If they choose to subscribe to all of them, we will need to turn all 10 of them on. So, we will use a while loop to cycle through our function 10 times if the Select All button has been clicked on the page. First, we created a variable called counter to use as a test for our while loop. Next, we created the framework for a while loop, which will run as long as counter is below 11, and because we have initialized counter to start with the value of 1, the loop will run through 10 times. The next step is to create the line of code that will select the individual checkboxes.

```
<script language="JavaScript1.2">
<!-- Code after this will be ignored by older browsers

function boxSelector() {
    var counter = 1;
    while(counter < 11) {

    eval("document.forms['promotion'].elements['content" +
counter + "'].checked = true");
            . . .
    }

}

// -->
</script>
```

Let's take a closer look at what we did. First, we used the eval() method to interpret the line of code that will actually make the change and select the box. Inside of the eval() method, we called first to the forms array and more specifically to the form named *promotion*, which holds our checkboxes. Next, we went into the elements array of the promotions form and called on the form element with the name contentx, where x is equal to the current value of counter. As the while loop cycles through counter, it will at one point hold the value that corresponds with each checkbox we need selected. The last thing we did in this line is set the value of the checked property of the current checkbox to the value true. This is the part that actually selects the current checkbox. The final thing we need to add to our function is a line that will increment the value of counter each time it goes through the loop.

```
<script language="JavaScript1.2">
<!-- Code after this will be ignored by older browsers

function boxSelector() {
```

```
        var counter = 1;
        while(counter < 11) {
            eval("document.forms['promotion'].elements[
        'content" + counter + "'].checked = true");
            ++counter;
        }
    }

    // -->
    </script>
```

Inserting the Event Handlers

The next step in our script is to insert the event handler into the HTML. We want our function to run if the user has clicked on the Select All button that is located with the content checkboxes, so we will place our event handler inside that button. Here is the line of code with the onClick() handler added to call our boxSelector() function when the user clicks on the button:

```
<input type="button" value="Select All"
onClick="boxSelector();"><br><br></td>
```

Reviewing the Script

With the previous step, we've added another notch in our JavaScript gun belt. This project was fairly straightforward, building on some of the concepts that we've already explored in the book. It is always good to look at the concepts that you've already mastered and find new and useful ways to implement them into your sites. Let's take a quick look at the completed script and the steps we took to create it. First, here is the boxSelector() function.

```
<script language="JavaScript1.2">
<!-- Code after this will be ignored by older browsers

function boxSelector() {
    var counter = 1;
    while(counter < 11) {
        eval("document.forms['promotion'].elements
    ['content" + counter + "'].checked = true");
        ++counter;
    }
}

// -->
</script>
```

1. We figured out how many checkboxes we would need our script to select, and created a `while` loop that would cycle through that many times.
2. We used the `eval()` function to interpret a line of code that would select the checkbox that was named with the same number as the current value of the variable `counter`.
3. We included a line that would increment our `counter` so we didn't end up in an infinite loop.

The last part of our script was to insert the event handler into the HTML:

```
<input type="button" value="Select All"
onClick="boxSelector();"><br><br></td>
```

This technique can be used in many ways. Not only can it select checkboxes or radio buttons, but with a little modification, it can be used to reset all of the fields in a form or populate all form entries with preconfigured answers. With the form finally complete, the marketing department wants to know if we are up to adding some error handling to the form, so let's take a look at exactly what they want.

◆ Project II: Error Handling of Forms

Chances are that most people will fill out the form correctly. However, some will mistype their responses, some will skip information the marketing folk desperately need, and some will fill in the boxes with garbage just to enter the contest.

If you include some JavaScript to error-check the form before it's submitted to the CGI script, the marketing people will have less incomplete or nonsensical data to sort through. Error checking will also make the CGI programmer's life easier, because you can guarantee that the data will arrive in certain forms. This is a pretty lengthy script, so we will break it up into a couple of sections: First we will check for empty form fields and erroneous data entered by the user. In the next project, we will go over how to let the user know what is wrong. Because both of these projects are part of the same script, we will postpone reviewing each part until the end when we have the completed script.

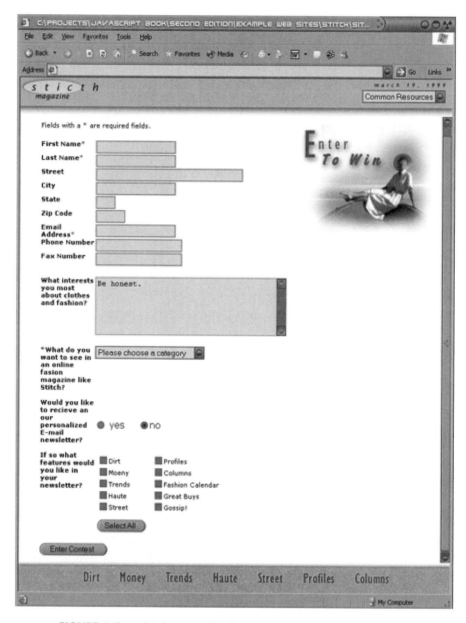

FIGURE 4–2   *Stitch* promotion form page.

The marketing folks obviously love for the users to fill in all of the boxes (see Figure 4–2), but only a few pieces of data are truly necessary to generate a lead. Generally, you should stick with name and email address as required entries. Avoid requiring a phone number unless it's absolutely necessary—people will assume you're going to sic a telemarketer on them and they may enter in the phone number of their ex-significant other instead. In our case, the marketing department really wants to know what people want to see in the magazine, so we are going to require that question be answered as well.

Here is the complete *promotion* form as it stands right now:

```
    <form action="/scripts/promotion.cgi" name="promotion"
method="post">
    <br>
    <table border="0" cellpadding="10" cellspacing="0">
        <tr>
            <td valign="top" align="left">
                  </td>
            <td valign="top" align="left"
class="blkText">
                Fields with a <font
class="redBldText">*</font> are required fields.
                <p>
    <table border="0" cellpadding="0" cellspacing="0">
        <tr>
            <td valign="top" align="left"
class="blkBldText">
                First Name<font class="redBldText">*
</font></td>
            <td>
                <input type="text" name="firstName">
</td>
        </tr>

        <tr>

            <td valign="top" align="left"
class="blkBldText">
                Last Name<font class="redBldText">*
</font></td>
            <td>
                <input type="text" name="lastName">
</td>
```

```
        </tr>

        <tr>
            <td valign="top" align="left"
class="blkBldText">
                Street</td>
            <td>
                <input type="text" size="40"
name="address"></td>
        </tr>

        <tr>
            <td valign="top" align="left"
class="blkBldText">
                City</td>
            <td>
                <input type="text" name="address"></td>
        </tr>

        <tr>
            <td valign="top" align="left"
class="blkBldText">
                State</td>
            <td  valign="top" align="left">
                <input type="text" name="address"
maxlength="2" size="2"></td>
        </tr>

        <tr>
            <td valign="top" align="left"
class="blkBldText">
                Zip Code</td>
            <td valign="top" align="left">
                <input type="text" name="zipCode"
maxlength="5" size="5"></td>
        </tr>

        <tr>


            <td valign="top" align="left"
class="blkBldText">
                Email Address<font
class="redBldText">*</font></td>
            <td>
                <input type="text" name="email"></td>
        </tr>
```

```
        <tr>
            <td valign="top" align="left"
class="blkBldText">
                    Phone Number</td>
            <td>
                    (<input type="text" name="areaCode"
size="3" maxlength="3">)
                    <input type="text" name="phoneNumber1"
size="3" maxlength="3">-
                    <input type="text" name="phoneNumber2"
size="4" maxlength="4"></td>
        </tr>

        <tr>
            <td valign="top" align="left"
class="blkBldText">
                    Fax Number</td>
            <td>
                    (<input type="text" name="faxareaCode"
size="3" maxlength="3">)
                    <input type="text" name="faxNumber1"
size="3" maxlength="3">-
                    <input type="text" name="faxNumber2"
size="4" maxlength="4"><br><br></td>
        </tr>

        <tr>
            <td valign="top" align="left"
class="blkBldText">
                    What interests you most about clothes
and fashion?<br><br></td>
            <td>
                    <textarea rows=6 cols=40>Be honest.</
textarea><br><br></td>
        </tr>

        <tr>
            <td valign="top" align="left"
class="blkBldText">
                    *What do you want to see in an online
fashion magazine like Stitch?<br><br></td>
            <td valign="top" align="left"
class="blkText">
                    <select name="whatTheyWant">
                        <option value="default">Please
choose a category
```

```
                        <option value="trends">Upcoming
trends
                        <option value="models">Information
about models
                        <option value="designers">
Information about designers
                        <option value="rage">What the
current rage is
                        <option value="gossip">Gossip!
                </select></td>
        </tr>

        <tr>
                <td valign="top" align="left"
class="blkBldText">
                        Would you like to receive our
personalized email newsletter?<br><br></td>
                <td>
                        <input type="radio" name="join"
value="yes"> yes    <input type="radio"
name="join" value="no" checked>no</td>
        </tr>

        <tr>
                <td valign="top" align="left"
class="blkBldText">
                        If so, what features would you like in
your newsletter?</td>
                <td class="blkText">
                        <table border="0" cellpadding="5"
cellspacing="0">
                                <tr>
                                        <td valign="top" align="left"
class="blkText">
                                                <input type="checkbox"
name="content1" value="trends">Dirt<br>
                                                <input type="checkbox"
name="content2" value="models">Money<br>
                                                <input type="checkbox"
name="content3" value="designers">Trends<br>
                                                <input type="checkbox"
name="content4" value="rage">Haute<br>
                                                <input type="checkbox"
name="content5" value="gossip">Street<br><br>
                                                <input type="button"
value="Select All" onClick="boxSelector();"><br><br></td>
```

```
                              <td valign="top" align="left"
class="blkText">
                                    <input type="checkbox"
name="content6" value="trends">Profiles<br>
                                    <input type="checkbox"
name="content7" value="models">Columns<br>
                                    <input type="checkbox"
name="content8" value="designers">Fashion Calendar<br>
                                    <input type="checkbox"
name="content9" value="rage">Great Buys<br>
                                    <input type="checkbox"
name="content10" value="gossip">Gossip!</td>
                              </tr>
                        </table></td>
            </tr>

            <tr>
                  <td colspan="2">
                        <input type="button" value="Enter
Contest" onClick="errorCheck()">
                  </td>
            </tr>

      </table></td>
                  <td valign="top" align="left">
                        <img src="images/promotion.jpg"
width=248 height=203 border=0 alt=""></td>
            </tr>
      </table>
      </form>
```

You will notice that at the end of the form the programmers have already inserted an `onClick` event handler into the Submit button within which they call the function `errorCheck()`. Since they went to the trouble of putting in the handler, we will use this for the name of the function that we create.

Checking Forms for Empty Text Box Fields

Following is the first bit of JavaScript we'll use to check the visitor's information. We insert it right after our `boxSelector()` function from the previous project.

```
// Required fields error checking

function errorCheck()
```

```
{


// Create some variables for our script
var requiredFieldsErrorMessage = "";
var firstNameEntered = "";
var lastNameEntered = "";
var emailEntered = "";
var areaCodeEntered = "";
var zipCodeEntered = "";
var pullDownErrorMessage = "";
var emailErrorMessage = "";
var areaCodeErrorMessage = "";
var zipCodeErrorMessage = "";


. . .

}

// Stop hiding the code here -->
</script>
```

We begin by setting some variables. We will use the first four in this project, and the others will be used in the next project. These variables will keep track of any specific error messages the user generates. At the end of the script, all the error messages will be patched together and one comprehensive error message will greet the site's visitor.

Next, we add the part of the function that will do the actual checking of the information.

```
// Required fields error checking

function errorCheck()
{


// Create some variables for our script
var requiredFieldsErrorMessage = "";
var firstNameEntered = "";
var lastNameEntered = "";
var emailEntered = "";
var areaCodeEntered = "";
var zipCodeEntered = "";
var pullDownErrorMessage = "";
var emailErrorMessage = "";
var areaCodeErrorMessage = "";
```

```
var zipCodeErrorMessage = "";

// gather values of First Name, Last Name and Email
firstNameEntered =
document.forms['promotion'].elements['firstName'].value;
lastNameEntered =
document.forms['promotion'].elements['lastName'].value;
emailEntered =
document.forms['promotion'].elements['email'].value;

. . .
}

// Stop hiding the code here -->
</script>
```

We require the visitor to enter information in three fields: first name, last name, and email address. In previous chapters, we learned how to access values from FORM elements on an HTML page. We use similar methods to get the values for the three fields we need to check. Thus, the line

```
firstNameEntered =
document.forms['promotion'].elements['firstName'].value
```

looks at what the visitor entered into the text field for first name and puts that value into the variable firstNameEntered. The two following statements work the same way for the other two fields. If the user didn't input information for any of these three questions, the variables will contain no value. Next, we set up a series of if statements to test these values.

```
// Required fields error checking

function errorCheck()
{

// Create some variables for our script
var requiredFieldsErrorMessage = "";
var firstNameEntered = "";
var lastNameEntered = "";
var emailEntered = "";
var areaCodeEntered = "";
var zipCodeEntered = "";
var pullDownErrorMessage = "";
```

```
var emailErrorMessage = "";
var areaCodeErrorMessage = "";
var zipCodeErrorMessage = "";

// gather values of First Name, Last Name and Email
firstNameEntered =
document.forms['promotion'].elements['firstName'].value;
lastNameEntered =
document.forms['promotion'].elements['lastName'].value;
emailEntered =
document.forms['promotion'].elements['email'].value;

// if statements to check if the user has entered data
if ((!firstNameEntered) || (!lastNameEntered) ||
(!emailEntered))
{

    if (!firstNameEntered)
    {
        requiredFieldsErrorMessage = "- your first
name\r";
    }
    if (!lastNameEntered)
    {
        requiredFieldsErrorMessage =
requiredFieldsErrorMessage + "- your last name\r";
    }
    if (!emailEntered)
    {
        requiredFieldsErrorMessage =
requiredFieldsErrorMessage + "- your email address\r";
    }
}

. . .
}

// Stop hiding the code here -->
</script>
```

The first line of the `if` statement is

```
if ((!firstNameEntered) || (!lastNameEntered) ||
(!emailEntered))
```

It means that if a visitor didn't enter a first name, last name, or email address, then the `if` statement will execute the code contained within it.

The double bar || is the symbol used for or in conditional statements. When an or operator is used in a conditional statement such as an if statement, if any of the conditions are met, then the if is seen as true and the statements that follow are executed. We have also used another operator in the preceding if statement, the ! comparison operator. In JavaScript (and most other programming languages), this symbol means not, so we are saying that if any of these variables do not have a value, then return a value of true and the engine will go on to execute the next statements. If all three fields were filled out correctly, our script will just skip over to the code following our if statement.

Chances are good that all three fields will not be filled out correctly, so we needed to put in some code that will be executed if there are any errors. We added three more if statements that will test the three fields individually and, if necessary, store a short message in the requiredFieldsErrorMessage variable that we will use later to tell the user that a field has been missed.

```
if (!firstNameEntered)
```

The preceding if statement means that if the visitor didn't enter anything in for a first name, the next line is executed:

```
requiredFieldsErrorMessage = "- your first name\r";
```

This line assigns the string - your first name to the variable requiredFieldsErrorMessage. You will notice the /r at the end of the string—as stated in previous chapters, the backward slash escapes the character that follows it and tells the JavaScript engine to execute it. The r value tells the engine to insert a line break, similar to hitting the Enter key.

There are two more if statements that check for the presence of a value in the two other fields we are concerned with and which will add information to the requiredFieldsErrorMessage variable if they are empty.

```
requiredFieldsErrorMessage =
requiredFieldsErrorMessage + "- your last name\r";
```

The preceding statement is executed if the last name test comes back empty. We want to add on to the visitor's existing error message because he or she may make more than one error. So, on the right-hand side of the expression, we say add - your last name\r to the existing value for requiredFieldsErrorMessage and then put them both back into the `requiredFieldsErrorMessage` variable. If more than one mistake is made, we want to list both of them, not just replace the first mistake with the next one. The third `while` loop follows the same syntax and checks for the presence of a value in the email address field.

Making Sure a Pull-Down Menu Option Was Chosen

The next thing we have to do is to make sure that an option was chosen from the pull-down menu that asks what the user wants to see in an online version of the magazine. Fortunately, the code to do this is almost exactly the same as looking at the value of a text field. We insert the JavaScript code to check the pull-down menu right below the code we created to test the text boxes.

```
    // check if the user has selected from the pull-down
menu
    var selectPos =
document.forms['promotion'].elements['whatTheyWant'].select
edIndex;
    . . .
    // Stop hiding the code here -->
</script>
```

We added a line that would reach into the pull-down menu object of our form and collect the value held in the `selectedIndex` property. This property holds the value of whichever option is currently selected from the menu. We assign this value to the variable `selectPos`. We now need to create a test that will check the value to make sure the user has selected an option.

```
    // check if the user has selected from the pull-down
menu
    var selectPos =
document.forms['promotion'].elements['whatTheyWant'].
selectedIndex;
    if(document.forms['promotion'].elements['whatTheyWant'].
options[selectPos].value == 'default'){
        pullDownErrorMessage = "- you didn't tell us what you
want to see in Stitch\r";

    }
    . . .
    }
```

```
// Stop hiding the code here -->
</script>
```

Because we are checking for only one form field, we can use just one `if` statement to accomplish our purposes. In the preceding `if` statement, we test the value of the selected option of the `whatTheyWant` pull-down menu against the value `default`. If you look at the HTML code for the pull-down menu, you will see that `default` is the value assigned to the first option in the menu. Therefore, if the user doesn't change it from its initial position and pick another option, the value will remain `default`, and the script will then assign a short message to the variable `pullDown-ErrorMessage`.

So far, we have written a script that will test for empty fields in the form; however, there are cases where that is not enough information. In certain instances, it would be useful to check for a bogus or erroneous response from the user. The next couple of sections cover several examples of just such cases.

Checking Email Addresses for . and @

You can never be 100 percent sure that someone is giving you a working email address. There's no formula or central database that keeps track of all the valid email addresses in the world. However, you can be sure that a person is giving you something that at least *looks* like an email address by checking for a . and an @. We add this new code right below our existing code, which is still within the `errorCheck()` function.

```
// email error checking

        emailValue = new String (emailEntered);
        emailHasAt = emailValue.indexOf("@");
        emailHasPeriod = emailValue.indexOf(".");

        if ((emailHasAt == -1) || (emailHasPeriod == -1)) {
        emailErrorMessage = "-your email address\r";
        }
    . . .
}
    // Stop hiding the code here -->
</script>
```

The first thing we did is to create a new object called `email-Value`—we do this the same way that we created the IMAGE objects we used in Chapter 2 for our image rollovers. Instead of creating an IMAGE object, however, we create a STRING object that holds the value that is held in our emailEntered variable:

```
emailValue = new String (emailEntered);
```

We put the field value into an object instead of simply keeping it in a regular variable as before because objects are more versatile and allow us access to methods that we can't use on variables. The method that we use in this script is indexOf(). This lets us look for specific characters that appear in the string; in this case, we look for a . and the @ symbol.

```
emailHasAt = emailValue.indexOf("@");
emailHasPeriod = emailValue.indexOf(".");
```

The first line looks for the character @ in the object email-Value and remembers where in the object that character occurred. For example, if emailValue was *book@smashingpixels.net*, the @ is in position 4 (remember, JavaScript starts counting with 0), emailHasAt would hold the value 4. If that character isn't found, you get a value of –1.

The second line is basically the same, but it checks for the existence of a . and stores its findings in the variable emailHasPeriod. Thus, the next lines

```
if ((emailHasAt == -1) || (emailHasPeriod == -1))
{
    emailErrorMessage = "-your email address\r";
}
```

mean that if the email address didn't have an @ symbol or a ., then create a new error message called emailErrorMessage. Next, we check the phone number fields for an area code.

Checking for Area Codes in Phone Numbers

The phone number isn't a required field; however, if a visitor does volunteer a phone number, you want to make sure that he or she gives the area code; after all, this is the Web and you have no idea where people are calling from. (We're ignoring international phone numbers on purpose for now. If the Web site ends up getting a lot of hits from locations outside the United States, we can change the phone number fields later.)

We are going to cheat a little bit here. We reformat the HTML of the form so we can more easily get at the information you want from the phone fields (see Figure 4–3). Instead of having one long field for the phone and fax numbers, we split them into three fields apiece: one for the area code, another for the first three digits, and one for the remaining four digits. Keep this trick in mind when you are creating scripts later on—there are often ways in which you can manipulate the HTML to make your scripts more efficient. Here is the new HTML code for the phone number fields.

```
(<input type="text" name="areaCode" size="3"
maxlength="3">)

<input type="text" name="phoneNumber1" size="3"
maxlength="3">-

<input type="text" name="phoneNumber2" size="4"
maxlength="4">
```

By separating the phone number into three separate fields, we can isolate the area code much easier. This way, you don't have to look at the entire phone number and try to figure out which part is the area code. This can be a problem because people write area codes differently; for example, (925)555-1212, 925-555-1212, 925/555.1212, or a hundred other combinations. Keep this in mind when writing scripts—there are often ways other than JavaScript solutions that are much easier to implement. Don't be afraid to explore these other avenues.

Because we have decided to use three different fields for the phone number, we can check the values in much the same way as we checked for the first name, last name, and email address fields.

```
// Area Code Check

areaCodeEntered =
document.forms['promotion'].elements['areaCode'].value

phoneNumber1Entered =
document.forms['promotion'].elements['phoneNumber1'].value

. . .

}
   // Stop hiding the code here -->
</script>
```

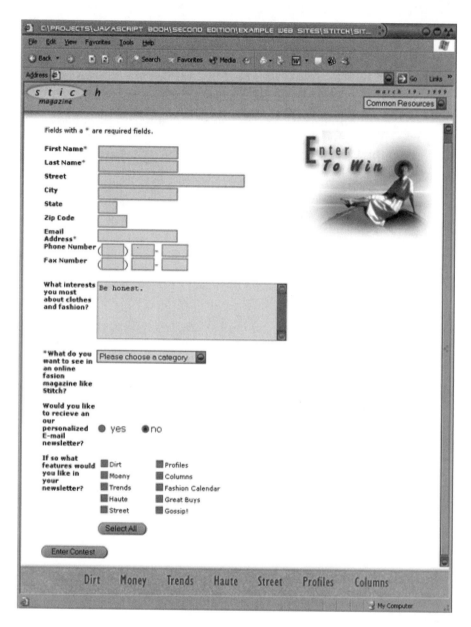

FIGURE 4–3 *Stitch* promotion form page with new phone number fields.

In the first two lines, we assign the values of both the area code field and the first phone number field to variables. Next, we use an `if` statement to tell us if what we need is there.

```
// Area Code Check

    areaCodeEntered =
document.forms['promotion'].elements['areaCode'].value

    phoneNumber1Entered =
document.forms['promotion'].elements['phoneNumber1'].value

    if ((!areaCodeEntered) && (phoneNumber1Entered))
    {
     areaCodeErrorMessage = "-please enter your area
code\r"
    }
. . .
}
    // Stop hiding the code here -->
</script>
```

If you haven't seen `&&` before, it is another logical operator like the `||` operator that we used previously in the script. The operator means that both conditions need to be met to return a `true` value in the statement. Therefore,

```
if ((!areaCodeEntered) && (phoneNumberEntered))
```

means if the variable `areaCodeEntered` has no value, but `phoneNumberEntered` does, then execute the next lines. This way, an error message is generated only if the visitor entered a phone number without an area code, or vice versa. Let's move on to the final field for which we have to test.

Making Sure Zip Codes Have Only Numbers

The JavaScript to make sure the visitor's zip code is just numbers is more complicated than what we've already seen and introduces a number of new features and functions. The overall plan is to look at the five-character string contained in the variable `zipCodeEntered` one character at a time and see if each character is actually a number. If it is, then we set a variable to yes and move on to the next character. If, however, anywhere along the line it finds a character that is not a number, then it will create an error message. This portion of the script begins like most of the others, by gathering the value of the field we need to check and assigning it to a variable.

```
// Zip Code Check

    zipCodeEntered =
document.forms['promotion'].elements['zipCode'].value;
      . . .
}
  // Stop hiding the code here -->
</script>
```

Next, because it is not required for the user to put in an address, we use an if statement to see if there is anything at all in the Zip Code field.

```
// Zip Code Check

    zipCodeEntered =
document.forms['promotion'].elements['zipCode'].value;

    if (zipCodeEntered) {
      . . .
    }
      . . .
}
  // Stop hiding the code here -->
</script>
```

If there is not a value in the Zip Code field, the script will ignore the rest of our zip code check and go on to the next part. However, if there is a value in the field, we need to create some variables and assign some of them a base value so that we can check for a proper zip code entry.

```
// Zip Code Check

    zipCodeEntered =
document.forms['promotion'].elements['zipCode'].value;

    if (zipCodeEntered) {
        numberCounter = 0;
```

```
            zipCounter = 0;
            foundNumber = "";
                . . .
        }
    . . .
}
   // Stop hiding the code here -->
      </script>
```

We have created two counter variables that we will use in while loops, and a third variable that we will use to store the outcome of our check.

Our next step is the creation of two while loops.

```
// Zip Code Check

        zipCodeEntered =
document.forms['promotion'].elements['zipCode'].value;

        if (zipCodeEntered) {
            numberCounter = 0;
            zipCounter = 0;
            foundNumber = "";

            while (zipCounter < 5) {
                . . .
                zipCounter++;
            }
        }
    . . .
}
   // Stop hiding the code here -->
</script>
```

Okay, there is the basis for our first while loop. What the script is saying is that *while* the variable zipCounter is less than 5, execute the statements that follow. At this point, there is only one statement that follows, but we will add to that in a moment. The statement that is there now, however, is the key to making sure we're not creating an infinite loop.

```
zipCounter++;
```

The preceding line takes the value of zipCounter and adds 1 to it, so that every time the loop is executed, zipCounter will have a value 1 higher than the previous pass until it reaches 5 and the condition is no longer met and the script can move on.

While the first `while` loop is used to cycle through all five of the characters in the Zip Code field, a second `while` loop located within the first will cycle through all 10 digits (0–9).

```
// Zip Code Check

    zipCodeEntered =
document.forms['promotion'].elements['zipCode'].value;

    if (zipCodeEntered) {
        numberCounter = 0;
        zipCounter = 0;
        foundNumber = "";

        while (zipCounter < 5) {
            while (numberCounter<10) {
                . . .
                numberCounter++;
            }
            if  (foundNumber != "yes" ) {
                zipCounter = 6;
            } else {
                zipCounter++;
                numberCounter = 0;
            }
        }
    }
. . .
}
    // Stop hiding the code here -->
</script>
```

What we have going on is that the second `while` loop will test for the numbers 0–9 for every time the first loop is run. For now, let's ignore the `if` statement at the end of the first loop and add the statements we need in the second loop.

```
// Zip Code Check

    zipCodeEntered =
document.forms['promotion'].elements['zipCode'].value;

    if (zipCodeEntered) {
        numberCounter = 0;
        zipCounter = 0;
```

```
foundNumber = "";

while (zipCounter < 5) {
    while (numberCounter<10) {
        if
    (zipCodeEntered.substr(zipCounter, 1)
    == numberCounter) {

            foundNumber = "yes";
            numberCounter = 11;
        } else {
            foundNumber = "no";
        }
        numberCounter++;
    }
    if    (foundNumber != "yes" ) {
        zipCounter = 6;
    } else {
        zipCounter++;
        numberCounter = 0;
    }
    }
  }
. . .
}
    // Stop hiding the code here -->
</script>
```

Now we have added an `if` statement to the inside of the second `while` loop. This `if` statement is the most important section of this part of the script—it does the actual testing of the values in the Zip Code field, so let's go over it in more detail. First, we set up the test of the value.

```
if (zipCodeEntered.substr(zipCounter, 1)   == numberCounter)
```

We use the `substr()` method in this statement to test a specific character in the Zip Code field. When we used this method in Chapter 1, we specified a range of characters that we wanted to gather; in this example, we check only a single character and we use the value of the variable `zipCounter` to tell the `substr()` method which character we want to check.

As the first loop cycles through, adding 1 to this variable each time it passes, we test the characters that are at positions 0–4 of the `zipCodeEntered` variable. Don't forget that when positioning,

JavaScript always starts with 0 instead of 1. In other words, it will test all five characters of the zip code.

We will compare these values one at a time to the value of the variable numberCounter. This is the variable that is the basis for the evaluation of our second loop, and as the second loop cycles through its life, numberCounter is also having the value of 1 added to it each time. So, while the second loop cycles, it tests to see if the character located at the position of zipCounter is the same as the value of numberCounter, which is cycling through the digits 0–9.

If it is a match, the if statement moves on to set the variable foundNumber to yes, and it sets the value of numberCounter to 11 so that on its next entry of the second while loop, the condition will be false and the script will move on. If it does not find a match, it sets the value of foundNumber to no, adds 1 to the value of number-Counter, and cycles through the second loop again searching for a match.

Once the second loop either runs through its 10 iterations or finds a match, the script continues on to the if statement we added to the first while loop a little bit ago. This if statement tests the value of foundNumber; if in the second while loop a number is not found, it sets the zipCounter to 6, which will kick us out of the first while loop on the next pass to create an error message. If a number was found in the second loop, then the if statement adds 1 to the value of zipCounter and lets it continue on to check the next character in the Zip Code field.

The final addition to this section of code is to create another error message if a nonnumber was found in the Zip Code field.

```
// Zip Code Check

    zipCodeEntered =
document.forms['promotion'].elements['zipCode'].value;

    if (zipCodeEntered) {
        numberCounter = 0;
        zipCounter = 0;
        foundNumber = "";

        while (zipCounter < 5) {
            while (numberCounter<10) {
```

```
        if
(zipCodeEntered.substr(zipCounter, 1)
== numberCounter) {

            foundNumber = "yes";
            numberCounter = 11;
        } else {
            foundNumber = "no";
        }
        numberCounter++;
    }
    if   (foundNumber != "yes" ) {
        zipCounter = 6;
    } else {
        zipCounter++;
        numberCounter = 0;
    }
}
if (foundNumber != "yes") {
    zipCodeErrorMessage = "-zip code has non-
numbers in it\r";
    }
}
. . .
}
  // Stop hiding the code here -->
</script>
```

In this section we have created some fairly difficult and advanced code. However, good news! We're almost finished! The only thing left to do is check if any error messages were created and display them to the user or, if none were created, submit the form to the CGI script.

◆ Project III: Letting the User Know What's Wrong

This final piece of code is nothing groundbreaking—we will be using methods that we covered earlier in the chapter. If the world were a perfect place, then the user would have filled out the form properly. However, this isn't always the case, so now that we have made the necessary checks for missing or erroneous data, we need to pass on what we have found to the user. We use a simple `if` statement to accomplish this.

```
// Letting the user know what was missed

    if ((requiredFieldsErrorMessage) ||
(pullDownErrorMessage) || (emailErrorMessage) ||
(areaCodeErrorMessage) || (zipCodeErrorMessage)) {
        . . .
    } else {
        . . .
    }
}
    // Stop hiding the code here -->
</script>
```

The first line of this section checks to see if any of our error message variables contain a value. If they do, that means that the user has missed something and we should go on to compose a comprehensive error message for the user. We do this by first assigning the beginning of a message to the variable `alertMessage`, and then add any error messages created by the checks we did on to the end.

```
// Letting the user know what was missed

    if ((requiredFieldsErrorMessage) ||
(pullDownErrorMessage) || (emailErrorMessage) ||
(areaCodeErrorMessage) || (zipCodeErrorMessage)) {
        alertMessage = "Oops! There's a little
trouble with the information you've provided\r";

        //build remainder of the alert message
        alertMessage = alertMessage +
requiredFieldsErrorMessage;
        alertMessage = alertMessage +
pullDownErrorMessage;
        alertMessage = alertMessage + emailErrorMessage;
        alertMessage = alertMessage +
areaCodeErrorMessage;
        alertMessage = alertMessage +
zipCodeErrorMessage;


        . . .
    } else {
        . . .
```

```
      }
  }
    // Stop hiding the code here -->
  </script>
```

After we add any other error messages we have to the message opening, all we have to do is use the `alert()` function to display our completed message to the user.

```
// Letting the user know what was missed

        if ((requiredFieldsErrorMessage) ||
(pullDownErrorMessage) || (emailErrorMessage) ||
(areaCodeErrorMessage) || (zipCodeErrorMessage)) {
            alertMessage = "Oops! There's a little trouble
with the information you've provided\r";

            //build remainder of the alert message
            alertMessage = alertMessage +
requiredFieldsErrorMessage;
            alertMessage = alertMessage +
pullDownErrorMessage;
            alertMessage = alertMessage + emailErrorMessage;
            alertMessage = alertMessage +
areaCodeErrorMessage;
            alertMessage = alertMessage +
zipCodeErrorMessage;

            alert (alertMessage);
        } else {
            . . .
        }
  }
    // Stop hiding the code here -->
  </script>
```

If there was nothing wrong with the user's answers, the `else` statement will submit the form data to the CGI script. We do this by calling the `submit` property of the Promotions form.

```
// Letting the user know what was missed

        if ((requiredFieldsErrorMessage) ||
(pullDownErrorMessage) || (emailErrorMessage) ||
(areaCodeErrorMessage) || (zipCodeErrorMessage)) {
            alertMessage = "Oops! There's a little trouble
with the information you've provided\r";
```

```
        //build remainder of the alert message
        alertMessage = alertMessage +
requiredFieldsErrorMessage;
        alertMessage = alertMessage +
pullDownErrorMessage;
        alertMessage = alertMessage + emailErrorMessage;
        alertMessage = alertMessage +
areaCodeErrorMessage;
        alertMessage = alertMessage +
zipCodeErrorMessage;

        alert (alertMessage);
    } else {
    document.forms['promotion'].submit();
    }
}
// Stop hiding the code here -->
</script>
```

Reviewing the Script

Well, if that isn't a mouthful, or should I say a page full, of Java-
Script, then I don't know what is. On the upside, though, we now
have a script that will have those marketing folks singing your
praises to your boss. Let's look over the script one last time and
review what we accomplished.

1. We created some variables to hold the values the user has
   entered into the required fields as well as variables to hold
   any error messages that need to be created.

```
//Create the errorCheck Function

function errorCheck() {

    // Create some variables for our script

    var requiredFieldsErrorMessage = "";
    var firstNameEntered = "";
    var lastNameEntered = "";
    var emailEntered = "";
    var areaCodeEntered = "";
    var zipCodeEntered = "";
    var pullDownErrorMessage = "";
    var emailErrorMessage = "";
```

```
var areaCodeErrorMessage = "";
var zipCodeErrorMessage = "";
```

2. We started to create the part of the function that will
    check for any omissions or errors in the user's answers
    and print out a message to let the user know what is
    wrong. The first step is to put the user's answers for the
    required fields into our new variables.

```
// Required fields error checking

firstNameEntered =
document.forms['promotion'].elements['firstName'].value;
    lastNameEntered =
document.forms['promotion'].elements['lastName'].value;
    emailEntered =
document.forms['promotion'].elements['email'].value;
```

3. We set up a series of `if` statements to make sure that vari-
    ables held data, and if not, to begin adding the omissions
    to the `requiredFieldsErrorMessage` variable.

```
    if ((!firstNameEntered) || (!lastNameEntered) ||
(!emailEntered)) {
        if (!firstNameEntered) {
            requiredFieldsErrorMessage = "- your
        first name\r";
        }
        if (!lastNameEntered) {
            requiredFieldsErrorMessage =
requiredFieldsErrorMessage + "- your last name\r";
        }
        if (!emailEntered) {
            requiredFieldsErrorMessage =
requiredFieldsErrorMessage + "- your email address\r";
        }
    }
```

4. To make sure the user selected an option other than the
    default from the required pull-down menu, we set up an
    `if` statement. If the user did not, our error message vari-
    able is added.

```
// check if the user has selected from the pull-down
// menu
```

```
    var selectPos =
document.forms['promotion'].elements['whatTheyWant'].
selectedIndex;

    if
document.forms['promotion'].elements['whatTheyWant'].
options[selectPos].value == 'default'){
            pullDownErrorMessage = "- you didn't tell us what
you want to see in Stitch\r";
    }
```

5. The next step in our `errorCheck()` function was to set up a series of `if` statements that would look at the string entered in the email form field and check for the presence of the @ symbol and a period (.).

```
// email error checking

if (emailEntered) {
        emailEntered =
document.forms['promotion'].elements['email'].value;
        emailValue = new String (emailEntered);
        emailHasAt = emailValue.indexOf("@");
        emailHasPeriod = emailValue.indexOf(".");


        if ((emailHasAt == -1) || (emailHasPeriod
== -1)) {
            emailErrorMessage = "-your email address\r";
        }
    }
```

6. If the user entered a phone number, we needed to be sure that an area code for that number was also entered. We set up another series of `if` statements, which tested the values held in both of the form fields.

```
// Area Code Check

areaCodeEntered =
document.forms['promotion'].elements['areaCode'].value;
    phoneNumber1Entered =
document.forms['promotion'].elements['phoneNumber1'].value;

    if ((!areaCodeEntered) && (phoneNumber1Entered)) {
        areaCodeErrorMessage = "-please enter your area
code\r";
    }
```

7. The last information we had to check was to make sure that the Zip Code field contained only numbers. To do this, we set up some `if` statements and a couple of `while` loops to look at each individual character of the string that was entered in the Zip Code field and test to make sure it was an integer.

```
// Zip Code Check

zipCodeEntered =
document.forms['promotion'].elements['zipCode'].value;

    // we don't want to do anything if the visitor hasn't
    // entered in anything for the zip code
    if (zipCodeEntered) {
        numberCounter = 0;
        zipLength =    5;
        zipCounter = 0;
        foundNumber = "";

        while (zipCounter < 5) {
            while (numberCounter<10) {
                if (zipCodeEntered.substr
(zipCounter, 1)   == numberCounter) {

                    foundNumber = "yes";
                    numberCounter = 11;
                } else {
                    foundNumber = "no";

                }
                numberCounter++;
            }

            if  (foundNumber != "yes" ) {
                zipCounter = 6;
            } else {
                zipCounter++;
                numberCounter = 0;
            }
        }

        if (foundNumber != "yes") {
            zipCodeErrorMessage = "-zip code has
non-numbers in it\r";
        }
    }
```

8. Finally, we set up some `if` statements to look at the values of the various error message variables. When we found that any of them held a value, we added that value to the `alertMessage` variable, and once all of the error messages were tested, we printed out the content of the final message for the user to see. If no error messages were found, we called the `submit()` function of the form.

```
// Letting the user know what was missed

     if ((requiredFieldsErrorMessage) ||
(pullDownErrorMessage) || (emailErrorMessage) ||
(areaCodeErrorMessage) || (zipCodeErrorMessage)) {
          alertMessage = "Oops! There's a little trouble
with the information you've provided\r";

          //build remainder of the alert message
          alertMessage = alertMessage +
requiredFieldsErrorMessage;
          alertMessage = alertMessage +
pullDownErrorMessage;
          alertMessage = alertMessage +
emailErrorMessage;
          alertMessage = alertMessage +
areaCodeErrorMessage;
          alertMessage = alertMessage +
zipCodeErrorMessage;

          // Now, display the error message
          alert ( alertMessage )
     } else {
          document.forms['promotion'].submit()
     }
}
</script>
```

We have learned the use of some new concepts in this chapter, as well as enhanced our knowledge of some concepts that we have already covered. Let's take a look at what we covered.

- We furthered our knowledge of the JavaScript hierarchy and our ability to access and manipulate its objects (especially form objects).
- We have a solid understanding of both `if` statements and `while` loops.
- We introduced the use of the `alert()` method as a means of delivering information to the user.

- We learned how to use several new logical operators: ||, &&, and !.
- We learned how to enter a hard line break using /r.
- The STRING object was introduced, along with some of its properties.

RECAP

We covered quite a lot of ground in this chapter, and if you can wrap your mind around these concepts and structures, then you have come a long way in mastering JavaScript. The understanding and use of if statements and while loops are key to advanced JavaScript solutions—as you continue to use JavaScript, this will become ever more apparent.

ADVANCED PROJECTS

Here are a few ideas that you can implement if you wish to further your understanding of the concepts covered in this chapter:

1. Try validating different form fields that weren't covered in this chapter, such as radio buttons.
2. Check text boxes for specific answers, possibly as a means to grade an online test.

5 JavaScript Windows and Frames

IN THIS CHAPTER

- A Look at the WINDOW Object
- Project I: Creating, Populating, and Closing Windows with JavaScript
- Project II: Using JavaScript to Talk Between Frames
- Project III: Making Sure Your Frames Site Shows up in Frames
- Recap
- Advanced Projects

We have done some pretty cool stuff with our newfound JavaScript knowledge. We've spent the last couple of projects working with forms, and now it is time to move on to something new. Except for the homepage, Stitch's site is created using frames, so in this chapter, we work on some of Stitch's secondary pages and bring you up to speed on how JavaScript handles frames and windows.

Before we get into any specific projects, however, we take a closer look at what windows and frames are and how they fall into JavaScript's object hierarchy. Dealing with frames and multiple windows can get quite complex and often seem very convoluted. By the end of this chapter, hopefully, you will have garnered a solid understanding of how windows and frames, when combined with JavaScript, can help you do some great things.

◆ A Look at the WINDOW Object

The WINDOW object in JavaScript is on the top of the JavaScript hierarchy; the DOCUMENT object and the objects below it are all descendants of the WINDOW object. The projects that we have done thus far have been contained within a single window, so we have never needed to deal with the WINDOW object or its properties. However, this is not always the case. There are many occasions when it is advantageous to create a new window or access objects contained within another window.

Because the window is an object, not only are we able to access the properties and objects contained within the window, but the window itself has properties of its own. Using JavaScript, we can modify a window's size, configure its toolbars, access its HISTORY array, and much more. Let's get into our first project and see exactly what we mean.

◆ Project I: Creating, Populating, and Closing Windows with JavaScript

On the *Stitch* Web site is a page that lists the companies that have placed ads in the current month's issue of the magazine. *Stitch is the* fashion magazine that attracts some huge companies as advertisers, and the ads themselves are often as groundbreaking as the fashion. Because the magazine is bombarded with requests of how to get in touch with the companies, the powers that be think having the ads on the Web site is a great idea. Therefore, the decision has been made to expand the functionality of the page and make the list of companies' links that will take the user to a page with the companies' contact information, a link to their Web site, and a link to a copy of their current ad.

Guess who they have come to with the job of making this a reality? That's right, you. No reason to fear, though. With your recent additions to the site, you are beginning to be known as the JavaScript guru in the office. So, after a quick planning meeting with your boss, you think you have come up with a great way to accomplish the task. The one problem that kept coming up was the fact that there will be at least 20 advertisers in each month's issue—this many pages added to the site will crowd the server and make for quite a few files to update each month. So, here is the plan: We're going to use JavaScript arrays on the existing list page to store all of the information we will need to dynamically create a page for each company, which we will then put into a new window. This will save space on the server, it will allow us to update one file a month, and it will give us one heck of a project for this chapter. There are three parts to creating this script. First, we will define and create the arrays for the companies' information; next, we will write the function that will open up our new window and populate it with the content; and finally, we will insert the proper event handlers into the HTML to make it all happen.

Creating and Defining the Arrays

The first thing we need to do is create the arrays to hold the company information. For each company, we need to store nine items: the company's name, street address, city, state, zip code, phone number, fax number, Web site if it has one, and the URL for the page with the company's ad on it. In Chapter 3 we used two arrays for each group, one to hold the name of the page and the other to hold the location of the URL. For the most part, we use the same idea here to store our company information; however, instead of two arrays for each group, we use only one for each company. Whereas before we assigned and referenced each element in the array by its position, in this project we give each element a name that we can use to reference it.

Let's start the script by defining the arrays for the companies. Because this page isn't going to be added until next month's issue, we don't know which companies will be placing ads yet, so we create arrays for two fictitious companies for now that will allow us to get our scripts working right away.

```
<script language="JavaScript1.2">
<!-- Code after this will be ignored by older browsers

// Arrays for Company Information
    //Define the arrays

Company1_info = new Array(9);
Company2_info = new Array(9);

. . .

// Stop hiding the code here -->
</script>
```

We have defined two arrays: one for company1 and the other for company2. Both have been given a length of nine elements. Next, we need to assign the companies' contact information to the arrays. Let's put the information for company1 into its array.

```
<script language="JavaScript1.2">
<!-- Code after this will be ignored by older browsers

// Arrays for Company Information
    //Define the arrays

Company1_info = new Array(9);
Company2_info = new Array(9);


    // Populate company1's array

    Company1_info['name'] = 'Company 1';
    Company1_info['street'] = '1235 company way #1';
    Company1_info['city'] = 'Smallsville';
    Company1_info['state'] = 'California';
    Company1_info['zip'] = '91367';
    Company1_info['phone'] = '818-555-1212';
    Company1_info['fax'] = '818-555-1213';
    Company1_info['website'] = 'http://www.company1.com';
    Company1_info['ads'] = 'company1_ads.html';



// Stop hiding the code here -->
</script>
```

When you are populating an array with as many elements as we are here, it is often easier to assign each element a name instead of using its numeric position. It is easy to forget where a specific element is located if you are only using its position number as a reference.

`Company1_info` array now holds all of the information we need to create a page for `Company1` later in the script. Let's fill in the array for `Company2`.

```
<script language="JavaScript1.2">
<!-- Code after this will be ignored by older browsers

// Arrays for Company Information
   //Define the arrays

Company1_info = new Array(9);
Company2_info = new Array(9);


   // Populate company1's array

   Company1_info['name'] = 'Company 1';
   Company1_info['street'] = '1235 company way #1';
   Company1_info['city'] = 'Smallsville';
   Company1_info['state'] = 'California';
   Company1_info['zip'] = '91367';
   Company1_info['phone'] = '818-555-1212';
   Company1_info['fax'] = '818-555-1213';
   Company1_info['website'] = 'http://www.company1.com';
   Company1_info['ads'] = 'company1_ads.html';



   // Populate company2's array

   Company2_info['name'] = 'Company 2';
   Company2_info['street'] = '4321 company way #2';
   Company2_info['city'] = 'Bigsville';
   Company2_info['state'] = 'California';
   Company2_info['zip'] = '91235';
   Company2_info['phone'] = '818-555-2121';
   Company2_info['fax'] = '818-555-2122';
   Company2_info['website'] = 'http://www.company2.com';
   Company2_info['ads'] = 'company2_ads.html';
```

```
// Stop hiding the code here -->
</script>
```

We now have all the information we need stored safely in our two arrays (if you need a refresher on the basics of arrays, check out Project II in Chapter 3). It's time to move on to the next step.

Creating the Function

The function for this script must do several things. First, it must decide which company was chosen and gather its information from the proper array. Next, it must open a new window, and finally, it must populate the new window with the information from the array. Let's first set up the framework for our function.

```
// Function to Create Advertiser Window

function PageCreator(selection)  {


. . .

}


// Stop hiding the code here -->
</script>
```

We've created a function `PageCreator()` and set up the variable `selection` to accept the value being passed to the function from the event handler. This value will be the name of the company that was chosen by the user. The next step is to find out which company that was and gather its information.

```
// Function to Create Advertiser Window

function PageCreator(selection)  {

var company = eval(selection + "_info['name']");
var street = eval(selection + "_info['street']");
var city = eval(selection + "_info['city']");
var state = eval(selection + "_info['state']");
var zip = eval(selection + "_info['zip']");
var phone = eval(selection + "_info['phone']");
var fax = eval(selection + "_info['fax']");
var website = eval(selection + "_info['website']");
var ads = eval(selection + "_info['ads']");
```

```
   .   .   .
}

// Stop hiding the code here -->
</script>
```

We know that the value of `selection` is going to be the name of the company, and we have used those names in the names of the arrays that store their information. In the preceding code, we used the `eval()` method to combine the variable value with a string, which when combined will call the information from the proper position of that company's array. After the information has been retrieved from the array, it is put into a variable that we will use later when printing the content of the popup window. This process is repeated for each of the nine different pieces of information that we need.

Now that we have the information for the selected company safely stored in our variables, we need to open up a new window to put that information into. Let's have a quick look at the syntax of the `open()` method of the `WINDOW` object.

```
window.open(URL, windowName, windowFeatures)
```

There are three elements that you include within the `open()` method: the URL of the page that you want to put into the new window; a string that contains the name that you want the window to use when it is being referenced as a `TARGET` in an anchor tag; and an optional list of standard window properties that you can customize, such as width, height, top location, left location, or the inclusion of various toolbars.

A window is not only able to carry the name that will be used as a `TARGET`, but it can also be associated to a name that you can use when referencing the `WINDOW` object using JavaScript. To assign it this second name, you use the following syntax, where `Name` is the name you wish to assign to the window.

```
Name = window.open(URL, windowName, windowFeatures)
```

Let's put in the code that will open up the window in our script.

```
// Creating the Function

function PageCreator(selection)  {
```

```
var company = eval(selection + "_info['name']");
var street = eval(selection + "_info['street']");
var city = eval(selection + "_info['city']");
var state = eval(selection + "_info['state']");
var zip = eval(selection + "_info['zip']");
var phone = eval(selection + "_info['phone']");
var fax = eval(selection + "_info['fax']");
var website = eval(selection + "_info['website']");
var ads = eval(selection + "_info['ads']");


    // Open the new Window
infowin =
window.open("blank.html","Company_Info","menubar=yes,width=
250,height=200,top=20,left=20");


. . .

}

// Stop hiding the code here -->
</script>
```

Let's go over the preceding code. First, we assign the new window the name `infowin`. Then we moved on to the `open()` method itself—the URL of the page we want to put in the window is `blank.html`. We will be populating the window dynamically with content from our arrays, so that HTML page is as blank as its name suggests. The next element of the code is the TARGET name we are assigning it, `Company_Info`. We won't be using this in our script, but it is a required element. Finally, the last element is our list of attributes that we want the window to take on. We included the toolbar that contains the menus, such as file, edit, view, and so forth. We gave the window a width of 250 pixels and a height of 200 pixels, and we told the window to open 20 pixels from the top left corner of the user's screen.

Now that we have opened our new window, we need to populate it with the information stored in our variables. To do this, we use the `document.write()` method. We have already used this method several times in this book, but this time we add a new little twist to its use. If we were to use the standard syntax

```
document.write('text to be written');
```

we would simply be rewriting the content to our company listing page and not in our new window. To write to our new window, we have to tell the JavaScript engine specifically where we want to write out our HTML. This can be accomplished by adding the name of the window that we want to write to in front of document, like so.

```
infowin.document.write('text to be written');
```

Now that we know how to write to our new window, let's add the code that will do just that.

```
// Creating the Function

function PageCreator(selection)  {

var company = eval(selection + "_info['name']");
var street = eval(selection + "_info['street']");
var city = eval(selection + "_info['city']");
var state = eval(selection + "_info['state']");
var zip = eval(selection + "_info['zip']");
var phone = eval(selection + "_info['phone']");
var fax = eval(selection + "_info['fax']");
var website = eval(selection + "_info['website']");
var ads = eval(selection + "_info['ads']");


    // Open the new Window
infowin =
window.open("blank.html","Company_Info","menubar=yes,width=
250,height=200,top=20,left=20");


    // Write content to new window
infowin.document.write("<html><head><title>Company
Information</title></head><body bgcolor='#FFFFFF'
topmargin='10' leftmargin='0' marginwidth='0'
marginheight='10'><center>");

infowin.document.write("<table border='0'' cellspacing='0'
cellpadding='0'><tr><td><b>" + company + "</b></td></tr>");

infowin.document.write("<tr><td>" + street + "</td></tr>");

infowin.document.write("<tr><td>" + city + ", " + state + "
"  + zip + "</td></tr>");
```

```
infowin.document.write("<tr><td>" + "phone - " + phone +
"</td></tr><tr><td>fax - " + fax + "</td></tr>");

infowin.document.write("<tr><td><a href='" + website + "'
target='_TOP'>" + website + "</a></td></tr>");

infowin.document.write("<tr><td align='center'><br><a
href='" + ads + "' target='Content'>View the Ad</a></td></
tr></table>");

infowin.document.write("<table border='0'' cellspacing='0'
cellpadding='0' width='249'><tr><td width='249'
valign='bottom' align='right'><br><a
href='javascript:window.close()'><img src='images/
closer.gif' border='0'></a></td></tr>");

infowin.document.write("<tr><td width='249'
bgcolor='#FFFF00'> </td></tr></table>");
}

// Stop hiding the code here -->
</script>
```

Okay, let's look at what's going on in this latest block of code. While it may seem like a lot, it really isn't. For the sake of legibility, we use multiple document.write(); methods to write out our new code. In the first line, we create a new HTML document and insert the head and body tags. In past uses of document.write(), we used a backward slash to escape quotes that we want to print out; in this example, we simply use two types of quotes. We use double quotes to signify the beginning and end of the content we want printed, while inside those quotes we use single quotes when we want them to actually be printed out in our code. Both this method and using the \ method work equally well; which one you use is a matter of personal preference.

In the rest of the document.write lines, we use a combination of a table template and the information we have stored in our variables to print out as content. The second-to-last document.write line contains some unfamiliar scripting, so let's take a closer look at what is going on there.

For the most part, the content we are printing out is pretty straightforward; however, if you look closely, you will see something new.

```
<a href='javascript:window.close()'>
```

The JavaScript link in this `href` can be thought of as an `onClick()` event handler—when the user clicks on the link, the JavaScript that follows the colon will be executed. In this case, the command will allow the user to close the new window once he or she has the necessary information from the page. Closing windows isn't something we've covered yet, so let's take a quick look at the `close()` method's syntax.

```
window.close();
```

By default, this line will close the window that the information is found in. If your goal was to close another browser window, you would simply call its name specifically, like so:

```
infowin.close()
```

The `document.write()` lines are the last part of our function. The only thing left to do in this script is insert the event handlers into the HTML, and we will be off and running.

Inserting the Event Handlers

As in the `close()` method used previously in the popup window content, we will put our event handlers directly into the `href` tags of the HTML. When the user clicks either of the companies' links (see Figure 5–1), the `PageCreator()` function will be called and passed the name of the company that was clicked. Here is the HTML containing the links with the handlers inserted into the `href` tags:

```
<tr>
    <td valign="top" align="left">
             </td>
    <td valign="top" align="left">
        <a href="javascript:PageCreator('Company1')"
class="prplLink">Company 1</a></td>

    <td valign="top" align="left">
        <a href="javascript:PageCreator('Company2')"
class="prplLink">Company 2</a></td>
</tr>
```

That about wraps it up for this project. Let's review what we did and look at the script as a whole.

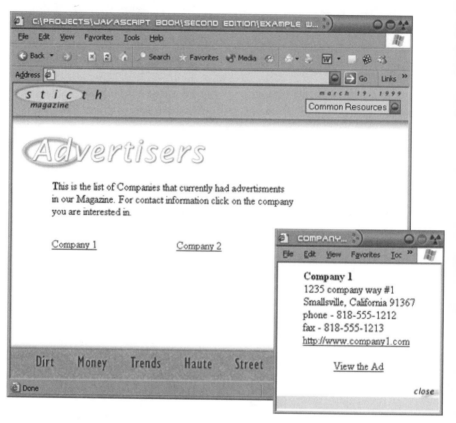

FIGURE 5–1 The Advertisers index page.

Reviewing the Script

1. First we defined and populated the arrays to hold the information for each company's contact information. Instead of using the position in the array that the information would hold, we assigned a name to the location so we can refer to the name instead of the numeric position.

```
<script language="JavaScript1.2">
<!-- Code after this will be ignored by older browsers

// Arrays for Company Information
    //Define the arrays
```

```
Company1_info = new Array(9);
Company2_info = new Array(9);


    // Populate company1's array

    Company1_info['name'] = 'Company 1';
    Company1_info['street'] = '1235 company way #1';
    Company1_info['city'] = 'Smallsville';
    Company1_info['state'] = 'California';
    Company1_info['zip'] = '91367';
    Company1_info['phone'] = '818-555-1212';
    Company1_info['fax'] = '818-555-1213';
    Company1_info['website'] = 'http://www.company1.com';
    Company1_info['ads'] = 'company1_ads.html';


    // Populate company1's array

    Company2_info['name'] = 'Company 2';
    Company2_info['street'] = '4321 company way #2';
    Company2_info['city'] = 'Bigsville';
    Company2_info['state'] = 'California';
    Company2_info['zip'] = '91235';
    Company2_info['phone'] = '818-555-2121';
    Company2_info['fax'] = '818-555-2122';
    Company2_info['website'] = 'http://www.company2.com';
    Company2_info['ads'] = 'company2_ads.html';
```

2. Our next step was to create the `PageCreator()` function.
   The first step was to set up a bunch of variables to hold
   the company's information and use the value passed into
   the function from the event handlers to call the information out of the proper array.

```
// Page Creator Function

function PageCreator(selection) {

var company = eval(selection + "_info['name']");
var street = eval(selection + "_info['street']");
var city = eval(selection + "_info['city']");
var state = eval(selection + "_info['state']");
var zip = eval(selection + "_info['zip']");
var phone = eval(selection + "_info['phone']");
```

```
var fax = eval(selection + "_info['fax']");
var website = eval(selection + "_info['website']");
var ads = eval(selection + "_info['ads']");
```

3. Once we put in the code to get the information out of the array, we used the open() method of the WINDOW object to create a new window to hold the company's information.

```
infowin =
window.open("blank.html","Company_Info","menubar=yes,width=
250,height=200,top=20,left=20");
```

4. With the new window created, we next used the write() method of the DOCUMENT object to print out our new content.

```
// Write content to new window
infowin.document.write("<html><head><title>Company
Information</title></head><body bgcolor='#FFFFFF'
topmargin='10' leftmargin='0' marginwidth='0'
marginheight='10'><center>");

infowin.document.write("<table border='0'' cellspacing='0'
cellpadding='0'><tr><td><b>" + company + "</b></td></tr>");

infowin.document.write("<tr><td>" + street + "</td></tr>");

infowin.document.write("<tr><td>" + city + ", " + state + "
" + zip + "</td></tr>");

infowin.document.write("<tr><td>" + "phone - " + phone +
"</td></tr><tr><td>fax - " + fax + "</td></tr>");

infowin.document.write("<tr><td><a href='" + website + "'
target='_TOP'>" + website + "</a></td></tr>");

infowin.document.write("<tr><td align='center'><br><a
href='" + ads + "' target='Content'>View the Ad</a></td></
tr></table>");

infowin.document.write("<table border='0'' cellspacing='0'
cellpadding='0' width='249'><tr><td width='249'
valign='bottom' align='right'><br><a
href='javascript:window.close()'><img src='images/
closer.gif' border='0'></a></td></tr>");

infowin.document.write("<tr><td width='249'
bgcolor='#FFFF00'> </td></tr></table>");
```

```
}

// Stop hiding the code here -->
</script>
```

5. The final step was to insert the event handlers into the `<a href>` tags of each company.

```
<tr>
    <td valign="top" align="left">
             </td>
    <td valign="top" align="left">
        <a href="javascript:PageCreator('Company1')"
class="prplLink">Company 1</a></td>

    <td valign="top" align="left">
        <a href="javascript:PageCreator('Company2')"
class="prplLink">Company 2</a></td>
</tr>
```

In writing this script, we used some features of JavaScript that are new to us. Let's take a look at those new features.

- We were introduced to the WINDOW object; we covered how to open, close, and populate windows.
- We learned that we could populate and access array information not just by the numeric position that the information occupied, but by user-defined labels.

We now have a clean and efficient way of dealing with what could otherwise have been a pretty tedious job. One of the great things about JavaScript is that it gives you the power to come up with solutions like this, which not only help handle the workload but are really cool uses of the technology.

Uh-oh, I think I hear the boss coming, no doubt with another project for you. What do you say we check out what we are going to be tackling next?

◆ Project II: Using JavaScript to Talk Between Frames

Sure enough, there is a new issue that the boss wants you to look at on the Web site. Currently, on the bottom frame of the site that

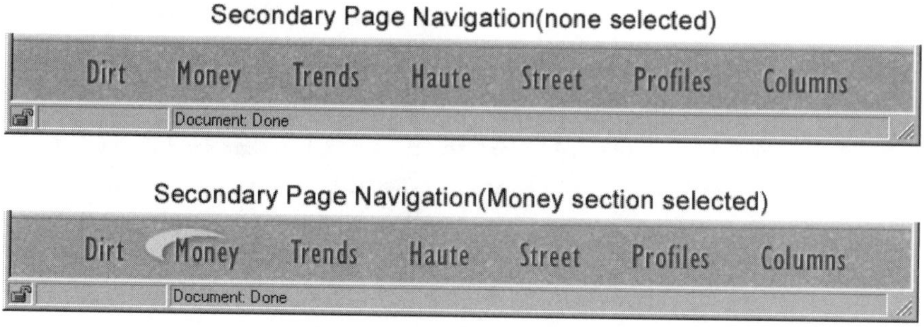

Secondary Page Navigation(none selected)

Secondary Page Navigation(Money section selected)

FIGURE 5–2   A *Stitch* secondary page's bottom navigation bar.

holds the main navigation, the graphics for the section you are in are highlighted (Figure 5–2). One of the other programmers has written the JavaScript to take care of changing the images when they are clicked on, but another problem has arisen that your boss needs you to take care of.

If the user clicks the forward or backward buttons of the browser instead of actually clicking on the navigation images, the graphics won't update. Therefore, we need to set up a script that will have the content frame talk to the navigation frame so that when a new page is loaded into the content frame, it will tell the navigation frame what graphic should be highlighted. To do this, we need a little more information on how JavaScript handles frames.

Figuring Out Your Frame Hierarchy

A frame can be thought of as sub-WINDOW object; like a window, it contains a DOCUMENT object as well as all of the descendant objects and properties that the HTML may create. If you look at the Java-Script hierarchy, however, you will see that the FRAME object sits below the WINDOW object; in fact, it is a property of the WINDOW object.

Each frame in a window can hold separate URLs. That can be very useful, such as in our *Stitch* site that uses three frames, one to hold that content and two others to hold navigation. This lets the user change or scroll in the content frame while always leaving the navigation in place.

When an HTML document with a FRAMESET is loaded into the browser, the JavaScript engine creates an array that holds all of the FRAME objects being made. This is very similar to the way in which JavaScript handles the images that it finds on a page. How we go about referencing the objects is similar as well. Let's take a look at what the FRAMESET looks like for the *Stitch* site and see how we go about referencing the various FRAME objects that are created.

```
<frameset rows="65,*,54" frameborder="0" border="0"
framespacing="NO">
        <frame name="Top Nav Bar" src="top_nav.html"
marginwidth="0" marginheight="0" scrolling="no"
frameborder="no" noresize>
        <frame name="Content" src="ad_index.html"
marginwidth="0" marginheight="0" scrolling="auto"
frameborder="no" noresize>
        <frame name="Bottom Nav Bar" src="bottom_nav.html"
marginwidth="0" marginheight="0" scrolling="no"
frameborder="no" noresize>
    </frameset>
```

The preceding code is the HTML that makes up the FRAMESET document; you can see that three frames are called into existence within the FRAMESET. The first is named Top_Nav_Bar, which holds the common navigation and the header logo. Next is a frame named Content; this frame holds all of the content for the sections of the site. Finally, a frame named Bottom_Nav_Bar is created that holds that navigation for the main sections of the site. Figure 5–3 shows you this FRAMESET's hierarchy.

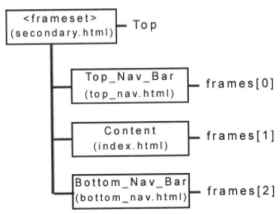

FIGURE 5–3 Our FRAME hierarchy.

As the FRAMESET page is loaded, the frames are put into the FRAMES array in the order in which they are created by the engine, so the Top_Nav_Bar will be frames[0], the Content frame is frames[1], and the Bottom_Nav_Bar is frames[2]. To access the FRAME objects, we use these position numbers when calling to the FRAMES array. For example, if we wanted to access the URL of the Content frame, the syntax would look like this:

```
frames[1].src
```

However, this will work only if we are requesting the information from the page holding the FRAMESET. If we were in one of the other frames, we would have to tell the JavaScript engine to first go back to the top level of the window and then go to the Content frame. There are two ways to do this. The line

```
top.frames[1].src
```

tells the engine to go to the very top level of the hierarchy and then move on to the second frame in the FRAMES array. You could also use parent instead of top to achieve the same effect, like so:

```
parent.frames[1].src
```

The difference between the two is that where top sends the engine to the top of the hierarchy, parent moves the pointer up only one level to the object that is the parent of the frame you are calling from. There will be times when there are nested frames; in other words, the HTML document that is called in a frame contains another FRAMESET instead of just HTML. This will add another set of layers on to the hierarchy, so to get to the top of the hierarchy, you would need to use parent multiple times, like this:

```
parent.parent.frames[1].src
```

Working with nested frames in JavaScript can get rather convoluted—luckily, the *Stitch* site contains no nested frames. With that said, let's get on with our project.

This project consists of two sections. First, we need to create a function in the Bottom_Nav_Bar that will change the highlighted graphic when Content page changes. Second, we need to insert event handlers that will be put into all of the pages that populate the Content frame to call the function that we will create in the first part of the project.

Creating a Function to Check Which Section You Are In

Before we get into writing our new function, it will be very helpful to take a look at the function that the other programmer wrote—it stands to reason that we may be able to use this function in our script. This function is located in the *bottom_nav.html* file and does basically two jobs. First, when it is called after the user has clicked on one of the navigation images, it goes through and turns all of the navigation images to the off state. Once it has done that, it looks to see what graphic the user clicked on and turns that image to the on state. Let's take a quick look at the function itself so we can get an idea of how this is accomplished.

```
function Highlighter(current) {

    var i = 1;
    while (i < 8) {
        document.images[i].src = eval("Pic" + i +
"Off.src");
        ++ i;
    }
    document.images[current].src = eval(current +
"On.src");
    able = current;

}
```

In the first line of the function the variable i is set to the value of 1—this value will be used as a test in the only loop that follows. The next line is the beginning of the while loop; as long as i is less than 8, the loop will keep cycling through. With i set to 1, when you enter the function, the loop will cycle seven times, once for each of the navigation images. We start the value of i at 1 instead of 0 because we are calling the images by their position in the IMAGE array as opposed to by the name that we assigned to it. So, the background image for the frame takes up the first position in the IMAGE array, and we need to skip over it when we are turning the images off.

Inside the loop, we change the source of the image located at the same position as the value of i to the off version of the graphic. When the while loop finishes, all of the navigation objects will have been turned to their default off condition.

Now that all of the images are off, it's time to turn the one the user has just clicked to the On position. The next line in the function takes care of this by setting the source of the image matching the value of the variable current to the rolled-over position.

The final line in the function sets the value of the variable able to the name of the category clicked on, which is held in the variable current. The variable able is used as a test in the off() function, one of the two functions that handles the rollovers on the page.

```
function off(pic) {
    if(document.images) {
        if (pic != able) {
            document.images[pic].src= eval(pic +
"Off.src");
        }
    }
}
```

This is done so that if you roll off of the graphic of the section you are currently in, it won't turn off. We will use this variable in our function as well.

Now that we have seen what's currently going on in the page, it's time to put our function in. Compared to the function the other programmer had to do, ours should be a walk in the park. Our new function will be called every time a new HTML page is loaded into the Content frame, but we want it to change an image only if the page that is loaded is from a different section than the previous page. To do this, we will pass a value into the function when it is called; that value will be the name of the section that the page is in. We test that value against the value of the variable able, which you will remember contains the name of the section that the user last clicked on. We want to run the rest of the function only if those values are not the same—in other words, if the section has changed. Let's get started with the function. We'll add it to the *bottom_nav.html* page right below the other programmer's functions.

```
function SectionChecker(content)
{

    if (content != able)  {

        . . .

    }
}
```

We now have the framework for our function as well as an `if` statement that will check if the new content page is in the same section as the one the user is currently in. If not, then the JavaScript engine will execute the rest of the function, which is the next thing we need to insert into our code.

```
function SectionChecker(content)
{
    if (content != able)  {
        Highlighter(content);
    }
}
```

Because the other programmer has already written the `Highlighter()` function that will turn off all seven of the graphics and then turn on the one with the name that we pass into the function, all we have to do is call that function and pass it the value that was given to our function by the content page.

As a result, if the page that is loaded into the `Content` frame passes the value `dirt` into our function, then our function will call the `Highlighter()` function and pass along that same value, which will in essence turn off all of the navigation images except for the `dirt` image. Now all we have to do is insert the event handlers into all of the pages that go into the `Content` frame.

Inserting the Event Handler

Up until now, we have relied on event handlers that were reacting to some interaction with the user: rolling over an image, clicking a button, or changing some form field. For this project, however, what we need is a handler that will trigger when an HTML page is loaded by the browser. Well, it's our lucky day; the `onLoad()` handler does just that. We place the `onLoad()` handler into the `<body>` tag of the HTML document. It is then triggered once the page has finished loading. Let's first insert it into our contest form page that we created in the last chapter, which is part of the `dirt` section of the site.

```
<body onLoad=". . . ">
```

Now that the handler is inserted, let's put in the call to the `SectionChecker()` function. Remember that because the `SectionChecker()` function is located in another frame, we have to specify the path to the function when calling it.

```
<body onLoad="top.frames[2].SectionChecker('dirt')">
```

Believe it or not, that's about it; all you need to do is put this handler in all of the HTML pages for the content frame. The only thing that will vary is the value that you pass to the SectionChecker() function; that value will be the name of the section in which the page resides.

Oops, just when we think we are done, one of the programmers who was helping Q.C. the new addition to the site has found what could be a potential problem with the script. It is possible that the onLoad() handler could trigger before the Bottom_Nav_Bar frame containing the function is loaded. If this happens, it will generate a JavaScript error.

To prevent this from happening, we want to make sure that the Bottom_Nav_Bar frame is loaded before calling the SectionChecker() function from the content frame. To do this, we need to add a little bit of code to the FRAMESET page, the Bottom_Nav_Bar page, and all of the content pages. First, let's insert the needed code into the FRAMESET page. We know that if either the content frame or the Bottom_Nav_Bar frame is loaded, the FRAMESET page itself must be loaded, so we will use a variable placed in the FRAMESET page to run our test.

```
<script language="JavaScript1.2">
<!-- Code after this will be ignored by older browsers

    var capable = 'no';

// -->
</script>
```

All we did in the preceding code was create a variable capable and assign it the default value of no. So, when the FRAMESET page is loaded, the capable variable will be created for us.

Next, let's put the code we need into the Bottom_Nav_Bar frame. All we need to do here is insert a line of code that will call the capable variable in the FRAMESET page and assign it the value yes—you can put it in right after our SectionChecker() function.

```
function SectionChecker(content)
{
    if (content != able)  {
        Highlighter(content);
    }
```

```
}

top.capable = 'yes';

// -->
</script>
```

Again, as in the onLoad() handler, we need to tell the browser how to get to variable in the hierarchy. When the Bottom_Nav_Bar frame is loaded, it will now change the capable variable to hold the value yes.

The last bit of code we need to put in is in the content pages. Let's make the change to the same dirt section page that we put the onLoad() handler in already. The first thing we need to do is change the onLoad() handler.

```
<body bgcolor="#FFFFFF" onLoad="Checker()">
```

Instead of calling the SectionChecker() frame directly, as we did before, we need to create a new function on the content page itself that will call the SectionChecker() function. This new Checker() function is the function that we will now be calling in the onLoad() event handler. The creation of the Checker() function is the last thing that we need to finish.

```
<script language="JavaScript1.2">
<!-- Code after this will be ignored by older browsers

function Checker() {
    if (top.capable='yes') {
        top.frames[2].SectionChecker('dirt');
    } else {
        setTimeout("Checker()", 2000);
    }
}

// -->
</script>
```

This function is quite simple. The first thing that happens when it is called is that we use an if statement to test the value of the capable variable located on the FRAMESET page. If the Bottom_Nav_Bar frame has been loaded, it will have changed the value of capable to yes, so the condition will be true and the function will go on and call the SectionChecker() function. However, if the `Bottom_Nav_Bar` frame hasn't been loaded, it will go down and run the timer, which will re-call the function after two seconds. So the `Checker()` function will continue to be called until the `Bottom_Nav_Bar` frame has been loaded and it is all right to call the `SectionChecker()` function.

Well, that's it. All you need to do now is insert the `onLoad()` handler and the `Checker()` function into all of the other pages that are located in the `Content` frame. Once that is done, you can use the Back and Forward buttons to your heart's content and always know what section you are in.

Reviewing the Script

Let's take a look at our script and how we accomplished it.

1. We were able to incorporate the functionality of an existing script into this project.

```
function Highlighter(current)
{

        var i = 1;
        while (i< 8) {
                document.images[test].src = eval("Pic" + test +
"Off.src");
                ++ i;
        }
        document.images[current].src = eval(current +
"On.src");
        able = current;

}
```

2. We added the `SectionChecker()` function to the page located in the `Bottom_Nav_Bar` frame. This will call the `Highlighter()` function and pass it the name of the section in which the page loaded into the `Content` frame belongs.

```
function SectionChecker(content)
{
        if (content != able) {
            Highlighter(content);
        }
}
```

3. We inserted the `onLoad()` event handler into all of the HTML pages that will show up in the `Content` frame. Within the handler, we put in a call to our `SectionChecker()` function and passed it the name of the section in which the page belongs.

```
<body onLoad="top.frames[2].SectionChecker('dirt')">
```

Once the event handlers were inserted, our script was functional; however, to make it a bit more robust, we decided to add a last little bit that would prevent us from getting errors if the `Botton_Nav_Bar` frame hadn't loaded before the `SectionChecker()` function was called.

1. We added a variable to the HTML page that held the FRAMESET. We will use this variable to test whether or not the `Bottom_Nav_Bar` frame has been loaded.

```
<script language="JavaScript1.2">
<!-- Code after this will be ignored by older browsers

    var capable = 'no';

// -->
</script>
```

2. We added a line of code into the HTML page in the `Bottom_Nav_Bar` frame that will change the value of the variable in the FRAMESET page to tell us that the bottom navigation page has indeed been loaded by the browser.

```
function SectionChecker(content)
{
    if (content != able)   {
        Highlighter(content);
    }
}

top.capable = 'yes';

// Stop hiding the code here -->
</script>
```

3. We added a function to all of the HTML that goes in the `Content` frame and modified the `onLoad()` handler to call this new function instead of calling our `SectionChecker()` function directly.

```
<script language="JavaScript1.2">
<!-- Code after this will be ignored by older browsers

function Checker() {
    if (top.capable='yes') {
        top.frames[2].SectionChecker('dirt');
    }
}


// -->
</script>

</head>
<body bgcolor="#FFFFFF" onLoad="Checker()">
```

◆ Project III: Making Sure Your Frames Site Shows Up in Frames

After working through a fairly complex project like the last one, you should enjoy working on this quick and easy project. One of the problems with building your site using frames is that people searching for your site on search engines are more often than not brought directly to the content page instead of to the frameset that contains the content page. They are often left looking at a page with no navigation and are unable to leave that individual page. There is a way around this problem, however, and it's going to be our next project for this site. As usual, the boss was the first person to find out about this problem through his AOL-using mother, and now he's throwing a small tizzy, so let's get cracking on it right away.

There are two parts to this project. First, we need to be able to tell if the user viewing the site is just looking at the content page sans the frames, and second, if that is the case, we need to reload the page within the proper frameset. Let's check out how we are going to tell if the user is looking at the site properly.

Checking for the Presence of Frames

How are we supposed to tell if they are looking at the site within the frames? It's actually rather easy; we know that when a frames site is created, the JavaScript engine creates a hierarchy that holds all of the different frames. In our site, when all is right with the world and the user is looking at the site within frames, the content page is here in the hierarchy.

```
top.frames[1]
```

However, if the user is looking at the content page outside of the frameset, then there are no levels to the hierarchy and the document will be at the top of the hierarchy. We can use this as a test in an `if` statement to check how the user is viewing the page. For our script to work site-wide, we need to put it in each of the content files on the site. To get our script up and running, let's first make the changes to the *ad_index.html* page that we used in the first project in this chapter. We'll insert our code at the bottom of the existing script tag.

```
// Used to check if page is being viewed within the
// frameset

if (window == top) {
. . .
}
// -->
</script>
```

The first thing we do is create an `if` statement that checks to see if the current page is located at the top of the window hierarchy. If it is, then the script will execute the next portion of our script.

Reloading the Page within the Frameset

The next portion of our script is the part that will reload the page within the proper frameset. This is done simply by changing the `location` property of the current page to that of the frameset we want to load.

```
// Used to check if page is being viewed within the
// frameset

if (window == top) {
document.location = 'advert_frameset.html';
}
// -->
</script>
```

Believe it or not, that's it for the most part with this script. The only thing left to do now is copy this script to the rest of the content pages within the site and change the frameset to the proper one for the content. That is the one drawback to using this method: Each content page needs its own frameset, but if you want people to view your site properly, it must be done.

Reviewing the Script

Let's take a look at our script and how we accomplished it.

1. We added an `if` statement to check the content page was being viewed within a frameset or not.

```
// Used to check if page is being viewed within the
// frameset

if (window == top) {
. . .
}
```

2. We added a statement to reload the page into the proper frameset if the user is in fact viewing the content page by itself.

```
<script language="Javascript">

// Used to check if page is being viewed within the
// frameset

if (window == top) {
    document.location = 'advert_frameset.html';
}
```

3. We needed to add this code snippet to each content page on the site and change the frameset being loaded to the proper one for the content.

RECAP

Working with windows and frames can greatly increase the functionality of your Web site—when used in conjunction with JavaScript, the sky is the limit as to what you can accomplish. In this chapter, we have just scratched the surface of what you can accomplish with these features of JavaScript.

The concept of frames and understanding how their hierarchy works is not an easy thing to grasp, but once you have the fundamentals down, it will open up a vast range of new applications.

ADVANCED PROJECTS

1. Use the section tracking technique we used in the second project in a site with nested frames and two sets of navigation images that need to be tracked.
2. Create a frames-based site with a set of nested frames where you can hide the navigation frame by changing the `location` property of the frame that holds the inner frames.

6 Advanced JavaScript

Now that you have the basics down, it's time to move on to some hard-core, complex crowd-pleasers, guaranteed to elicit oohs and aahs from clients and friends. There are two different projects that have been on the back burner here at Stitch for quite some time, just waiting for the right person to come along to tackle them. The first is an interactive slideshow that will allow users to check out photos from the latest fashion shows from around the world. Second, as a service to the site's users, the powers that be want to add a searchable designer database to the site that will let users find out information about their favorite designers. The slideshow seems to have the most people backing the project, so let's start there.

Both of these projects are rather advanced; they rely heavily on subject matter that has been covered earlier in the book, so if you've skipped ahead to get to the "good" stuff, just be fore-warned that we won't be pulling any punches for these projects. If you're just starting out, it's a good idea to go back and cut your teeth on some of the simpler projects in the book. With that said, let's get on with the first project.

◆ Project I: Interactive Photo Slideshow

Stitch, being the top-notch fashion magazine that it is, always sends reporters and photographers to all of the major fashion shows. Because of the limited space in the print version of the magazine, tons of great photos from the shows go unseen, so the idea is to create a place on the Web site where readers can go to see them. At first, it was thought that a typical photo gallery would be fine, but after kicking around some ideas, it was decided that it would be great if the photos could be displayed as a slide-show. That way, the users could see all of the pictures on one page, and if the slideshow could be made to run automatically, that would be even better.

Now that we've become adept at manipulating images with JavaScript, this should be a walk in the park. The first thing that needs to be done is to get together with one of the designers and work out a layout and figure what features need to be included on the page. After a quick brainstorming session over lunch and a couple of hours noodling around in Photoshop, it looks like we've got a good idea going (see Figure 6–1).

We want the slideshow to be able to run in two different ways. First, the users will be able to cycle through the photos using the next and previous buttons. Or, if they choose to, they can click on the Start Slideshow button and let the pictures cycle through automatically with a short delay between each. To achieve this dual purpose, we need to create three different functions, one to control the "next" functionality, one to control the "previous" functionality, and one to control the "self-running slideshow" functionality. But first, we need to create some IMAGE objects as well as some arrays to hold the information for our photos.

FIGURE 6–1 The photo slideshow page layout.

Creating and Inserting the Image Objects

Let's start off with creating the IMAGE objects that we'll need for our project. Because the photos of the fashion show are quite large, we will treat them differently than the images in our previous image replacement scripts, so we don't have to worry about creating IMAGE objects for them. We will, however, be modifying the Next, Previous, and Start Slideshow images in our script. The

FIGURE 6–2 The versions of the navigation images.

designer has created two versions of each graphic (see Figure 6–2). One version is a fully visible "on" version, while the other is a grayed-out "off" version. We will use the different versions as we reach different sections of the slideshow. For instance, when the user is at the beginning of the slideshow, the Previous button will not do anything, so it will be grayed out. Likewise, when the user reaches the last photo in the slideshow, we want to gray out the Next button to let them know that they've reached the end. When the user selects to watch the self-running slideshow, we will use the grayed-out versions of all three navigation images to let them know they don't need to do anything but sit back and enjoy the show. Let's insert our script into the <head> of the *fashion_show.html* file and insert our IMAGE objects.

```
<script language="Javascript1.2">
<!-- Code after this will be ignored by older browsers

// Next Previous and Slideshow Button Image Objects

nextOn=new Image(71, 35);
nextOn.src="images/fashion_show/next_on.gif";
nextOff=new Image(71, 35);
nextOff.src="images/fashion_show/next_off.gif";

previousOn=new Image(96, 35);
previousOn.src="images/fashion_show/previous_on.gif";
previousOff=new Image(96, 35);
previousOff.src="images/fashion_show/previous_off.gif";

slideshowOn=new Image(96, 35);
slideshowOn.src="images/fashion_show/slideshow_on.gif";
slideshowOff=new Image(96, 35);
slideshowOff.src="images/fashion_show/slideshow_off.gif";

. . .
```

```
//  -->
</script>
```

We now have two IMAGE objects for each navigation image, one for the on state and one for the off state. Let's move on and see how we are going to store the information for the actual photos that go in the slideshow.

Creating the Photo Arrays

The main problem with creating individual IMAGE objects for each slideshow photo is that they are rather large. Not in width or height, but in file size. Each photo is on average 20 kb. If there were, let's say, eight photos in the slideshow, that would mean preloading an extra 160 kb of files. This would make the page load awfully slowly for those not on a fast connection. If this was the only issue with creating IMAGE objects for all the photos, we still might just bite the bullet and let the preloading happen in the background. However, there is another issue that is pushing us away from that solution. The functional specification for the project calls for a caption to be displayed for each photo. These captions are not part of the photos; they are text that needs to be displayed when each photo is brought up. After looking around, you've decided that the best way to store the captions is in an array, which we will access each time the photo changes. Because we are already making the arrays to hold the captions, it's been decided that we will store the URL to each photo in the array as well; this will negate the need of creating IMAGE objects for each of them.

After some discussion, it has been decided that we should create an array for each photo. Each array will have two entries: the URL of the photo and the caption for it. We haven't received either the number of photos or their names for this month's fashion show yet, so our designer buddy has created eight temporary images that we can use to build our script. Let's define the eight different arrays we'll need for our script.

```
// Arrays for Photo Information

    //Define the arrays

picture1 = new Array(2);
picture2 = new Array(2);
```

```
picture3 = new Array(2);
picture4 = new Array(2);
picture5 = new Array(2);
picture6 = new Array(2);
picture7 = new Array(2);
picture8 = new Array(2);
```

We now have eight new arrays defined, named `picture1` through `picture8`, and each is two entries long. Now that we have them defined, it's time to create the entries for them. We'll start with the entries for `picture1`. We label the first entry `caption` and the second entry `url`.

```
// Populate the picture arrays array

picture1['caption'] = 'This is picture #1';
picture1['url'] = 'images/fashion_show/photo_1.jpg';
```

As with the pictures, these captions are just placeholders. The first thing we did was insert a placeholder caption. For `picture1` we inserted a caption "This is picture #1." No doubt the copywriters will come up with a better caption when the real photo arrives. Next, we inserted the path by which the first photo can be found from the Fashion Show page. Now that you see how we created the entries for the first photo, let's create the entries for the remaining seven photos.

```
// Populate the picture arrays array

picture1['caption'] = 'This is picture #1';
picture1['url'] = 'images/fashion_show/photo_1.jpg';

picture2['caption'] = 'This is picture #2';
picture2['url'] = 'images/fashion_show/photo_2.jpg';

picture3['caption'] = 'This is picture #3';
picture3['url'] = 'images/fashion_show/photo_3.jpg';

picture4['caption'] = 'This is picture #4';
picture4['url'] = 'images/fashion_show/photo_4.jpg';

picture5['caption'] = 'This is picture #5';
picture5['url'] = 'images/fashion_show/photo_5.jpg';

picture6['caption'] = 'This is picture #6';
```

```
picture6['url'] = 'images/fashion_show/photo_6.jpg';

picture7['caption'] = 'This is picture #7';
picture7['url'] = 'images/fashion_show/photo_7.jpg';

picture8['caption'] = 'This is picture #8';
picture8['url'] = 'images/fashion_show/photo_8.jpg';
```

All right, we now have not only the image objects we'll need created, but all the information we'll need for each of the slideshow photos. Let's move on to the functions that will run our script.

Creating the Slideshow Functions

We now need the three functions to run our slideshow. First, we create the `next` function, which will bring up the next photo in the slideshow when the user clicks on the Next button. We place our function directly below our photo arrays, but first we need to define some variables that we will be using in our functions.

```
var currentPic = 0;
var slideshow = 'off';
var browser = navigator.appName;
```

We declared three different variables. First, we created a variable called `currentPic`. This will hold the number of the picture that is currently being displayed. We set its initial value to 0, because when the user first comes to the page, the photo that is showing is just an introductory graphic and not part of the slideshow. Next, we created a variable called `slideshow`. This variable will hold either the value `on` or `off` depending on if the self-running slideshow is playing. It of course defaults to the value `off`. Finally, as we have done for other scripts, we need to do some cloaking, so we created a variable called `browser` to hold the name of the browser the user is viewing the site with. With our variables defined, let's start the `next` function.

```
// function that switches to next photo in the slideshow

function photoNext() {
    if ((currentPic < 8) && (slideshow != 'on')) {

    }
}
```

We defined a function called photoNext() and we added an if statement inside of it. Let's see what we are accomplishing with the if statement. If the user clicks on the Next button, the event handler on the button calls this function, which we then want to change out the photo being displayed to the next photo in our arrays. This is true in all but two cases: first, if the user is looking at the last photo in the set, and second, if currently viewing the self-running slideshow. In both of these instances, we don't want this function to do anything, so we wrap the main functionality of our function within this if statement. Now that we have that out of the way, we'll move on to the meat of our function.

The first thing we want to accomplish when we enter our function is to take stock of where the user is at in the slideshow and see if anything special needs to be done before we actually change the photo and the caption. There are two things in particular that we need to check for. First, you will notice that when the page is first loaded, the Previous button is grayed out and not functional. This makes sense because we are at the beginning of the slideshow and there are no previous photos to show. However, once the user gets to the second photo in the slideshow, he or she may way want to go back and view the previous photos in the show. So, when the user gets to the second photo in the show, we want to turn the Previous button to its on state to let the user know that he or she can go backwards in the show.

The other stage that we need to take special note of is when the user comes to the last photo in the show. Here we want to turn the Next button to its off state to let the user know that he or she has reached the end of the slideshow. We will keep an eye out for these two scenarios using if statements that test the value of currentPic. When the photoNext() function is first called, the value of currentPic should hold the value of the picture being currently displayed, so if there are eight photos in the show, as the function is called to bring up the final photo, currentPic's value should be 7. Likewise, when the user moves on to the second photo in the slideshow, the value of currentPic should be 1. These are the values we will use as conditions in our if statements.

```
// function that switches to next photo in the slideshow

function photoNext() {
    if ((currentPic < 8) && (slideshow != 'on')) {
        if(currentPic == 7) {
```

```
           . . .
      }
      if(currentPic == 1) {
             . . .

      }
          . . .

   }
}
```

Now we have two `if` statements, one that will execute if the user is going to the last photo in the show and one that will execute if the user is going to the second photo in the show. Let's insert the code that we want both of these `if` statements to execute if their conditions come up `true`.

```
// function that switches to next photo in the slideshow

function photoNext() {
     if ((currentPic < 8) && (slideshow != 'on')) {
          if(currentPic == 7) {
               document.images['next'].src = nextOff.src;
          }
          if(currentPic == 1) {
               document.images['previous'].src =
previousOn.src;
          }
             . . .

     }
}
```

In each `if` statement, we add a single line of code that will change the state of one of the navigation images. The first `if` statement turns the Next button to its `off` state if the user comes to the end of the slideshow, while the second `if` statement turns the Previous button to its `on` state when the user reaches the second photo in the show. Now that we have the "housekeeping" aspects of this function out of the way, let's move on to the next portion of our function.

Next, we want our function to change both the photo and the caption to the next in the set of arrays. First, we'll take care of changing the photo. As was mentioned above, when the `photoNext()` function is called, `currentPic` holds the value that corresponds to the photo currently being shown, so if we are going to use `currentPic` to call up our next photo, then we need to increment its value by 1.

```
// function that switches to next photo in the slideshow

function photoNext() {
    if ((currentPic < 8) && (slideshow != 'on')) {
        if(currentPic == 7) {
            document.images['next'].src = nextOff.src;
        }
        if(currentPic == 1) {
            document.images['previous'].src =
previousOn.src;
        }
        ++currentPic;
        . . .
    }
}
```

With `currentPic` now holding the value that corresponds to the next photo in the set, let's swap in that photo.

```
// function that switches to next photo in the slideshow

function photoNext() {
    if ((currentPic < 8) && (slideshow != 'on')) {
        if(currentPic == 7) {
            document.images['next'].src = nextOff.src;
        }
        if(currentPic == 1) {
            document.images['previous'].src =
previousOn.src;
        }
        ++currentPic;
        document.images['fashionPics'].src =
    eval('picture' + currentPic + '["url"]');
        . . .
    }
}
```

We've had quite a bit of experience with changing out images using JavaScript, so this should look pretty familiar. There is one slight twist to the way we did it here. Usually, we would use a variable being passed in to the function combined with the rest of the name of an IMAGE object to specify which IMAGE object should be used for the new picture. However, because we are simply storing the paths to the photos in our arrays, all we need to do is call on the location in the array that holds the path of the photo we wish to display. So, on the left-hand side of the assignment operator, we have the typical call to the source property of the image we wish to change. But on the right-hand side, we use the `eval()` function to combine the value of `currentPic` with a call to the `url` entry in the array of the next photo we wish to display. When this line is executed, presto, the new image is displayed. Now we need to tackle displaying the caption that goes along with it.

The idea to change the caption came from one of the marketing department people who had seen it on another site. After visiting the site to see how they accomplished it, we've run into a slight snag. It seems that this technique will work only in Internet Explorer, and not in Netscape. After checking the Web server logs, you've found out that approximately 87 percent of the users who visit the site are using Internet Explorer, so it wouldn't be the end of the world if we went ahead and used this technique for the captions, as long as the users on Netscape could still view the photos. A good rule to follow when creating a Web site is the 80/20 rule, which says it's okay to implement something that 80 percent of your visitors have the capability to view but that may exclude the remaining 20 percent. Obviously, there are limits; I mean, you wouldn't want to have the main navigation of the site only viewable to some users, no matter the percentage, but as long as not having the new feature doesn't negatively impact the user too much, it should be fine. After much discussion, it's decided that our changing captions are such an instance. So the next thing we have to include in the function is some cloaking for the different types of browsers.

```
// function that switches to next photo in the slideshow

function photoNext() {
    if ((currentPic < 8) && (slideshow != 'on')) {
        if(currentPic == 7) {
            document.images['next'].src = nextOff.src;
        }
        if(currentPic == 1) {
            document.images['previous'].src =
previousOn.src;
        }
        ++currentPic;
        document.images['fashionPics'].src =
    eval('picture' + currentPic + '["url"]');
        if (browser == 'Microsoft Internet
    Explorer') {
```

. . .

```
            }
        }
}
```

We added an `if` statement that will execute only if the user is on Internet Explorer. To see how this portion works, let's first look at the area of HTML that holds the text that we want to change.

```
<br>
Use the controls below to view the photos either in a
slideshow or at your own pace using the "next" and
"previous" buttons.</td>
```

This is the text as it is when the page first loads; it tells the user how to use the slideshow. For us to have the ability to change the text as each new photo is displayed, we need to put this text into a block of CSS-defined content, much as we did in our project with CSS menus. Whereas we used a `<div>` tag to hold our menus, here we wrap our text in a `<span>` tag, like so.

```
<span id="captionText">Use the controls below to view the
photos either in a slideshow or at your own pace using the
"next" and "previous" buttons.</span>
```

We have not only wrapped our text in a `<span>` tag, but we have given the `<span>` an ID of `captionText`. The last step to make this text accessible through JavaScript is to assign it to a CSS selector. Let's open up the *styles_default.css* file and create one.

```
#captionText  {
color : #8E1C1C;
font : 8pt Verdana;
font-weight : normal;
}
```

Now that our text is assigned to a specific selector, an object has been created through which we can access and modify the text with our script. The property of the `captionText` object that we need to access is the `innerText` property. This property contains all of the text held inside our `<span>` tag. The line of code to change the text is very similar to the line that we used to change the photo. Let's take a look at it.

```
// function that switches to next photo in the slideshow

function photoNext() {
```

```
if ((currentPic < 8) && (slideshow != 'on')) {
    if(currentPic == 7) {
        document.images['next'].src = nextOff.src;
    }
    if(currentPic == 1) {
        document.images['previous'].src =
previousOn.src;
    }
    ++currentPic;
    document.images['fashionPics'].src =
eval('picture' + currentPic + '["url"]');
    if (browser == 'Microsoft Internet Explorer') {
        captionText.innerText= eval('picture'
+ currentPic + '["caption"]');}


}
}
```

On the right-hand side of the assignment operator, we use the
eval() function and the currentPic variable to make a call into
our photo arrays, this time to the caption entry of the proper
photo. We then assign the returned value to the innerText property of our captionText object.

That wraps it up for the photoNext() function. We now have a
function that will keep track of the states for the Previous and
Next buttons and will change out the photo and caption to the
next in the list. Now we need to create the function that will take
the user back a photo in the slideshow.

We will call this function photoPrevious(). It will contain for
the most part the same functionality as our photoNext() function,
but it will travel the other way in the list of photos. Let's get
started on it.

```
// function that switches to previous photo in the
slideshow

function photoPrevious() {
    if ((currentPic > 1) && (slideshow != 'on')) {
        . . .
    }
}
```

Again, as in the photoNext() function, the first thing we need
to do is make sure that the function should actually be run. For
this function, we don't want to change the photo if the show is

currently displaying the first photo in the slideshow or if the self-running slideshow has been selected.

With our `if` statement in place to make sure the function should actually run, we can move on to the housekeeping aspect of this function. Like in the `photoNext()` function, there are two points at which we need to make changes to one of the navigation images: When the user moves from the last photo to the second to last photo we need to turn the Next button to its `on` state, and when the user moves from the second photo to the first, we need to turn the Previous button to its `off` state. The values of `currentPic` at those times are 8 and 2. Let's set up a couple of `if` statements to catch the users at that point.

```
// function that switches to previous photo in the
// slideshow

function photoPrevious() {
    if ((currentPic > 1) && (slideshow != 'on')) {
        if(currentPic == 8) {
            . . .
        }
        if(currentPic == 2) {
            . . .
        }
        . . .
    }
}
```

With that done, let's insert the code that we want each `if` statement to execute.

```
// function that switches to previous photo in the
// slideshow

function photoPrevious() {
    if ((currentPic > 1) && (slideshow != 'on')) {
        if(currentPic == 8) {
            document.images['next'].src = nextOn.src;
        }
        if(currentPic == 2) {
            document.images['previous'].src =
previousOff.src;
        }
        . . .
    }
}
```

If `currentPic` is set to 8 when the function is called, that means the Next button is currently grayed out, but as the function runs, the user will be taken to the second to last photo and may want to move ahead again. So, in the first `if` statement, we change the state of the Next button to its `on` state. Likewise, if the user is moving from the second photo back to the first photo in the slideshow, we change the state of the Previous button to its `off` state, which is what we do in the second `if` statement. Keep in mind that if you change the number of pictures in the slideshow, you will need to change the value that is being tested in both of the first housekeeping `if` statements in the `photoNext()` and `photoPrevious()` functions to work with the new number of pictures.

Let's now move on to the photo and caption changing portions of the function.

```
// function that switches to previous photo in the
// slideshow

function photoPrevious() {
    if ((currentPic > 1) && (slideshow != 'on')) {
        if(currentPic == 8) {
            document.images['next'].src = nextOn.src;
        }
        if(currentPic == 2) {
            document.images['previous'].src =
previousOff.src;
        }
        --currentPic;
        currentUrl =
        document.images['fashionPics'].src =
eval('picture' + currentPic + '["url"]');
        if (browser == 'Microsoft Internet Explorer') {
            captionText.innerText= eval('picture' +
currentPic + '["caption"]');
        }
    }
}
```

These lines are the same as the ones from the `photoNext()` function, albeit with one exception. Because we are moving backwards in the list of photos, we need to subtract a value of 1 from `currentPic` each time the function is run, which is what we do in the first line in the new section of code.

Well, two functions down, one more to go. Let's move on to the function that will power the self-running slideshow. We'll call it `slideShow()`.

```
// function that powers the self running slideshow

function slideShow() {
    . . .
}
```

The first thing we need to do when this function is called is determine if the user has just started the self-running slideshow. If this is the case, then the value of the variable `slideshow` should be `off`. We use this as a test in an `if` statement to hold some code that needs to be executed when the slideshow is first started.

```
// function that powers the self running slideshow

function slideShow() {
    if (slideshow == 'off') {
        . . .
    }
    . . .
}
```

There are three things that need to happen when the slideshow is first started. First, we need to turn all three of the navigation buttons to their grayed-out `off` state.

```
// function that powers the self running slideshow

function slideShow() {
    if (slideshow == 'off') {
        document.images['next'].src = nextOff.src;
        document.images['previous'].src =
previousOff.src;
        document.images['slideshow'].src =
slideshowOff.src;
        . . .
    }
    . . .
}
```

Next, we need to set the variable `showcase` equal to `on` so that our function will know that the `slideshow` is already running. Finally, we need to reset the variable `currentPic` equal to `0`. This way, if the user has started the slideshow after already having gone part way through it manually, the slideshow will start from the beginning.

```
// function that powers the self running slideshow

function slideShow() {
    if (slideshow == 'off') {
        document.images['next'].src = nextOff.src;
        document.images['previous'].src =
previousOff.src;
        document.images['slideshow'].src =
slideshowOff.src;
        slideshow = 'on';
        currentPic = 0
    }
    . . .
}
```

Now that we've got the slideshow initialized and ready to run, we need to add the code that will change the photos and captions. We want this code to run each time this function is called, with the exception of when the slideshow reaches the last photo in the set. Let's set up an `if` statement that will let us do this.

```
// function that powers the self running slideshow

function slideShow() {
    if (slideshow == 'off') {
        document.images['next'].src = nextOff.src;
        document.images['previous'].src =
previousOff.src;
        document.images['slideshow'].src =
slideshowOff.src;
        slideshow = 'on';
        currentPic = 0
    }
    if (currentPic < 8) {
        . . .
    } else {
        . . .
    }
}
```

If the function is called at any time other than when the last photo is already displayed, the condition of our latest `if` statement will evaluate `true` and the code that follows will be executed. If, however, the show is already on the last photo, the code following the `else` portion of the statement will execute. The code contained within the `if` portion of the statement is the exact same code that changes the photo and caption in the `photoNext()` function, so there isn't really a need for a long flowery explanation. Here is the function with this chunk of code added.

```
// function that powers the self running slideshow

function slideShow() {
    if (slideshow == 'off') {
        document.images['next'].src = nextOff.src;
        document.images['previous'].src =
previousOff.src;
        document.images['slideshow'].src =
slideshowOff.src;
        slideshow = 'on';
        currentPic = 0
    }
    if (currentPic < 8) {
        ++currentPic;
        document.images['fashionPics'].src = currentUrl =
eval('picture' + currentPic + '["url"]');
        if (browser == 'Microsoft Internet Explorer') {
            captionText.innerText= eval('picture' +
currentPic + '["caption"]');
        }
        . . .
    } else {
        . . .
    }
}
```

Here's the short and sweet explanation of what this code does, for those of you who weren't paying attention during the `photoNext()` function. We added the line of code that increments the `currentPic` variable, then the next line changes the photo being displayed. Finally, we added the code that will change the caption if the user is viewing the site with Internet Explorer. There is one thing we need to add to this section of code that varies for the `photoNext()` function. Because this is the self-running slideshow, we need to insert a mechanism to call this function again after a short delay. To do this, we use the `setTimeout()` function. We've already used this in several of our projects, so it should be familiar.

```
// function that powers the self running slideshow

function slideShow() {
```

```
if (slideshow == 'off') {
        document.images['next'].src = nextOff.src;
        document.images['previous'].src =
previousOff.src;
        document.images['slideshow'].src =
slideshowOff.src;
        slideshow = 'on';
        currentPic = 0
}
if (currentPic < 8) {
        ++currentPic;
        document.images['fashionPics'].src = currentUrl =
eval('picture' + currentPic + '["url"]');
            if (browser == 'Microsoft Internet Explorer') {
                captionText.innerText= eval('picture' +
currentPic + '["caption"]');
            }
            setTimeout("slideShow()", 8000);
        } else {
            . . .
        }
}
```

We inserted a timer that will re-call the `slideshow()` function after a pause of 8 seconds. Eight seconds should give not only the computer time to download the next photo, but the user time to give it a good looking over.

We now move on to the section of code that goes in the `else` portion of the statement that will be executed when the slideshow has reached the last picture. In this section of code, we need to let the user know that the slideshow is over, so we reset the photo to the introductory photo that is displayed when the page is first loaded. We also turn both the Next and Start Slideshow buttons to their `on` state.

```
// function that powers the self running slideshow

function slideShow() {
    if (slideshow == 'off') {
        document.images['next'].src = nextOff.src;
        document.images['previous'].src =
previousOff.src;
        document.images['slideshow'].src =
slideshowOff.src;
        slideshow = 'on';
        currentPic = 0
```

```
        }
    if (currentPic < 8) {
        ++currentPic;
            document.images['fashionPics'].src = currentUrl =
eval('picture' + currentPic + '["url"]');
            if (browser == 'Microsoft Internet Explorer') {
                captionText.innerText= eval('picture' +
currentPic + '["caption"]');
            }
            setTimeout("slideShow()", 8000);
    } else {
            document.images['next'].src = nextOn.src;
            document.images['slideshow'].src =
slideshowOn.src;
            document.images['fashionPics'].src = 'images/
fashion_show/start_pic.gif';
                . . .
    }
}
```

The last thing we need to do in this section of code is reset the currentPic and slideshow variables to their default state. This resets the slideshow and makes it ready to run again, either automatically or manually.

```
// function that powers the self running slideshow

function slideShow() {
    if (slideshow == 'off') {
            document.images['next'].src = nextOff.src;
            document.images['previous'].src =
previousOff.src;
            document.images['slideshow'].src =
slideshowOff.src;
            slideshow = 'on';
            currentPic = 0
    }
    if (currentPic < 8) {
        ++currentPic;
            document.images['fashionPics'].src = currentUrl =
eval('picture' + currentPic + '["url"]');
            if (browser == 'Microsoft Internet Explorer') {
                captionText.innerText= eval('picture' +
currentPic + '["caption"]');
            }
            setTimeout("slideShow()", 8000);
    } else {
```

```
        document.images['next'].src = nextOn.src;
        document.images['slideshow'].src =
slideshowOn.src;
        document.images['fashionPics'].src = 'images/
fashion_show/start_pic.gif';
        slideshow = 'off';
        currentPic = 0;
    }
}
```

With that, we are done with our functions; the only thing left to do is insert the event handlers that will call our functions.

Inserting the Event Handlers

To make our slideshow run, each of the three navigation buttons need event handlers. Let's take a quick look at the HTML for these three buttons.

```
<td valign="top" align="left">
    <br><a href=" "><img
src="images/fashion_show/previous_off.gif" alt=""
name="previous" width="96" height="35"
border="0"></a></td>

<td valign="top" align="left">
    <a href=" "><img
src="images/fashion_show/slideshow_on.gif" alt=""
width="133" height="38" border="0"
name="slideshow"></a></td>

<td valign="top" align="left">
    <a href=" "><img
src="images/fashion_show/next_on.gif" alt=""
name="next" id="next" width="71" height="35"
border="0"></a></td>
```

Each button has an anchor tag wrapped around it, so let's place our handlers directly into the HREFs so they will trigger when the button is clicked on by the user. Here is the code with the handlers inserted into each anchor tag.

```
<td valign="top" align="left">
    <br><a href="javascript:photoPrevious();"><img
src="images/fashion_show/previous_off.gif" alt=""
name="previous" width="96" height="35"
border="0"></a></td>
```

```
<td valign="top" align="left">
    <a href="javascript:slideShow();"><img
src="images/fashion_show/slideshow_on.gif" alt=""
width="133" height="38" border="0"
name="slideshow"></a></td>

<td valign="top" align="left">
    <br><a href="javascript:photoNext();"><img
src="images/fashion_show/next_on.gif" alt=""
name="next" id="next" width="71" height="35"
border="0"></a></td>
```

The final thing we need to do is insert the name property into the image that we want to swap out for the actual fashion show pictures. Here is that <img> tag with the name attribute inserted.

```
<img src="images/fashion_show/start_pic.gif" width="400"
height="300" alt="" name="fashionPics">
```

With that, we have ourselves an interactive photo slideshow that our users are going to love. Let's take a quick peek back at how we wrote our script.

Reviewing the Script

The first thing we did was create some IMAGE objects.

```
<script language="Javascript1.2">
<!-- Code after this will be ignored by older browsers


// Next Previous and Slideshow Button Image Objects

nextOn=new Image(71, 35);
nextOn.src="images/fashion_show/next_on.gif";
nextOff=new Image(71, 35);
nextOff.src="images/fashion_show/next_off.gif";

previousOn=new Image(96, 35);
previousOn.src="images/fashion_show/previous_on.gif";
previousOff=new Image(96, 35);
previousOff.src="images/fashion_show/previous_off.gif";

slideshowOn=new Image(96, 35);
slideshowOn.src="images/fashion_show/slideshow_on.gif";
```

```
slideshowOff=new Image(96, 35);
slideshowOff.src="images/fashion_show/slideshow_off.gif";
```

We created both an on and off IMAGE object for each of the three navigation buttons on the page.

Next, we created the arrays that would hold the information on the photos to be displayed by the slideshow.

```
// Arrays for Photo Information

    //Define the arrays

picture1 = new Array(2);
picture2 = new Array(2);
picture3 = new Array(2);
picture4 = new Array(2);
picture5 = new Array(2);
picture6 = new Array(2);
picture7 = new Array(2);
picture8 = new Array(2);
```

We created eight different arrays that have two entries each. We named them picture1 through picture8.

Next, we populated these arrays with information about the photos.

```
// Populate the picture arrays array

    picture1['caption'] = 'This is picture #1';
    picture1['url'] = 'images/fashion_show/photo_1.jpg';

    picture2['caption'] = 'This is picture #2';
    picture2['url'] = 'images/fashion_show/photo_2.jpg';

    picture3['caption'] = 'This is picture #3';
    picture3['url'] = 'images/fashion_show/photo_3.jpg';

    picture4['caption'] = 'This is picture #4';
    picture4['url'] = 'images/fashion_show/photo_4.jpg';

    picture5['caption'] = 'This is picture #5';
    picture5['url'] = 'images/fashion_show/photo_5.jpg';

    picture6['caption'] = 'This is picture #6';
    picture6['url'] = 'images/fashion_show/photo_6.jpg';
```

```
picture7['caption'] = 'This is picture #7';
picture7['url'] = 'images/fashion_show/photo_7.jpg';

picture8['caption'] = 'This is picture #8';
picture8['url'] = 'images/fashion_show/photo_8.jpg';
```

For each array, we created two entries: one labeled `caption` and the other labeled `url`.

- In the `caption` field, we stored the caption we wish to be displayed with the picture.
- In the `url` field, we stored the path of the photo that we want displayed.

The next step was to define and assign values to several variables that our functions would use.

```
var currentPic = 0;
var slideshow = 'off';
var browser = navigator.appName;
```

1. We created the variable `currentPic` to hold the number associated with the photo that is currently being displayed. As only the introductory picture is displayed when the page is first loaded, we assigned it a value of 0.
2. We created the variable `slideshow`. This variable holds either the value `on` or `off`, depending on if the self-running slideshow is currently running. We gave it the default value of `off`.
3. We created the variable `browser`, which holds the name of the browser that the user is viewing the site with. This variable will be used later to help with some cloaking issues.

Next, we created the three functions that will power the slideshow. First, we created the `photoNext()` function, which is called each time the user clicks on the Next button.

```
// function that switches to next photo in the slideshow

function photoNext() {
    if ((currentPic < 8) && (slideshow != 'on')) {
        if(currentPic == 7) {
            document.images['next'].src = nextOff.src;
        }
        if(currentPic == 1) {
            document.images['previous'].src =
previousOn.src;
```

```
        }
        ++currentPic;
        document.images['fashionPics'].src =
eval('picture' + currentPic + '["url"]');
        if (browser == 'Microsoft Internet Explorer') {
            captionText.innerText= eval('picture' +
currentPic + '["caption"]');
        }
    }
}
```

1. We set up an `if` statement which would test two values: `currentPic` to make sure we aren't already viewing the last picture and `slideshow` to make sure the self-running slideshow isn't already going. If both of these conditions are `true`, then the function executes the code contained within the `if` statement.

2. Inside the `if` statement, we inserted some housekeeping functionality to turn the Next button to its `off` state when the user reaches the last photo, and turn the Previous button to its `on` state once the user reaches the second photo in the slideshow.

3. We started the code that would actually change the photo and the caption; first, we incremented the value of `currentPic` by one to advance to the value associated with the next photo. We then made a call to the proper photo array, grabbed the path to the photo we want to display, and assigned it to the source property of the `fashionPics` image.

4. We set an `if` statement to change the caption being shown for those users browsing the site with Internet Explorer. To do this, we again reached into the proper array and this time selected the text from the `caption` field, which we assigned to the `innerText` property of the `captionText` object.

Once we completed the `photoNext()` function, we moved on to the `photoPrevious()` function.

```
// function that switches to previous photo in the
// slideshow

function photoPrevious() {
    if ((currentPic > 1) && (slideshow != 'on')) {
        if(currentPic == 8) {
```

```
                    document.images['next'].src = nextOn.src;
            }
            if(currentPic == 2) {
                    document.images['previous'].src =
    previousOff.src;
            }
            --currentPic;
            currentUrl =
            document.images['fashionPics'].src =
    eval('picture' + currentPic + '["url"]');
            if (browser == 'Microsoft Internet Explorer') {
                    captionText.innerText= eval('picture' +
    currentPic + '["caption"]');
            }
        }
    }
}
```

1. This function is similar in structure to the `photoNext()` function, so the first step was to make sure that we actually wanted the function to execute. We did this by setting up an `if` statement to test the values of `currentPic` and `slideshow`.

2. We took care of the housekeeping functions that either turn the Next button to its `on` state when the user moves away from the last photo or turn the Previous button to its `off` state once the user reaches the first photo in the slideshow.

3. Instead of adding a value of 1 to `currentPic`, in this function we inserted a line to subtract a value of 1 from `currentPic` in order to move backwards in the group of photos.

4. We inserted the code that will change the photo as well as the caption for those using Internet Explorer.

The final function we created was to power the self-running slideshow.

```
// function that powers the self running slideshow

function slideShow() {
    if (slideshow == 'off') {
            document.images['next'].src = nextOff.src;
            document.images['previous'].src =
    previousOff.src;
```

```
                document.images['slideshow'].src =
slideshowOff.src;
                slideshow = 'on';
                currentPic = 0
        }
        if (currentPic < 8) {
                ++currentPic;
                document.images['fashionPics'].src = currentUrl =
eval('picture' + currentPic + '["url"]');
                if (browser == 'Microsoft Internet Explorer') {
                        captionText.innerText= eval('picture' +
currentPic + '["caption"]');
                }
                setTimeout("slideShow()", 8000);
        } else {
                document.images['next'].src = nextOn.src;
                document.images['slideshow'].src =
slideshowOn.src;
                document.images['fashionPics'].src = 'images/
fashion_show/start_pic.gif';
                slideshow = 'off';
                currentPic = 0;
        }
}
```

1. We inserted some code that would execute if the slideshow was just starting, and this is the first time the function is called. So, we created an `if` statement that tests the value of `slideshow` to make sure it is still `off`. If that is the case, we inserted code that would turn all three of the navigation buttons to their grayed-out `off` state. We also set the value of slideshow to `on` and reset the value of `currentPic` to 0 so that the slideshow would start from the beginning.

2. We created an `if else` statement that, if `true`, should change the photos, since the user has not reached the end of the slideshow. However, if it evaluates `false`, it should not change the photo because it has reached the end.

   - The code we inserted into the `if` portion of the statement is a copy of the functionality that changes the picture and caption in the `photoNext()` function, with one exception. At the end of the code, we added a timer to re-call the function after a delay of 8 seconds; this will keep the slideshow moving along.

- The code that we inserted into the `else` portion of the statement executes when the user has reached the end of the slideshow. We first turn each of the three navigation buttons to their `on` state and then set the `slideshow` variable to `off` and reset the `currentPic` variable to 0.

The last thing we did in this project was insert the event handlers that will call our functions.

```
<td valign="top" align="left">
    <br><a href="javascript:photoPrevious();"><img
src="images/fashion_show/previous_off.gif" alt=""
name="previous" width="96" height="35"
border="0"></a></td>

<td valign="top" align="left">
    <a href="javascript:slideShow();"><img
src="images/fashion_show/slideshow_on.gif" alt=""
width="133" height="38" border="0"
name="slideshow"></a></td>

<td valign="top" align="left">
    <br><a href="javascript:photoNext();"><img
src="images/fashion_show/next_on.gif" alt=""
name="next" id="next" width="71" height="35"
border="0"></a></td>
```

We inserted the handlers directly into the HREFs of each anchor tag that wraps around the three navigation buttons.

We have learned the use of some new concepts during this project as well as enhanced our knowledge of some concepts that we have already covered.

- We explored a new way of handling image replacement, using custom arrays as opposed to IMAGE objects. Custom arrays let us store not only the path to the image but a caption for the photo.
- We introduced the `innerText` property.

◆ Project II: Searchable Designer Database

Now that we've knocked off the first of the two projects that we wanted to tackle, it's time to take a look at the other one. The idea behind this project is that *Stitch*, being the top-notch fashion magazine that it is, has information on all of the top designers in the world. It would be great if we had some way to get that information to our readers, who are constantly asking for more information on their favorite designers. The idea came up of creating a page on the site where a user could go to search for information on designers. When the idea was originally conceived, the thought was to store all of the information in a database and write the search functionality in a language like PHP or Cold Fusion. This, unfortunately, has proved to be quite out of the price range that the powers that be are comfortable with, and this is the main reason the project has been kicking around for so long; no one has figured out a way to do it cheaply. After thinking about the problem for a bit, you've decided that you could probably pull off a version of the project using just JavaScript. The idea is to create a page where users select from several criteria and, with each selection, narrow down the list of designers to a point where the user can find the designer he or she is looking for. This wouldn't allow for the full-blown functionality of the original ideal, but hey, the price tag is certainly right. So after running the idea up the ladder and getting approval to work on the project, it's time to figure out exactly what we can accomplish.

Functional Specification

Since this project is going to be a little complicated, we're going to take time to plan out exactly what we want to happen before we start coding. It's tempting to skip this step and just jump into the code, but control yourself. Thinking through the project before you start will always save you time and usually results in a better end product. Let's first take a look at the data and choose the different criteria we might want the user to be able to sort the designers by.

After talking to some of the more fashion-minded people in the company, it looks like there are several top-level criteria that designers are usually associated with: where they are based and what they design (clothes, hats, lingerie). We have a lot more information on each designer, but it looks like these two criteria will serve us best as the basis for our search parameters. Now, because we don't have access to a language that is designed for creating search functionality, we will arrange these criteria so that the user must follow a "trail" to generate their results.

1. The user will choose from a location pull-down menu.
2. This will populate a pull-down menu that holds the different types of designers from the region.

3. Once the user selects a type of designer, a list of the designers that are of that type and from that region selected will appear in a menu.
4. The user may select a designer from the list and click on a button to open a page that holds the rest of the information we have on that designer.

This means we need to create a page with a Location pull-down menu, a Type pull-down menu, a Select box that we can populate with the designers' names, and a button that opens the designer's information page. Now that we know the fields that we need to include on the search page, it's time to sit down with a designer and work on what the page will look like (see Figure 6–3).

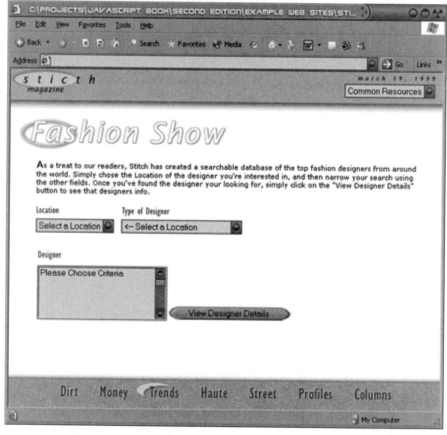

FIGURE 6–3   Designer search page.

After nailing down the look and feel of the page, it's time to figure out how the script will work. The first thing we need to figure out is how to store all of the data we need to use in our script. It seems the best way to store the information would be in arrays. We have created arrays for several of our projects; we've always created an array for each item that we wanted to store data on. If we were to create an array for each location and then an array for each type and then an array for each designer, we would end up with 50 million arrays that would be very hard to group without resorting to some archaic naming convention. It would be nice if we could create one array that would hold all of our information. Well, it's our lucky day: Enter multidimensional arrays.

Multidimensional Arrays

Up until now we have used only single-dimensional arrays. Multidimensional arrays work in much the same way but give us expanded capabilities. They let us create arrays that can store other arrays inside of them. A good way to think of a single-dimensional array is as a filing cabinet and each entry into the array as a drawer that holds a single piece of information. A multidimensional array adds another layer onto that; it would also have several file folders in each drawer. This would make each drawer within the main filing cabinet kind of a filing cabinet itself. Let's look at an example of a case where we would want to create a multidimensional array. Let's say you're a car dealer and you want to write a script that will hold information on all the cars on your lot. You could create an array that would hold the make and model of each car. Now, what if you not only wanted to be able to access the make and model, but you also wanted to be able to store a list of the features for each car. This is a perfect place to use a multidimensional array, so let's create one for our fictitious car dealer.

When we created arrays in previous projects, we always first explicitly defined the array and the number of entries each array would hold. With newer versions of JavaScript, there is a much easier way to create arrays. You simply create the array and fill it with its information all at once. Here is an example of how you would do this with a simple single-dimensional array.

```
CarList = ['Nissan Xterra', 'Volkswagen Jetta']
```

We have now created an array called `CarList`, which holds entries of two cars. To define a multidimensional array, you simply insert another as an entry in the first array. Here's the same array converted into a multidimensional array, which holds not only the car make and model, but the vehicle's features as well.

```
CarList = [
            // Car 1
            ['Nissan Xterra', '2002', '5000
        miles', 'Blue'],

            //Car 2
            ['Volkswagen Jetta, '1999', '30000
        miles', 'Green']
        ]
```

We now have a multidimensional array called `CarList`, which has two entries that are themselves arrays that hold the individual cars' information. We don't have to stop there—we could keep adding arrays, nesting them deeper and deeper. We will use this method to hold all of the information we will need to fill out our search criteria menus.

With cases like this, where the array structure can get fairly complicated, it's a good idea to sketch out on paper what the structure of the arrays is actually going to be, so after sitting down and working at it for a while, it looks like you've come up with a pretty solid diagram of the array structure (see Figure 6–4).

We have now finished the functional specification portion of our project. We figured out how the page will function, came up with a look and feel for the page, and sketched out the array structure that will hold our data. With this portion of the project done, we can move forward with the creation of this page. We start by using placeholder information instead of hunting down the actual information for each criteria. Once we have the functionality of the page working, we can fill in our arrays with the proper information.

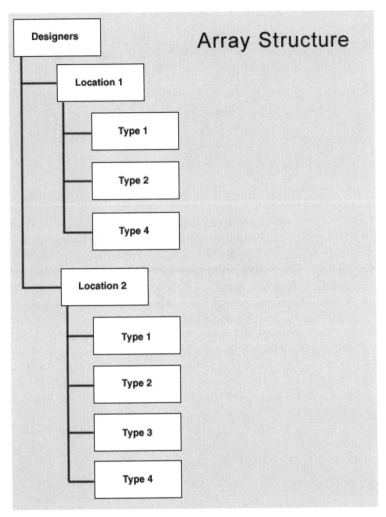

FIGURE 6–4 The array structure.

Creating and Filling the Arrays

Now that we know how to create our arrays and the structure that they need to follow, let's get cracking with their creation. We start with the first two levels of our array.

```
designers = [
            // location 1
            [ ],

            // location 2
            [ ]

        ]
```

We defined an array called `designers`, which has two nested arrays located inside of it, one for each location where a designer might be found. Since we are using placeholder information, we need only two locations to get our script up and going. Once the script is complete, we'll add in the true locations where designers are found. All we'll need to do is add another array for each location.

Now we add the next level of arrays, which will hold the types of designers found in each location.

```
designers = [
            // location 1
            [
                // type 1
                [ 'Type 1'],

                // type 2
                [ 'Type 2'],

                // type 4
                [ 'Type 4']],
            ],

            // location 2
            [
                // type 1
                [ 'Type 1'],

                // type 2
                [ 'Type 2'],
```

```
                    // type 3
                    [ 'Type 3'],

                    // type 4
                    [ 'Type 4']
              ]


        ]
```

You will notice that we entered an initial entry into each `type` array; this entry holds a string that specifies the type of designer that will be listed in the array. This entry is used to fill out the Type pull-down menu once a location has been chosen.

Our next step is to nest arrays into each of the `type` arrays that will hold the actual designers' information. Let's first insert them for the designers in `location1`.

```
designers = [
                    // location 1
                    [
                    // type 1
                    [ 'Type 1',
                        // designer 1
                        ["designer.html", "Joe", "Abrams"],
                        // designer 2
                        ["designer.html", "Roger", "Dennis"],
                        // designer 3
                        ["designer.html", "Missy", "Johnson"],
                        // designer 4
                        ["designer.html", "Sarah", "Leonard"]
                    ],
                    // type 2
                    [ 'Type 2',
                        // designer 1
                        ["designer.html", "Mike", "Bunker"],
                        // designer 2
                        ["designer.html", "Tara",
"Cartwright"],
                        // designer 3
                        ["designer.html", "Ashley", "Trakker"]
                    ],
                    // type 4
                    [ 'Type 4',
                        // designer 1
                        ["designer.html", "Caitlin",
"Archibold"],
```

```
                    // designer 2
                    ["designer.html", "Giovonni",
"Filnelli"]
                    ]

                ],
```

In each `type` array directly following the initial label entry, we nested new arrays, which hold three entries themselves. The first entry is the name of the HTML page that holds the detailed information about the designer; the second entry holds the designer's first name and last; the third entry holds his or her last name. You will also notice that the name of the HTML page is all `designer.html`. This again is because we don't have each designer page created yet. Using just a single page it makes it easier for us to get the script up and running.

Let's enter the `designer` arrays for `location2`.

```
            // location 2
            [
            // type 1
            [ 'Type 1',
                // designer 1
                ["designer.html", "Scott", "Jaspers"],
                // designer 2
                ["designer.html", "Lisa", "Lee"],
                // designer 3
                ["designer.html", "Mary", "Marker"],
                // designer 4
                ["designer.html", "Joel", "Schwartz"]
            ],
            // type 2
            [ 'Type 2',
                // designer 1
                ["designer.html", "Mia", "Adams"],
                // designer 2
                ["designer.html", "Ashlyn", "Deerborn"]
            ],
            // type 3
            [ 'Type 3',
                // designer 1
                ["designer.html", "Justine",
"Andrews"],
                // designer 2
                ["designer.html", "Lauren", "Bishop"],
                // designer 3
```

```
                        ["designer.html", "Laura", "Michaels"],
                        // designer 4
                        ["designer.html", "Kristin", "Sanger"]
                    ],
                    // type 4
                    [ 'Type 4',
                        // designer 1
                        ["designer.html", "Caitlin",
"Archibold"],
                        // designer 2
                        ["designer.html", "Giovonni",
"Filnelli"],
                        // designer 3
                        ["designer.html", "Pat", "Micelli"]
                    ]
                ]
            ]
```

We now have all of our data stored in arrays; our next step is to create functions that can pull out the data that is requested from them.

Creating the Search Functions

With our current plan, there are two different mechanisms that a user must use to narrow the choices for designers that are shown, so it makes sense to create a function for each of them. We will create a function called updateLocation(), which is called when the user makes a selection from the Location pull-down menu as well as a function called updateType(), which is called when the user makes a selection from the Type pull-down menu. We also need a function that sends the user to the proper HTML page once he or she has selected the designer. But first, as usual, we need to define some variables that we will use in our functions.

```
// variables needed for our functions
var whichLocation = '';
var designerType = '';
var designerListSize = 20;
var typeSize = 4;
```

We created four variables that we will need later on. Let's take a look at each of them. First, we created the whichLocation variable, which will hold a number corresponding to the position in the designers array that holds the location array that was selected by the user. Next, we created the variable designerType; this variable holds a number that corresponds to the position in the location array, which holds the type array the user has selected. Next, we created a variable called designerListSize, which holds a number that specifies the maximum number of designers that we will display. Finally, we created a variable called typeSize, which holds a number that specifies the maximum number of types that will be listed for the Type menu. Now that we have the variables we'll need defined, we can start on our functions.

The first function we create is updateLocation(), which will be called when the user makes a selection from the Location pull-down menu. Its main purpose is to populate the Type pull-down menu with all of the designer types for the location chosen. When the user makes a selection from the Location menu and this function is called, a number that corresponds to the position of that location in the designers array will be passed into the function.

Let's define the function.

```
// Populates the Type Field
function updateLocation(whichLoc) {

        .  .  .

}
```

The first thing we need to do inside of the function is make sure that the user actually selected a location and not just the first entry in the menu, which tells the user to "Select a Location." If the user has chosen the first option, we don't want to run this function. Instead, we want to alert the user that a location must be selected from the list. We achieve this by adding an if statement that checks to make sure a value is actually passed into the function.

```
// Populates the Type Field
function updateLocation(whichLoc) {
        if(whichLoc) {
        .  .  .
        } else {
                alert('Please Choose a Location');
        }
}
```

If the user has selected a location and a value is passed in to the function, the `if` portion of the statement will evaluate to `true` and it will do its work. If not, then it will display an alert telling the user to "Please Choose a Location."

The location number passed into the function will be needed later on by the other functions in our script, so we need to assign the value of `whichLoc` to a variable defined outside of the function, thereby making it accessible by all functions within our script. The `whichLocation` variable was created for this purpose.

```
// Populates the Type Field
function updateLocation(whichLoc) {
    if(whichLoc) {
        // set whichLocation variable to the value passed
into the function
        whichLocation = whichLoc;
    . . .
    } else {
        alert('Please Choose a Location');
    }
}
```

Next, we need to create some housekeeping functionality. If the user has already made a search and brought up some designers before choosing a new location, it is a good chance that the other fields on our page are already filled with data. This data must be cleared away when a new location is displayed, so we need to insert some code that will clear out the type of designer field and the designer list field. Let's start with clearing out the designer list field.

```
// Populates the Type Field
function updateLocation(whichLoc) {
    if(whichLoc) {
        // set whichLocation varaible to the value passed
into the function
        whichLocation = whichLoc;

        //clear out the Designer select box

        var listCounter = 0;
        while(listCounter <= designerListSize) {
            document.searchForm.designer.options
[listCounter].text = '';
            document.searchForm.designer.options
[listCounter].value = '';
         ++listCounter;
```

```
     }
         . . .
 } else {
     alert('Please Choose a Location');
 }


}
```

Because we have set the maximum number of designers that can be shown in the variable `designerListSize`, we can use that variable in a `while` loop to cycle through every possible position in the designers list. The first thing we did was create a variable called `listCounter`, which we can use as a counter in our `while` loop. Next, we created a `while` loop, which will run as long as `listCounter` is less than or equal to the number held within the `designerListSize` variable, which we assigned a value of 20. As the `while` loop cycles through, each time we will reset the `text` property as well as the `value` property of the menu location that corresponds to the current value of the `listCounter` variable. Once the designers list has been cleared out, we reinsert our message telling the user to "Please Choose Criteria" into the first position of the menu and set it to be the selected choice within the menu. We do this by first specifying a new `text` value for the first option in the menu and then making the selected property of that option equal to `true`.

```
// Populates the Type Field
function updateLocation(whichLoc) {
     if(whichLoc) {
          // set whichLocation variable to the value passed
into the function
          whichLocation = whichLoc;

          //clear out the Designer select box

          var listCounter = 0;
          while(listCounter <= designerListSize) {
              document.searchForm.designer.options
          [listCounter].text = '';
              document.searchForm.designer.options
          [listCounter].value = '';
           ++listCounter;
          }
```

```
//snap designers list to the first slot and
//repopulate it with criteria message
document.searchForm.designer.options[0].text =
"Please Choose Criteria              ";
document.searchForm.designer.options[0].
selected = true;
    . . .
} else {
    alert('Please Choose a Location');
}
}
```

We've taken care of clearing out the designers list; now let's clear out the Type pull-down menu. We'll use the same technique that we used for the designers list. First, we'll create a counter variable and then add a `while` loop to run through and reset all of the options in the menu.

```
// Populates the Type Field
function updateLocation(whichLoc) {
    if(whichLoc) {
        // set whichLocation variable to the value passed
        // into the function
        whichLocation = whichLoc;

        //clear out the Designer select box

        var listCounter = 0;
        while(listCounter <= designerListSize) {
            document.searchForm.designer.options
        [listCounter].text = '';
            document.searchForm.designer.options
        [listCounter].value = '';
            ++listCounter;
        }
        //snap designers list to the first slot and
        //repopulate it withh criteria message
        document.searchForm.designer.options[0].text
    = "Please Choose Criteria              ";
        document.searchForm.designer.options[0].
    selected = true;

        //clear out the Type pull down

        var typeCount = 0;
        while(typeCount <= typeSize) {
```

```
                document.searchForm.type.options[typeCount].
            text = '';
                document.searchForm.type.options[typeCount].
            value = '';
                ++typeCount;
            }
            . . .
    } else {
            alert('Please Choose a Location');
    }

}
```

This time, we use the `typeSize` variable as the high number in the condition of our `while` loop, so this loop will cycle through five times, clearing out all of the currently displayed menu options. We don't need to worry about resetting the Select a Type message, because we will be refilling this menu with a new type list a little later on in the function. There is one other thing, however, we need to do regarding the Type menu: We need to reset the value of the variable `designerType`, which may be holding a previously selected designer type.

```
// Populates the Type Field
function updateLocation(whichLoc) {
    if(whichLoc) {
        // set whichLocation varaible to the value
        // passed into the function
        whichLocation = whichLoc;

        //clear out the Designer select box

        var listCounter = 0;
        while(listCounter <= designerListSize) {
            document.searchForm.designer.options
        [listCounter].text = '';
            document.searchForm.designer.options
        [listCounter].value = '';
        ++listCounter;
        }
        // snap designers list to the first slot and
        // repopulate it with criteria message
        document.searchForm.designer.options[0].text =
    "Please Choose Criteria              ";
        document.searchForm.designer.options
    [0].selected = true;
```

```
//clear out the Type pull down

var typeCount = 0;
while(typeCount <= typeSize) {
    document.searchForm.type.options
[typeCount].text = '';
    document.searchForm.type.options
[typeCount].value = '';
    ++typeCount;
}
designerType = '';
. . .
} else {
    alert('Please Choose a Location');
}
}
```

Okay, we've finished our housekeeping. Let's move on to the section of code that populates the Type menu with the types associated with the location chosen by the user.

We need to set a new message into the first option of the Type menu. When the page is first loaded, this message is displayed in the first option:

```
<-- Select a Location
```

Now that the user has selected a location, we need to change that message:

```
Select a Type
```

We also want to make sure that this first option is the one that shows in the pull-down menu.

```
// Populates the Type Field
function updateLocation(whichLoc) {
    if(whichLoc) {
        // set whichLocation varaible to the value passed
        // into the function
        whichLocation = whichLoc;

        //clear out the Designer select box

        var listCounter = 0;
        while(listCounter <= designerListSize) {
            document.searchForm.designer.options
[listCounter].text = '';
```

```
    document.searchForm.designer.options
[listCounter].value = '';
++listCounter;
}
//snap designers list to the first slot and
repopulate it with criteria message
    document.searchForm.designer.options[0].text =
"Please Choose Criteria              ";
    document.searchForm.designer.options
[0].selected = true;

    //clear out the Type pull down

    var typeCount = 0;
    while(typeCount <= typeSize) {
        document.searchForm.type.options
    [typeCount].text = '';
        document.searchForm.type.options
    [typeCount].value = '';
            ++typeCount;
    }
    designerType = '';


    // Populate type pull down with new choices
    document.searchForm.type.options
[0].text = 'Select a Type';
    document.searchForm.type.options
[0].selected = true;
        . . .
} else {
        alert('Please Choose a Location');
}
}
```

In the first line, we reassign the `text` property of the first option in the menu to our new message, and in the next line, we set the selected property of that option to `true`. Next, we define a variable to hold the position of the menu option we will want to access each time a new type is inserted into the menu.

```
// Populates the Type Field
function updateLocation(whichLoc) {
    if(whichLoc) {
        // set whichLocation varaible to the value passed
into the function
        whichLocation = whichLoc;
```

```
//clear out the Designer select box

var listCounter = 0;
while(listCounter <= designerListSize) {
    document.searchForm.designer.options
[listCounter].text = '';
    document.searchForm.designer.options
[listCounter].value = '';
    ++listCounter;
}

//snap designers list to the first slot and
//repopulate it with criteria message
document.searchForm.designer.options[0].text =
"Please Choose Criteria              ";
    document.searchForm.designer.options[0].selected
= true;

//clear out the Type pull down

var typeCount = 0;
while(typeCount <= typeSize) {
document.searchForm.type.options[typeCount].text
= '';
    document.searchForm.type.options[typeCount].value
= '';
    ++typeCount;
}
designerType = '';


// Populate type pull down with new choices

document.searchForm.type.options[0].text =
'Select a Type';
    document.searchForm.type.options[0].selected =
true;
    var typeLocation = 1;
    . . .
} else {
    alert('Please Choose a Location');
}
}
```

We now have a variable named typeLocation, which holds
the default value of 1. We have assigned it 1 because we have
already created an entry for the first option in the menu. There-

fore, we must add the various types starting with the second position in the menu.

Now that we've displayed a new message in the menu and
created our typeLocation variable, we need to populate the menu
with the various types of designers found in the selected location.

We use a for loop to cycle through and pull out the type
labels for each type located within the chosen locations array.
We haven't used a for loop yet, so let's take a look at the syntax
for creating one.

```
for (initial-expression; condition; increment-expression) {
     statements
}
```

A for loop consists of three expressions, separated by semicolons, followed by one or more statements that are executed if the
condition within the loop proves true. In previous projects that
required while loops, we have had to create a counter variable
that increments each time the loop is executed. The for loop lets
us do this right inside the initial declaration of the loop. The initial-expression is where we declare a counter variable and set it
to its default value. The condition is the same as in a while loop:
a statement that can be evaluated as either true or false. Finally,
the increment-expression is where we increment the value of the
initial-expression each time the loop is cycled through.

In our case, we want a loop that will cycle through as many
times as there are type arrays held within the chosen location
array. This is accomplished like so.

```
// Populates the Type Field
function updateLocation(whichLoc) {
     if(whichLoc) {
          // set whichLocation variable to the value passed
          // into the function
          whichLocation = whichLoc;

          //clear out the Designer select box

          var listCounter = 0;
          while(listCounter <= designerListSize) {
               document.searchForm.designer.options
          [listCounter].text = '';
               document.searchForm.designer.options
          [listCounter].value = '';
          ++listCounter;
```

```
    }
    //snap designers list to the first slot and
    //repopulate it with criteria message
    document.searchForm.designer.options[0].text
= "Please Choose Criteria              ";
    document.searchForm.designer.options[0].selected
= true;

    //clear out the Type pull down

    var typeCount = 0;
    while(typeCount <= typeSize) {
        document.searchForm.type.options[typeCount].
    text = '';
        document.searchForm.type.options[typeCount].
    value = '';
        ++typeCount;
    }
    designerType = '';


    // Populate type pull down with new choices

    document.searchForm.type.options[0].text =
'Select a Type';
    document.searchForm.type.options[0].selected =
true;
    var typeLocation = 1;
    for (var i = 0; i <
designers[whichLocation].length; i++) {
        . . .
    }
    . . .
} else {
    alert('Please Choose a Location');
}
}
```

In our `for` loop, we have set the `initial-expression` to declare a variable name `i` and set its default value to 0. The condition in the statement will evaluate `true` as long as `i` is less than the number of `type` arrays in the `location` array located at the position held in the variable `whichLocation`. Let's take a closer look at the condition.

```
i < designers[whichLocation].length
```

The right-hand side of the less-than comparison operator is where all the fun is really happening. What we are doing is going in to the designers array and accessing the length property of the nested array, which is located at the position held within the whichLocation property. So, if the user has selected location1 from the Location pull-down, the value of whichLocation will hold the value 0. This means that this statement will gather the length of the array that sits in the first position in the designers array. This array is the one that holds the three nested type arrays for that location, so the value returned should be 3. This means that our for loop will execute three times until the variable i is equal to the length of the location array. If the user had chosen location2 from the pull-down, the loop would again run until i reached the length of the second location array. We now have a loop that will execute as many times as there are types for whichever location was chosen by the user. We now need to insert the code that the loop will execute on each pass.

```
// Populates the Type Field
function updateLocation(whichLoc) {
    if(whichLoc) {
        // set whichLocation varaible to the value passed
        // into the function
        whichLocation = whichLoc;

        //clear out the Designer select box

        var listCounter = 0;
        while(listCounter <= designerListSize) {
            document.searchForm.designer.options
        [listCounter].text = '';
            document.searchForm.designer.options
        [listCounter].value = '';
        ++listCounter;
        }
        //snap designers list to the first slot and
        //repopulate it with criteria message
        document.searchForm.designer.options[0].
    text = "Please Choose Criteria          ";
        document.searchForm.designer.options[0].
    selected = true;

        //clear out the Type pull down

        var typeCount = 0;
```

```
while(typeCount <= typeSize) {
        document.searchForm.type.options
[typeCount].text = '';
        document.searchForm.type.options
[typeCount].value = '';
        ++typeCount;
    }
    designerType = '';


    // Populate type pull down with new choices

        document.searchForm.type.options[0].
    text = 'Select a Type';
        document.searchForm.type.options[0].
    selected = true;
        var typeLocation = 1;
        for (var i = 0; i <
    designers[whichLocation].length; i++) {
            document.searchForm.type.options[type
        Location].text = designers[whichLocation][i][0];
            document.searchForm.type.options
    [typeLocation].value = i
            ++typeLocation;
        }
    } else {
        alert('Please Choose a Location');
    }
}
```

We created three new lines of code to populate the Type menu with the types of designers located within the chosen location. The first line set the `text` property of the first blank pull-down menu option to the type label held within each `type` array. Let's take a closer look.

```
document.searchForm.type.options[typeLocation].text =
designers[whichLocation][i][0];
```

On the left-hand side of the assignment operator, we call the `text` property of the option with the location equal to the value of the variable `typeLocation`. You will remember that we gave this variable a default value of 1, so the first time the loop is called, we will be changing the `text` property of the second option in the Type menu. To stop the script from constantly writing to the same option, we increment this variable each time through the loop. So as the left-hand side calls the `text` property of the next blank menu option, the right-hand side sets that property to the first entry in the `type` array at the location specified by the value of the variable `i`. So, if the user has chosen `location1`, then the first time the loop is run, it calls the first entry of the array located at the position `0` in the first `type` array. This returns a value of `Type 1`, which is stored in the `text` property of the first blank option in the Type menu. This happens each time the loop is executed until all of the types of designers in `location1` have been listed in the Type menu.

The second line of code sets the `value` property of the menu option that our first line changed the `text` property of. It assigns it the number value currently held in the variable `i`. This number value is the same as the position of that option's `type` array within the selected location's array. This value is used in our next function to access the `designer` arrays when a specific designer type is selected from the Type menu.

Finally, we increment the `typeLocation` variable so that each time the loop is run, the next blank option in the Type menu is updated.

With that, we've finished our first function. Now it's time to move on to the function that is called when the user selects from the Type menu. We'll call this function `updateType()`, and the first thing we want to do is, again, make sure that the code inside the function should be run. We want to run the code only if the user has already selected from the Location menu and has picked an option in the Type menu other than the initial Select a Type message. We do that by inserting an `if` statement, which makes sure that the `whichLocation` variable as well as the variable being passed into the function has a value.

```
// update the Type List and Fill in Designers List
function updateType(whichType)
{
    if ((whichLocation) && (whichType)) {
        . . .
    else {
        if (whichLocation) {
            alert("Please choose a type of designer.");
        } else {
            alert("Please choose a location.");
        }
        document.searchForm.type.options[0].selected =
    true;
    }
}
```

Because there are two possible reasons that we may not want to run this function, we have inserted an extra `if` statement in the `else` portion of our main `if` statement. The first one takes care of when the user hasn't selected a location yet. It will print out an alert telling the user to do so. If the user has already chosen a location but selected the initial message in the Type menu, then it will print out an alert to choose a type of designer. Now that we've set up the mechanism to weed out those instances when we don't want to run the function, let's get started with the code that needs to be executed when we do.

As in our last function, the first step is to assign the value that is passed into our function to a variable that was defined outside of the function so that other functions can access it. This time, we assign the value passed into the variable `designerType`.

```
// update the Type List and Fill in Designers List
function updateType(whichType)
{
        if ((whichLocation) && (whichType)) {

                // set designerType variable to the value passed
                // into the function
                designerType = whichType;

                . . .

        } else {
            if (whichLocation) {
                alert("Please choose a type of designer.");
            } else {
                alert("Please choose a location.");
            }
            document.searchForm.type.options[0].selected
        = true;
        }
}
```

Next, we take care of the housekeeping functionality for this function. In this function, we need to clear out only the designers list field. We won't want to clear out the Type menu, because it already holds the types for the selected location. The code we use is the same as the code we used to clear out this field in our first function.

```
// update the Type List and Fill in Designers List
function updateType(whichType)
```

```
{
    if ((whichLocation) && (whichType)) {

        // set designerType variable to the value passed
        // into the function
        designerType = whichType;

        //clear out the Designer select box

        var listCounter = 0;
        while(listCounter <= designerListSize) {
            document.searchForm.designer.options
[listCounter].text = '';
            document.searchForm.designer.options
[listCounter].value = '';
            ++listCounter;
        }


            . . .

    } else {
        if (whichLocation) {
            alert("Please choose a type of designer.");
        } else {
            alert("Please choose a location.");
        }
        document.searchForm.type.options[0].
selected = true;
    }
}
```

Now that we've got our housekeeping functionality out of the way, we can populate the Designer menu with a list of designers that are from the location and of the type selected.

As in our last function, we use a `for` loop to cycle through and print out all of the designers that meet our search criteria. This is a bit simpler, however. Whereas we had to leave the initial Select a Type message when we populated the Type menu, for the Designer menu, we simply print out the designer's name starting from the first option in the menu. There is no need for us to keep track of an extra variable that holds the position at which we want to print out a designer's name. We can use the `i` variable that is running the `for` loop. Let's insert our loop and take a look at what we've got.

```
// update the Type List and Fill in Designers List
function updateType(whichType)
{
    if ((whichLocation) && (whichType)) {

        // set designerType variable to the value passed
        // into the function
        designerType = whichType;

        //clear out the Designer select box

        var listCounter = 0;
        while(listCounter <= designerListSize) {
            document.searchForm.designer.options
        [listCounter].text = '';
            document.searchForm.designer.options
        [listCounter].value = '';
            ++listCounter;
        }


        // Populate the designers list box
        for (var i = 1; i <
designers[whichLocation][designerType].length; i++) {
            . . .
        }

    } else {
        if (whichLocation) {
            alert("Please choose a type of designer.");
        } else {
            alert("Please choose a location.");
        }
        document.searchForm.type.options[0].selected
    = true;
    }
}
```

Again, we have set up a loop that compares the value of a variable i with the length of an array. This time we are checking the length of the type array that corresponds with the designer type chosen from the Type menu. Let's take a closer look at the right-hand side of the less-than comparison operator that gathers this value.

```
designers[whichLocation][designerType].length
```

We first go into the `location` array that corresponds with the location the user has selected from the Location menu, and then we get the length of the array that corresponds with the type of designer chosen from the Type menu. So, if the user first selected `location1` and then chose `type2`, the value returned would be 3, because that `type` array holds information on three designers. So, if this is the case, our `for` loop will cycle through three times, each time assigning a menu option the name of a designer. Let's add the code that will assign the menu options.

```
// update the Type List and Fill in Designers List
function updateType(whichType)
{
        if ((whichLocation) && (whichType)) {

                // set designerType varaible to the value passed
                // into the function
                designerType = whichType;

                //clear out the Designer select box

                var listCounter = 0;
                while(listCounter <= designerListSize) {
                        document.searchForm.designer.options
                [listCounter].text = '';
                        document.searchForm.designer.options
                [listCounter].value = '';
                        ++listCounter;
                }


                for (var i = 1; i <
        designers[whichLocation][designerType].length; i++) {
                        document.searchForm.designer.options
                [i-1].text =
                designers[whichLocation][designerType][i][1]
                + ' ' +
                designers[whichLocation][designerType][i][2];
                        document.searchForm.designer.options
                [i-1].value =
                designers[whichLocation][designerType][i][0];
                }

        } else {
                if (whichLocation) {
                        alert("Please choose a type of designer.");
```

```
    } else {
        alert("Please choose a location.");
    }
    document.searchForm.type.options[0].selected
 = true;
    }
}
```

As in our first function, the first line of code changes the `text` property of the menu option to that of a designer held within our arrays. Because we store the designers' first and last names in separate fields in our arrays, on the right-hand side of the assignment operator we combine the first and last name with a space in between them. This way, the whole name gets placed into the `text` property of the menu option. On the second line, we assign the name of the HTML page that holds the detailed information about the designer to the `value` property of the current menu option. This value will be used to send the user to the proper page once he or she has selected a designer from the list.

That wraps it up for our second function. With our first two functions complete, the user can now select a location and then a type that will display a list of designers who meet both criteria. The next step is to write the function that takes the user to the detailed information page of the selected designer.

This function is called `viewDesigner()`, and it should be really straightforward. Once the user has selected a designer and clicked on the View Designer Details button, this function will be called and passed in the name of the HTML page of the designer that the user has selected from the Designer menu. The first thing we want to make sure of when the function is called is that the user has already selected a location and type of designer, and has a designer highlighted. We use an `if` statement to check the variables `whichLocation` and `designerType` for a value and to make sure that the value that is passed into the function matches that of the designer that is currently selected in the designers list.

```
// send the user to the proper designer detail page
function viewDesigner(newLoc) {
    if ((whichLocation) && (designerType) &&
(document.searchForm.designer.options[document.searchForm.
designer.selectedIndex].value)) {
        . . .
    } else {
```

```
        alert("Please choose a location and type of
designer");
    }
}
```

If any of our conditions are not met, then the `if` statement will display an alert telling the user to select a location and a type of designer. If all of them are met, then we want our script to take the user to the location stored in `newLoc`, so we set the `location` property of the `document` object to the value held in `newLoc`.

```
// send the user to the proper designer detail page
function viewDesigner(newLoc) {
    if ((whichLocation) && (designerType) &&
(document.searchForm.designer.options[document.searchForm.
designer.selectedIndex].value)) {
        document.location = newLoc;
    } else {
        alert("Please choose a location and type of
designer");
    }
}
```

With that, we are done with our functions for our script. The next step is to insert the event handlers into the HTML to call our functions.

Inserting the Event Handlers

Before we get into inserting the handlers, let's look at the code for the form as it stands now.

```
<form name="searchForm">
    <td>
        <select name=location>
            <option value="">Select a Location
            <option value="0">Location 1
            <option value="1">Location 2
        </select></td>
    <td>
        <select name=type>
            <option><-- Select a
Location       &nb
sp;        
            <option>
            <option>
```

```
                    <option>
                    <option>
                </select></td>
        </tr>
    </table>
    <table border="0">
        <tr>
            <td>
                <br>
                <img src="images/search/
designer.gif"></td>
                <td rowspan="2" valign="bottom">
                    <input type=button name=viewit
value="View Designer Details"></td>
        </tr>
        <tr>
            <td>
                <select name=designer size="5">
                <option>Please Choose
Criteria        &nb
sp;        
                    <option>
                    <option>
                    <option>
                    <option>
                    <option>
                    <option>
                    <option>
                    <option>
                    <option>
                    <option>
                    <option>
                    <option>
                    <option>
                    <option>
                    <option>
                    <option>
                    <option>
                    <option>
                    <option>
                </select></td>
        </tr>
    </table>
    </form>
```

You will notice that the form is named `searchForm` and that it contains three pull-down (select) menus as well as a button to launch a designer's Web page. In our functions, we have been referencing this form and the three pull-down menus, so it should be no surprise that they are named Location, Type, and Designer. What may take a little explaining, however, is why we have blank `<option>` fields for the Type and Designer menus. Because we are dynamically populating these two menus, we need to have blank menu spaces for us to insert types and designer names into. For our example, we know that there are four possible types of designers, so we placed four blank `<option>` tags into the Type menu. We also know that we have set a limit of 20 designers to be shown in the Designer menu, so we placed 20 blank `<option>` tags into that menu. Now that we know how to set up our form, let's move on to the event handlers.

We need to insert event handlers in three places: in the Location pull-down menu, the Type pull-down menu, and the View Designer Details button. For the two pull-down menus, we use `onChange()` handlers, and we use an `onClick()` handler for the button. Let's first insert the `onChange()` handler for the Location pull-down menu.

```
<select name=location
onChange="updateLocation(this.options[this.selectedIndex].
value); return true;">
```

In this event handler, we call our `updateLocation()` function and pass it the value held in the option that the user has chosen. Next, let's put in the event handler for the Type menu.

```
<select name=type
onChange="updateType(this.options[this.selectedIndex].value
); return true;">
```

We have the handler call the `updateType()` function and pass the value held in the option the user has chosen. Finally, let's insert the `onClick()` handler into the View Designer Details button.

```
<input type=button name=viewit value="View Designer
Details" onClick="viewDesigner(); return true;">
```

This handler calls the `viewDesigner()` function when the button is clicked. With the insertion of the event handlers, we have now completed our script. Let's review the steps taken to complete this project.

Reviewing the Script

The first thing we did for this project was lay out a functional specification. This forced us to figure out several key issues: what we wanted to include in the project, the best way to lay it out, and a structure for our arrays, which would hold the data we would need in our script. Once we had a firm grasp on how to accomplish the project, we created and filled our arrays.

```
designers = [
                // location 1
                [
                // type 1
                [ 'Type 1',
                    // designer 1
                    ["designer.html", "Joe", "Abrams"],
                    // designer 2
                    ["designer.html", "Roger", "Dennis"],
                    // designer 3
                    ["designer.html", "Missy", "Johnson"],
                    // designer 4
                    ["designer.html", "Sarah", "Leonard"]
                ],
                 // type 2
                 [ 'Type 2',
                    // designer 1
                    ["designer.html", "Mike", "Bunker"],
                    // designer 2
                    ["designer.html", "Tara",
"Cartwright"],
                    // designer 3
                    ["designer.html", "Ashley", "Trakker"]
                ],
                // type 4
                [ 'Type 4',
                    // designer 1
                    ["designer.html", "Caitlin",
"Archibold"],
                    // designer 2
                    ["designer.html", "Giovonni",
"Filnelli"]
                ]
            ],
```

```
                        // location 2
                        [
                        // type 1
                        [ 'Type 1',
                            // designer 1
                            ["designer.html", "Scott", "Jasper"],
                            // designer 2
                            ["designer.html", "Lisa", "Lee"],
                            // designer 3
                            ["designer.html", "Mary", "Marker"],
                            // designer 4
                            ["designer.html", "Joel", "Schwartz"]
                        ],
                        // type 2
                        [ 'Type 2',
                            // designer 1
                            ["designer.html", "Mia", "Adams"],
                            // designer 2
                            ["designer.html", "Ashlyn", "Deerborn"]
                        ],
                        // type 3
                        [ 'Type 3',
                            // desighner 1
                            ["designer.html", "Justine",
      "Andrews"],
                            // designer 2
                            ["designer.html", "Lauren", "Bishop"],
                            // desighner 3
                            ["designer.html", "Laura", "Michaels"],
                            // designer 4
                            ["designer.html", "Kristin", "Sanger"]
                        ],
                        // type 4
                        [ 'Type 4',
                            // designer 1
                            ["designer.html", "Caitlin",
      "Archibold"],
                            // designer 2
                            ["designer.html", "Giovonni",
      "Filnelli"],
                            // designer 3
                            ["designer.html", "Pat", "Micelli"]
                        ]
                    ]
                ]
```

1. We created the main `designers` array and nested two new arrays within it, one for each location that a user would be able to select from.
2. We nested the correct number of `type` arrays into each `location` array, with each `type` array holding the label for that type as its first entry.
3. We inserted an array for each designer to hold the designer's HTML page, first name, and last name.

With the array complete, we defined four variables that our functions will use later in the script.

```
// variables needed for our functions
var whichLocation = '';
var designerType = '';
var designerListSize = 20;
var typeSize = 4;
```

1. We defined the first variable `whichLocation` to hold a numerical value that corresponds to the position of one of the `location` arrays.
2. We created the variable `designerType` to hold a numerical value that corresponds to the position of one of the `type` arrays.
3. The final two variables, `designerListSize` and `typeSize`, were created and set to hold a numerical value that represents the maximum allowed options in the Designer menu and Type menu, respectively.

With the variables defined, we moved on to create our functions. The first of our three functions is called `updateLocation()`. This function is called when the user selects an option from the Location pull-down menu.

```
// Populates the Type Field
function updateLocation(whichLoc) {
    if(whichLoc) {
        // set whichLocation variable to the value passed
        // into the function
        whichLocation = whichLoc;

        //clear out the Designer select box
        var listCounter = 0;
        while(listCounter <= designerListSize) {
            document.searchForm.designer.options
            [listCounter].text = '';
```

```
            document.searchForm.designer.options
        [listCounter].value = '';
            ++listCounter;
        }

        //snap designers list to the first slot and
        //repopulate it with criteria message
        document.searchForm.designer.options[0].text =
"Please Choose Criteria              ";
        document.searchForm.designer.options[0].selected
= true;

        //clear out the Type pull down
        var typeCount = 0;
        while(typeCount <= typeSize) {
            document.searchForm.type.options
        [typeCount].text = '';
            document.searchForm.type.options
        [typeCount].value = '';
            ++typeCount;
        }
        designerType = '';

        // Populate type pull down with new choices
        document.searchForm.type.options[0].text =
    'Select a Type';
        document.searchForm.type.options[0].selected =
    true;
        var typeLocation = 1;
        for (var i = 0; i <
designers[whichLocation].length; i++) {
            document.searchForm.type.options
        [typeLocation].text =
        designers[whichLocation][i][0];
            document.searchForm.type.options
        [typeLocation].value = i
            ++typeLocation;
        }
    } else {
        alert('Please Choose a Location');
    }
}
```

1. The first step in the updateLoction() function was to set up an if statement to make sure the user has chosen a location and a valid value has been passed into the func-

tion. If not, then we have the function display an alert telling the user to choose a location.

2. If the user selected a location, we assigned the variable whichLocation equal to the value passed into the function so our other functions can access to this value.

3. We cleared out the Type menu and the Designer menu of any existing information.

   - We used a while statement to cycle through all of the available options in the Designer menu and reset each to be blank.

   - We reinserted the initial Please Choose Criteria message into the first menu option of the Designer menu and made sure it was the selected option.

   - We used a while loop to cycle through all available options in the Designer menu and reset each to be blank.

4. With housekeeping chores out of the way, we wrote the code to populate the Type menu based on the location the user selected.

   - We changed the initial message that said Select a Location to Choose a Type.

   - We used a for loop to go into the location array the user specified and grab the label entry from each type array nested within it. We set it up to place those names into the Type menu as choices. We assigned the position of each type array to be the value for each option.

With the first function finished, we created a function called updateType() that would be called when the user selects a designer type from the Type pull-down.

```
// update the Type List and Fill in Designers List
function updateType(whichType) {
    if ((whichLocation) && (whichType)) {

        // set designerType variable to the value passed
        // into the function
        designerType = whichType;

        //clear out the Designer select box
        var listCounter = 0;
        while(listCounter <= designerListSize) {
            document.searchForm.designer.options
        [listCounter].text = '';
```

```
                document.searchForm.designer.options
        [listCounter].value = '';
                ++listCounter;
        }

        // Populate the designers list box

        for (var i = 1; i <
designers[whichLocation][designerType].length; i++) {
                document.searchForm.designer.options
        [i-1].text =
        designers[whichLocation][designerType][i][1] + '
        ' + designers[whichLocation][designerType][i][2];
                document.searchForm.designer.options[i-1].
        value =designers[whichLocation][designerType]
        [i][0];

        }
    } else {
        if (whichLocation) {
                alert("Please choose a type of designer.");
        } else {
                alert("Please choose a location.");
        }
    document.searchForm.type.options[0].selected = true;
    }
}
```

1. As in our `updateLocation()` function, the first thing we did was set up an `if` statement to see if we should run the code contained within. This time, we checked to make sure two conditions had been met: first, that the user had already selected from the Location pull-down, and second, that the user had selected an option from the Type pull-down other than the initial Choose a Type message. If one or both of the conditions proved to be false, we set up an `if` statement that would display an alert telling the user to take the appropriate action.

2. We took care of the housekeeping functionality as we did in the first function. This time, however, we only needed to clear out the Designer menu. We inserted the same while loop we used in the `updateLocation()` function.

3. With the Designer menu now clear, we moved on to the section of code that populates the Designer menu with all of the designers from the selected type. Again, as in

the `updateLocation()` function, we used a `for` loop to cycle through as many times as there are designers for the chosen type. We inserted code that would reach into a specified `designers` array and assign the `text` field of the next blank menu option to hold the first and last names of the designer. We also added a line of code that assigned the designer's HTML page to the value of that same menu option.

With those two functions complete, the only function left to write was the `viewDesigner()` function, which sends the user to the HTML page of the designer selected from the Designer menu.

```
// send the user to the proper designer detail page
function viewDesigner(newLoc) {
        if ((whichLocation) && (designerType) &&
(document.searchForm.designer.options[document.searchForm.
designer.selectedIndex].value)) {
                document.location = newLoc;
        } else {
                alert("Please choose a location and type of
designer");
        }
}
```

This function was fairly straightforward after the previous two functions. The first thing we did was make sure the user had already chosen a location and a type, and that the value being passed into the function matched the value of the currently selected option in the Designer menu. We then inserted a line of code that assigns the `location` property of the `document` object to the value that was passed into the function. This line of code would be executed only if all three of our conditions evaluated `true`.

The final step in the project was to insert the event handlers into the three form elements.

```
<select name=location
onChange="updateLocation(this.options[this.selectedIndex].
value); return true;">
```

First we inserted an `onChange()` handler into the Location pull-down menu. When triggered, this handler calls the `update-Location()` function and passes it the value of the currently selected option.

Next, we inserted the handler for the Type pull-down menu.

```
<select name=type
onChange="updateType(this.options[this.selectedIndex].value
); return true;">
```

As for the Location pull-down, we also inserted an `onChange()` handler into the Type pull-down menu. This handler is set up to call the `updateType()` function and pass it the value of the currently selected option in the Type menu.

Finally, we inserted the handler into the View Designer Details button.

```
<input type=button name=viewit value="View Designer
Details" onClick="viewDesigner(); return true;">
```

In the View Designer Details button, we inserted an `onClick()` handler, which calls the `viewDesigner()` function when the user clicks on it. This of course is the function that sends the user to the individual designer's information page.

We now have quite a nice feature for the *Stitch* site. We covered quite a lot of ground in this project, including some new concepts:

- We created a functional specification for the project.
- We learned how to define and access multidimensional arrays.
- We were introduced to the `for` conditional statement.

RECAP

One look at the two new projects that you put together for the site and everyone in the office is bowing to you in submission as you pass them in the halls. For both of these projects, we were able to take basic concepts and combine them with a few new twists and a little creative thinking to engineer some truly advanced functionality for the site. But don't think that these are the coolest or most complex things you can achieve with JavaScript—far from it. With CSS/DHTML deeply entrenched in the industry, the new features and capabilities that are being added to JavaScript are truly amazing.

Well, we have come a long way and created some great scripts, even if they were for two fictitious companies—now here is where the true fun begins. It's time to take what you have learned and use that knowledge to work on your own sites.

ADVANCED PROJECTS

1. Add a field to our designer database page that lets the user further narrow down the options shown by inserting the first letter of the designer's last name.
2. Create a script that will set up a secure form submission by encrypting the data from the fields on a form.
3. Create a script to save user information data to a file on the Web server so you can serve up a customized page when the user returns.

A Event Handlers

JavaScript is a language that is inherently event-driven; that is to say that scripts created in JavaScript usually are executed as a result of an event caused either by the user or the browser itself. The way that we harness these events is through the use of event handlers. This appendix was created to give you a place where you can check out all of the different event handlers, their syntax, and a description of their uses.

◆ onAbort

Description: This handler is triggered when the user aborts the loading of an image either by clicking on a link or hitting the Stop button.
Syntax: onAbort="code to be executed"
Implemented in: Navigator 3.0
Used within: Image

◆ onBlur

Description: This handler is triggered when a frame, window, or form element loses focus.
Syntax: onBlur="code to be executed"
Implemented in: Navigator 2.0/3.0
Used within: Button, Checkbox, FileUpload, Layer, Password, Radio, Reset, Select, Submit, Text, Textarea, Window

◆ onChange

Description: This handler is triggered when a Select, Text, or Textarea form field loses focus and its value is changed.
Syntax: onChange="code to be executed"
Implemented in: Navigator 2.0/3.0
Used within: FileUpload, Select, Text, Textarea

◆ onClick

Description: This handler is triggered when either a Form object is clicked upon or the handler is placed within an <href> tag and the image or text link is clicked on.
Syntax: onClick="code to be executed"
Implemented in: Navigator 2.0/3.0
Used within: Button, Document, Checkbox, Link, Radio, Reset, Submit

◆ onDblClick

Description: This handler is triggered when either a Form object is double-clicked on, or if the handler is placed within an <href> tag and the link is double-clicked on.
Syntax: onDblClick="code to be executed"
Implemented in: Navigator 4.0
Used within: Document, Link

◆ onDragDrop

Description: This handler is triggered when the user drops an object, such as a file, onto the Navigator window.
Syntax: onDragDrop ="code to be executed"
Implemented in: Navigator 4.0
Used within: Window

◆ onError

Description: This handler is triggered when the loading of a document or an image causes an error.
Syntax: onError ="code to be executed"
Implemented in: Navigator 3.0
Used within: Image, Window

◆ onFocus

Description: This handler is triggered when a Window, Frame, Frameset, or Form element receives focus.
Syntax: onFocus ="code to be executed"
Implemented in: Navigator 2.0/3.0/4.0
Used within: Button, Checkbox, FileUpload, Layer, Password, Radio, Reset, Select, Submit, Text, Textarea, Window

◆ onKeyDown

Description: This handler is triggered when the user presses a key.
Syntax: onKeyDown ="code to be executed"
Implemented in: Navigator 4.0
Used within: Document, Image, Link, Textarea

◆ onKeyPress

Description: This handler is triggered when the user presses down or holds down a key.
Syntax: onKeyPress ="code to be executed"
Implemented in: Navigator 4.0
Used within: Document, Image, Link, Textarea

◆ onKeyUp

Description: This handler is triggered when the user releases a key.

Syntax: onKeyUp ="code to be executed"

Implemented in: Navigator 4.0

Used within: Document, Image, Link, Textarea

◆ onLoad

Description: This handler is triggered when all of the content is finished loading into a window or all of the frames within a frameset. It can also be triggered by the loading of an image.

Syntax: onLoad ="code to be executed"

Implemented in: Navigator 2.0/3.0

Used within: Image, Layer, Window

◆ onMouseDown

Description: This handler is triggered when the user presses the mouse button.

Syntax: onMouseDown ="code to be executed"

Implemented in: Navigator 4.0

Used within: Button, Document, Link

◆ onMouseMove

Description: This handler is triggered when the user moves the cursor.

Syntax: onMouseMove ="code to be executed"

Implemented in: Navigator 4.0

Used within: None

◆ onMouseOut

Description: This handler is triggered when the user moves the cursor off of the object.

Syntax: onMouseOut ="code to be executed"

Implemented in: Navigator 3.0

Used within: Layer, Link

◆ onMouseOver

Description: This handler is triggered when the user moves the cursor over the object.

Syntax: onMouseOver ="code to be executed"

Implemented in: Navigator 2.0/3.0

Used within: Layer, Link

◆ onMouseUp

Description: This handler is triggered when the user releases the mouse button.

Syntax: onMouseUp ="code to be executed"

Implemented in: Navigator 4.0

Used within: Button, Document, Link

◆ onMove

Description: This handler is triggered when a script or the user moves the window or a frame.

Syntax: onMove ="code to be executed"

Implemented in: Navigator 4.0

Used within: Window

◆ onReset

Description: This handler is triggered when the user resets a form.

Syntax: onReset ="code to be executed"

Implemented in: Navigator 3.0

Used within: Form

◆ OnResize

Description: This handler is triggered when the user resizes the window or a frame.

Syntax: onResize ="code to be executed"

Implemented in: Navigator 4.0

Used within: Window

◆ onSelect

Description: This handler is triggered when the user selects some text either from a Text or Textarea form field.

Syntax: onSelect ="code to be executed"

Implemented in: Navigator 2.0

Used within: Text, Textarea

◆ onSubmit

Description: This handler is triggered when the user submits a form.

Syntax: onSubmit ="code to be executed"

Implemented in: Navigator 2.0

Used within: Form

◆ onUnload

Description: This handler is triggered when the user exits the document.

Syntax: onUnload ="code to be executed"

Implemented in: Navigator 2.0

Used within: Window

B JavaScript Objects

Because JavaScript is an object-oriented language, and it's kind of hard to do much without knowing the objects supported in the language, we have decided to include this reference. This appendix breaks down the objects in JavaScript into five different categories and gives you their objects along with their properties and methods.

◆ Core Objects

The core objects are objects that aren't associated with the Java-Script object hierarchy and are available to both client-side and server-side applications.

Array

Description: An array is an object that lets you store sets of data, with each element of the data set stored in its own unique position, which in turn can be referenced or retrieved.

Syntax for creating:
```
new Array(arrayLength) or
new Array(element0, element1, ..., elementN)
```

Parameters:

arrayLength—the desired initial length of the array

elementN—This is the initial set of values that will be stored in the array. The array length will be set to the number of arguments.

Implemented in: Navigator 3.0
Properties: index, input, length, prototype
Methods: concat, join, pop, push, reverse, shift, slice, splice, toString, unshift

Boolean

Description: The Boolean object is used as a container for a Boolean value.
Syntax for creating:
```
new Boolean(value)
```
Parameters:
value—the initial value of the Boolean object
Implemented in: Navigator 3.0/4.06
Properties: prototype
Methods: toString, toSource

Date

Description: The Date object gives you the capability to work with dates and times.
Syntax for creating:
```
new Date() or
new Date("month day, year hours:minutes:sec-
onds") or
new Date(yr_num, mo_num, day_num, hr_num,
min_num, sec_num)
```
Parameters:
day, hours, minutes, month, seconds, year—If used, these various parts of the date will be string values.

day_num, hr_num, min_num, mo_num, sec_num, yr_num—If used, these various parts of the date will be integers.
Implemented in: Navigator 2.0/3.0/4.06
Properties: prototype
Methods: getDate, getDay, getFullYear, getMilliseconds, getHours, getMinutes, getMonth, getSeconds, getTime, getTimezoneOffset, getYear, parse, setDate, setFullYear, setMilliseconds, setHours, setMinutes, setMonth, setSeconds, setTime, setYear, toGMTString, toLocaleString, toSource UTC

Function

Description: This object contains lines of JavaScript, which is executed when the object is accessed.
Syntax for creating:

    new Function(arg1, arg2, …, argN, functionBody)

Parameters:
arg1, arg2, …, argN—a set of string values that can be used to store data passed into the function
Functionbody—the set of JavaScript commands to be interpreted by the function
Implemented in: Navigator 3.0/4.06
Properties: arguments, arity, caller, prototype
Methods: apply, call, toSource, toString

Java

Description: This object is used to access any Java class in the package java.*.
Syntax for creating: This object is a top-level, pre-defined object that is automatically created by the JavaScript engine.
Implemented in: Navigator 3.0

Math

Description: This object contains methods and properties that help in doing advanced math.
Syntax for creating: None; the math object is a built-in part of the JavaScript engine and can be called or referenced without having to be created.
Implemented in: Navigator 2.0
Properties: E, LN10, LN2, LOG10E, LOG2E, PI, SQRT1 2, SQRT2
Methods: abs, acos, asin, atan, atan2, ceil, cos, exp, floor, log, max, min, pow, random, round, sin, sqrt, tan

Netscape

Description: This object is used to access any Java class in the package netscape.*.

Syntax for creating: This object is a top-level, predefined object that is automatically created by the JavaScript engine.
Implemented in: Navigator 3.0

Number

Description: This object contains primitive numeric values; it is useful in dealing with numeric values.
Syntax for creating:

```
new Number(value)
```

Parameters:
value—This is the numeric value to be contained within the object.
Implemented in: Navigator 3.0/4.0/4.06
Properties: MAX VALUE, MIN VALUE, NaN, NEGATIVE INFINITY, POSITIVE INFINITY, prototype
Methods: toSource, toString

Object

Description: This is the built-in JavaScript object that all objects within JavaScript are descended from.
Syntax for creating: `new object()`
Parameters: None
Implemented in: Navigator 2.0/3.0/4.06
Properties: constructor, prototype
Methods: eval, toSource, toString, unwatch, valueOf, watch

RegExp

Description: This object contains a regular expression that can be used to find, replace, and manipulate matches in strings.
Syntax for creating:

```
new RegExp("pattern," "flags")
```

Parameters:
pattern—the text contained within the regular expression
flags—There are three possible values for a flag: global match(g), ignore case(i), both global match and ignore case(gi).

Implemented in: Navigator 4.0/4.0g
Properties: $n, $, $*, $&, $+, &`, $', global, ignoreCase, input, lastIndex, lastMatch, lastParen, leftContext, multi-line, rightContext, source
Methods: compile, exec, test, toSource

String

Description: This object contains a series of characters that make up a string.
Syntax for creating:
```
new String(string)
```
Parameters:
String—a string
Implemented in: Navigator 2.0/3.0/4.0/4.0g
Properties: length, prototype
Methods: anchor, big, blink, bold, charAt, charCodeAt, concat, fixed, fontcolor, fontsize, fromCharCode, indexOf, italics, lastIndexOf, link, match, replace, search, slice, small, split, strike, sub, substr, substring, sup, toLowerCase, toSource, toUpperCase

◆ Document Objects

This section covers the Document object and all of its related objects.

Anchor

Description: This object specifies a place in a document that is a target for a hypertext-link.
Syntax for creating: This is created by using the HTML <a> tag or calling the String.anchor method.
Implemented in: Navigator 2.0/4.0
Properties: name, text, x, y
Methods: This object inherits the watch and unWatch methods from Object.

Applet

Description: This object contains any Java applets contained within an HTML page.

Syntax for creating: NA
Created by: the HTML applet tag
Implemented in: Navigator 3.0
Properties: All of the public properties of the applet are available through the object.
Methods: all public methods

Area

Description: This object represents an area of an image map. For more information on its properties, see the Link object.
Implemented in: Navigator 3.0

Document

Description: This object contains the properties of the current document.
Syntax for creating: NA
Created by: This object is created by the <body> tag of an HTML document as the runtime engine reads the page.
Implemented in: Navigator 2.0/3.0/4.0
Event Handlers: onClick, onDblClick, onKeyDown, onKeyPress, onKeyUp, onMouseDown, onMouseUp
Properties: alinkColor, anchors, applets, bgColor, cookie, domain, embeds, fgColor, formName, forms, images, lastModified, layers, linkColor, links, plugins, referrer, title, URL, vlinkColor
Methods: captureEvents, close, getSelection, handleEvent, open, releaseEvents, routeEvent, write, writeln

Image

Description: This object contains an image and permits access to the image's properties.
Syntax for creating:
```
new Image(width, height)
```
Parameters:
> width—the width of the image
> height—the height of the image

Created by: the image constructor or an <img> tag found within an HTML document

Implemented in: Navigator 3.0/4.0
Event Handlers: onAbort, onError, onKeyDown, onKeyPress, onKeyUp, onLoad
Properties: border, complete, height, hspace, lowsrc, name, prototype, src, vspace, width
Methods: handleEvent

Layer

Description: This object contains a layer from an HTML document and permits access to the layer's properties.
Syntax for creating: NA
Created by: Either the `<layer>` or `<ilayer>` tag in an HTML document will create a layer object.
Implemented in: Navigator 4.0
Event Handlers: onMouseOver, onMouseOut, onLoad, onFocus, onBlur
Properties: above, background, bgColor, below, clip.bottom, clip.height, clip.left, clip.right, clip.top, clip.width, document, left, name, pageX, pageY, parentLayer, siblingAbove, siblingBelow, src, top, visibility, zIndex
Methods: captureEvents, handleEvent, load, moveAbove, moveBelow, moveBy, moveTo, moveToAbsolute, releaseEvents, resizeBy, resizeTo, routeEvent

Link

Description: This object contains a link from an HTML document and permits access to the link's properties.
Syntax for creating:
```
theString.link(href)
```
Parameters:
theString —a string object
Href—a string that specifies URL
Created by: Either the `<a href>` or `<area>` tag in an HTML document or a call to the String.link method will create a link object.
Implemented in: Navigator 2.0/3.0/4.0
Event Handlers: onClick, onDblClick, onKeyDown, onKeyPress, onKeyUp, onMouseDown, onMouseOut, onMouseOver, onMouseUp

Properties: hash, host, hostname, href, pathname, port, protocol, search, target, text
Methods: handleEvent

Style

Description: This object specifies the style of CSS-defined HTML elements.
Created by: A style can be defined by any of the following methods or properties of the document object:
 document.classes
 document.contextual
 document.ids
 document.tags
Implemented in: Navigator 4.0
Properties: align, backgroundColor, backgroundImage, borderBottomWidth, borderColor, borderLeftWidth, borderRightWidth, borderStyle, borderTopWidth, clear, color, display, fontFamily, fontSize, fontStyle, fontWeight, lineHeight, lstStyleType, marginBottom, marginLeft, marginRight, marginTop, paddingBottom, paddingLeft, paddingRight, paddingTop, textAlign, textDecoration, textIndent, textTransform, whiteSpace, width
Methods: borderWidths, margins, paddings

◆ **Window Objects**

This section covers the Window object and all of its related objects.

Frame

Description: This object contains a frame, which is specified in an HTML frameset. Every frame is in reality a Window object; the frame object is just used for convenience.
Syntax for creating: NA
Created by: Either the <frame> or <frameset> tag in an HTML document will create a frame object.
Implemented in: Navigator 2.0/3.0
Event Handlers: See the Window object.

Properties: See the Window object.
Methods: See the Window object.

History

Description: This object contains an array that holds all of the URLs that the user has visited within that window.
Syntax for creating: NA
Created by: This is a built-in JavaScript object.
Implemented in: Navigator 2.0/3.0
Event Handlers: NA
Properties: current, length, next, previous
Methods: back, forward, go

Location

Description: This object contains the current URL.
Syntax for creating: NA
Created by: This is a built-in JavaScript object.
Implemented in: Navigator 2.0/3.0
Event Handlers: NA
Properties: hash, host, hostname, href, pathname, port, protocol, search
Methods: reload, replace

Screen

Description: This object contains information on the display screen and colors.
Syntax for creating: NA
Created by: This is a built-in JavaScript object that the runtime engine creates for you.
Implemented in: Navigator 4.0
Event Handlers: NA
Properties: availHeight, availWidth, height, pixelDepth, width
Methods: NA

Window

Description: This object delineates a browser or frame.
Syntax for creating: NA

Created by: This object is created by each `<body>`, `<frameset>`, or `<frame>` HTML tag or by the open method of the Window object.
Implemented in: Navigator 2.0/3.0/4.0
Event Handlers: onBlur, onDragDrop, onError, onFocus, onLoad, onMove, onResize, onUnload
Properties: closed, defaultStatus, document, frames, history, innerHeight, innerWidth, length, location, menubar, name, opener, outerHeight, outerWidth, pageXOffset, pageYOffset, parent, personalbar, scrollbars, self, status, statusbar, toolbar, top, window
Methods: alert, back, blur, captureEvents, clearInterval, clearTimeout, close, confirm, disableExternalCapture, enableExternalCapture, find, focus, forward, handleEvent, home, moveBy, moveTo, open, print, prompt, releaseEvents, resizeBy, resizeTo, routeEvent, scroll, scrollBy, scrollTo, setInterval, setTimeout, stop

◆ Form Objects

This section covers the Form object and all of its related objects.

Button

Description: This object contains a push-button from an HTML form.
Syntax for creating: NA
Created by: the `<input>` tag with "button" specified as the TYPE attribute
Implemented in: Navigator 2.0/3.0/4.0
Event Handlers: onBlur, onClick, onFocus, onMouseDown, onMouseUP
Properties: form, name, type, value
Methods: blur, click, focus, handleEvent

Checkbox

Description: This object contains a checkbox from an HTML form.
Syntax for creating: NA
Created by: the `<input>` tag with "checkbox" specified as the TYPE attribute

Implemented in: Navigator 2.0/3.0/4.0
Event Handlers: onBlur, onClick, onFocus
Properties: checked, defaultChecked, form, name, type, value
Methods: blur, click, focus, handleEvent

FileUpload

Description: This object contains a file upload element from an HTML form.
Syntax for creating: NA
Created by: the `<input>` tag with "file" specified as the TYPE attribute
Implemented in: Navigator 2.0/3.0/4.0
Event Handlers: onBlur, onChange, onFocus
Properties: form, name, type, value
Methods: blur, focus, handleEvent, select

Form

Description: This object contains an HTML form and all of the objects contained within that form.
Syntax for creating: NA
Created by: The runtime engine creates this object when it comes across a `<form>` tag in an HTML document.
Implemented in: Navigator 2.0/3.0/4.0
Event Handlers: onReset, onSubmit
Properties: action, elements, encoding, length, method, name, target
Methods: handleEvent, reset, submit

Hidden

Description: This object contains a hidden text object from an HTML form.
Syntax for creating: NA
Created by: the `<input>` tag with "hidden" specified as the TYPE attribute
Implemented in: Navigator 2.0/3.0
Event Handlers: NA
Properties: form, name, type, value
Methods: NA

Option

Description: This object contains individual options from a selection pull-down menu.

Syntax for creating:
```
new    Option(text,    value,    defaultSelected,
selected)
```

Parameters:

text—sets the text to be displayed in the menu list

value—sets the value returned to the server when the form is submitted with that option chosen

defaultSelected—sets the option that is initially true or selected

selected—sets the current state of the option

Created by: the `<option>` tag or the use of the Option constructor

Implemented in: Navigator 2.0/3.0

Event Handlers: NA

Properties: defaultSelected, selected, text, value

Methods: NA

Password

Description: This object contains a text field from an HTML form that conceals its value.

Syntax for creating: NA

Created by: the `<input>` tag with "password" specified as the TYPE attribute

Implemented in: Navigator 2.0/3.0/4.0

Event Handlers: onBlur, onFocus

Properties: defaultValue, form, name, type, value

Methods: blur, focus, handleEvent, select

Radio

Description: This object contains a single radio button from a set of buttons on an HTML form.

Syntax for creating: NA

Created by: the `<input>` tag with "radio" specified as the TYPE attribute

Implemented in: Navigator 2.0/3.0/4.0

Event Handlers: onBlur, onClick, onFocus

Properties: checked, defaultChecked, form, name, type, value

Methods: blur, click, focus, handleEvent

Reset

Description: This object contains a reset button from an HTML form.

Syntax for creating: NA

Created by: the `<input>` tag with "reset" specified as the TYPE attribute

Implemented in: Navigator 2.0/3.0/4.0

Event Handlers: onBlur, onClick, onFocus

Properties: form, name, type, value

Methods: blur, click, focus, handleEvent

Select

Description: This object contains a selection pull-down menu from an HTML form.

Syntax for creating: NA

Created by: the `<select>` inserted into an HTML form

Implemented in: Navigator 2.0/3.0/4.0

Event Handlers: onBlur, onChange, onFocus

Properties: form, length, name, options, selectedIndex, type

Methods: blur, focus, handleEvent

Submit

Description: This object contains a submit button from a HTML form.

Syntax for creating: NA

Created by: the `<input>` tag with "submit" specified as the TYPE attribute

Implemented in: Navigator 2.0/3.0/4.0

Event Handlers: onBlur, onClick, onFocus

Properties: form, name, type, value

Methods: blur, click, foucs, handleEvent

Text

Description: This object contains a text field from an HTML form.
Syntax for creating: NA
Created by: the `<input>` tag with "text" specified as the TYPE attribute
Implemented in: Navigator 2.0/3.0/4.0
Event Handlers: onBlur, onChange, onFocus, onSelect
Properties: defaultValue, form, name, type, value
Methods: blur, focus, handleEvent, select

Textarea

Description: This object contains a multiple input text field from an HTML form.
Syntax for creating: NA
Created by: the `<textarea>` tag
Implemented in: Navigator 2.0/3.0/4.0
Event Handlers: onBlur, onChange, onFocus, onKeyDown, onKeyPress, onKeyUp, onSelect
Properties: defaultValue, form, name, type, value
Methods: blur, focus, handleEvent, select

◆ Browser Objects

This section covers the objects that contain the properties specific to the browser.

Navigator

Description: This object contains information about the user's browser.
Syntax for creating: NA
Created by: This object is automatically created when the browser is loaded.
Implemented in: Navigator 2.0/3.0/4.0
Properties: appCodeName, appName, appVersion, language, mimeTypes, platform, plugins, userAgent
Methods: javaEnabled, plugins.refresh, preference, taintEnabled

MimeType

Description: This object contains a MIME type supported by the browser.
Syntax for creating: NA
Created by: This object is automatically created when the browser is loaded.
Implemented in: Navigator 3.0
Properties: description, enabledPlugin, suffixes, type
Methods: NA

Plugin

Description: This object contains a plug-in installed on the user's browser.
Syntax for creating: NA
Created by: This object is automatically created when the browser is loaded.
Implemented in: Navigator 3.0
Properties: description, filename, length, name
Methods: NA

Index